AF568088

Beyond A Billion Ballots

Beyond A Billion Ballots

Democratic Reforms for a Resurgent India

Vinay Sahasrabuddhe, PhD

First published 2013

ISBN 978-81-8328-322-9

Published by

Wisdom Tree
4779/23, Ansari Road
Darya Ganj, New Delhi-110 002
Ph.: 23247966/67/68
wisdomtreebooks@gmail.com

Printed in India

This book is dedicated to the
anonymous, unsung, unrecognised political activist—
an endangered species still found in almost all
ideology-driven parties—
who has been working untiringly for the victory
of his or her ideology. For, it is such an activist who
needs to be protected and saved from extinction,
for the empowerment of parties and success of democracy.

Contents

Preface

About democracy in India, a lot has already been stated and a lot more will be written in the days to come. The year 2012 marked the completion of six decades after independent India voted to elect its first Lok Sabha, the lower house of its Parliament. In 2010, we had celebrated the sixtieth anniversary of India becoming a republic.

Against this backdrop, it makes sense to analyse the performance of the Indian democracy. Analysts and researchers will apply their own yardsticks to measure the success of democracy and draw their own conclusions. However, one particular question that nobody can possibly escape is, 'How serious are people in India about the quality and result-orientation of democracy in the country?' *Beyond a Billion Ballots* explores the answers to this question, the focus being the political parties in India.

Over the years, a point that is being almost unmistakably raised in the context of democracy in India is that of the failure of, or the unimpressive performance of, its institutions. In India, while institutions are working, the process of institutionalisation of democracy itself appears to have been bogged down. Elections take place in a fairly conducive atmosphere, parliament is functioning despite several hiccups, state legislatures conduct their meetings regularly, courts are delivering judgments even if too tardily every so often, political parties are indulging in party-competition and voters too are queuing up at the polling booths. Yet, many question whether the Indian democracy is delivering at all.

Many new entrants join politics and form new political parties with the hope of making a difference. From the alumni of the renowned Indian Institutes of Technology and business management graduates to the likes of Lok Satta Movement's Jayprakash Narayan (JN) and social worker Medha Patkar, all those who want to transform Indian politics have toyed with the idea of establishing a new political party. Arvind Kejriwal is the latest contender. And yet, many of them seem to have lost their way as partisan electoral politics in India almost compels all the players to fall in line and succumb to populist pressures. To use the words of noted policy analyst and commentator, Pratap Bhanu Mehta, 'unless this "present mould of politics" is changed, parties cannot really bring about any true transformation'. Thankfully, politicians have realised that transformation is what the restive people of India are seeking. It was not for no reason that, at the February 2008 annual meeting of the Federation of Indian Chamber of Commerce and Industry (FICCI), veteran Bharatiya Janata Party (BJP) leader and former Deputy Prime Minister LK Advani had observed, 'People are hungry for change, but they are not looking only for a change in government, with some new faces replacing old ones...people want to see a change in the culture and efficacy of governance. They want to see a big change in the way government functions at all levels'.

Beyond a Billion Ballots enquires as to why this expectation continues to be unfulfilled, more often than not. In the process, it tries to establish that the twin factors of populism and electoral compulsions are mainly to blame for this 'present mould of politics' which imprisons political parties. It also advocates a systemic solution to this crisis, through change in the electoral system.

This study comes as a work pursued through a practitioner's view point. Over the past twenty-five years, I have had the privilege of working as the founder-director of the Rambhau Mhalgi Prabodhini (RMP). The RMP is a unique academy—established in the memory of late Rambhau Mhalgi, one of the most illustrious Members of Parliament—working for the capacity building of elected representatives, political party activists and voluntary social workers.

In the process of conceiving, planning and executing human resource development programmes mainly for political workers, I gained a fund of experience. On several occasions, I interacted with politicians of different hues. Although RMP mainly works for the BJP, other parties like the Shiv Sena and many individual leaders belonging to the Nationalist Congress Party (NCP), the Peasants and Workers Party (PWP), etc. have also used our facility and sought help from us in conducting training programmes for their respective party cadres.

Sadly, I found a number of well-meaning, socially conscious and scrupulous political workers not succeeding in bringing about any significant change in the way electoral politics operates in our country. One could easily see how human frailties prevented many of them from achieving their objectives. In most cases, their will to transform evaporated with the realisation that it is the system that conditions one's response to a particular issue, both as an individual and as a political party. Many explained to me how systemic changes are easier said than done. In many instances, I wondered: Has the inertia of some politicians got anything to do with developing a vested interest in the very system that they had promised to transform?

I remember my dialogue with a political leader some years ago. He is a friend from my college days and is known for his strong patriotic fervour. I asked him whether he had conclusively accepted that without exploiting social backgrounds, harnessing money power, learning the art of managing what appears in the media and cultivating individuals with muscle power, one really cannot climb up in politics? Sadly, he shied away from answering in a straightforward manner. This made me realise that no amount of experiments with new political parties, new charismatic leaders, new alluring promises and new enchanting issues is really going to make any big difference. At a particular point, I also wondered like the hero of Ernest Hemingway's *A Farewell to Arms*: Are all of us trapped in the system? Can this not be changed at all?

At the end of the day, I realised that the system is the great leveler. This realisation made me restless. The turbulence within motivated me to undertake this study, examine my premises and suggest possible systemic solutions. To conduct this study in a structured manner, I registered myself for a PhD and completed my research in 2008. My desire to undertake this study was primarily with a view to developing an insight into the whole gamut of issues concerning systemic change. After my thesis was submitted, which eventually brought me a PhD, many suggested that I should convert it into a book. By accepting their suggestion, I believed that the work would give a fair amount of impetus to the discussion about systemic changes.

From Tiananmen in China to Taksim in Turkey via Tahrir in Egypt and Jantar Mantar in India, popular unrest is making a powerful statement. Dictatorships and democracies, both have been caught off guard.

Against this backdrop, a series of recently unearthed scams, unending criminalisation of electoral politics and umpteen numbers of unresolved issues are the symptoms of ailing systems. Once accustomed to such flawed systems, reason deserts one's thinking. No wonder that a section of political parties is opposed to the inclusion of parties under the Right to Information Act. The urgent requirement is, therefore, a right diagnosis of what ails the system and a firm resolve to restore health to our body politic. To that end, I only hope this book will be able to generate a debate and enhance the awareness of people.

This study would not have been possible without the continued inspiration, valuable guidance and support of my guide Dr Maneesha Tikekar. My lack of academic background in Political Science was a lacunae but she helped me overcome it. I am, indeed, extremely grateful to Dr Maneesha Tikekar.

I would also like to express deep gratitude towards Dr PM Kamath, Dr Ashok Modak, Dr Atmaram Kulkarni and Dr Aroon Tikekar who always encouraged me in my efforts to complete this study. I must thank Dr Pippa Norris of the Kennedy School of Government, Boston, who allowed me to audit (attend) some of her lectures and gave me time to discuss this project with her when I met her in 1999. I must also mention that my participation at the Session 388 of the Salzburg Seminar in 2001 on 'Sustaining Democracy in the Modern World', and my interactions with resource persons like David S Broder helped me gain valuable insights.

In 1998, I was selected for the Rotary Ambassadorial Scholarship. This scholarship facilitated my travel to Europe and a brief supervised research at the Arms Control and Disarmament and International Studies (ACDIS) unit of the University of Illinois, Urbana-Champaign (UIUC), and the USA for about eight months. I am thankful to all those who were working at this unit during 1998-99 for their support.

I must also thank my publisher Shobit Arya of Wisdom Tree and all his colleagues handling the editorial department. Without him, this study could not have been published in this form.

Lastly, the encouragement given and the patience shown by all my family members; more particularly, my mother who breathed her last immediately after I completed my study, my wife Nayana and son Ashay, need a mention.

Vinay Sahasrabuddhe
Mumbai, 16 June 2013

List of Abbreviations Used

ABVP	Akhil Bharatiya Vidyarthi Parishad (All India Students Council)
AGP	Asom Gana Parishad
AIADMK	All-India Anna Dravida Munnetra Kazhagam
BJD	Biju Janata Dal
BJP	Bharatiya Janata Party
BJYM	Bharatiya Janata Yuva Morcha (Youth wing of the BJP)
BKD	Bharatiya Kranti Dal
BSP	Bahujan Samaj Party
CM	Chief Minister
CPI	Communist Party of India
CPI (M)	Communist Party of India (Marxist)
DMK	Dravida Munnetra Kazhagam
EPIC	Election Process Information Collection, a project
FPTP	First-Past-The-Post
HVP	Haryana Vikas Party
IFES	International Foundation for Electoral Systems
IIDEA	International Institute for Democracy and Electoral Assistance
INC	Indian National Congress
MLA	Member of Legislative Assembly
MMP	Mixed Member Proportional
NCP	Nationalist Congress Party
NDA	National Democratic Alliance
OBC	Other Backward Classes
PMK	Pattali Makkal Katchi
PR	Proportional Representation
PSP	Praja Socialist Party
RJD	Rashtriya Janata Dal
RSS	Rashtriya Swayamsevak Sangha (National Organisation of Volunteers)
SPD	Socialist Democratic Party
SSP	Samyukta Socialist Party
TDP	Telugu Desam Party
UPA	United Progressive Alliance
VHP	Vishwa Hindu Parishad

CHAPTER 1

The Democratic World

The Economist Intelligence Unit of *The Economist* magazine has come out with a report, 'Democracy Index 2012: Democracy at a Standstill'. The report focuses on certain key features of the contemporary scenario of the democratic world. They include the unprecedented rise of movements for democratic change across the Arab world, the sovereign debt crises and weak political leadership in the developing world. They also include the decline of popular confidence in political institutions in Europe, institutional crisis in the UK, political brinkmanship and paralysis in the USA, as also the negative impact of violence and drug trafficking in Latin America.

If one analyses what is central to this stagnation of democracy leading to a potential decline, it is the lack of strong and decisive political leadership. Such lack of leadership is essentially the product of weak and un-delivering democratic institutions, particularly, the political parties. What causes deep concern is the fact that individuals manning democratic institutions that need to be fixed, occasionally do talk about reforms but very rarely walk the talk. This has made democracies hollow from within. Complacency, myopia, lack of vision and mostly, an all-encompassing crisis of ownership are the key factors that are weakening democratic institutions. The level of performance often falls woefully short of the expectations of those for whom they claim to be working.

Although India is at the centre of the discussion here, at the backdrop is the state of democracy the world over. More than ever in the past, perhaps it is today that when one thinks about democracy, it is not just about sustaining it. Any discussion about this institution has to address a fundamental question: Are democracies delivering? Are they making any significant change in the lives of people, especially when compared to nations where there is no democracy?

Democracy all over the world appears to be passing through a critical period. On the face of it, as a system of government, it seems to be well entrenched. Unlike in the middle of the last century, people no longer debate whether a particular newly-independent country can afford to be a democracy or not. In the year 2000, when East Timor became an independent country, no questions were raised about the suitability of democracy for this newborn island nation. Similarly, recent developments towards democratisation of Bhutan and consolidation of the institution in Nepal are also ungrudgingly welcomed all over the world. It is now taken for granted that people everywhere are in favour of democracy, almost as if humanity does not know an alternative to it.

Not very long ago, the world witnessed a trend of newly-democratic countries relapsing into dictatorship or military rule, as pointed out by Samuel P Huntington.[1] However, after the latest and the third wave[2], this trend seems to have receded. This may

---

[1]Samuel P Huntington, *The Third Wave: Democratization in the Late Twentieth Century*, p.16.

[2]Samuel P Huntington has termed three phases of the spread of democracy as three distinct waves. 'A wave of democratisation is a group of transitions from non-democratic to democratic regimes that occur within a specified period of time and that significantly outnumber transitions in the opposite direction during that period of time. A wave also usually involves liberalisation or partial democratisation in political systems that do not become fully democratic.' (*The Third Wave,* p15). The chronology of these waves as stated by Huntington is as follows: First wave, (long) 1828-1926, First reverse wave 1922-1942, Second, (short) 1943-1962, Second reverse wave 1958-1975 and finally the Third wave 1974-present.

sound like a welcome development towards greater consolidation of democracy. But this inference may prove to be an oversimplification since democracy is being promoted primarily because of several ulterior reasons. Efforts for promoting it do not always reflect a true commitment to democratic values.

Democracy is always welcomed also because going against the democratic aspirations of the people is rightly considered as anti-people and hence, politically incorrect. Besides, there is a universal acceptance of the fact that democracy is an unparalleled model of governance, in spite of all its shortcomings.

This leaves enough room to infer that politicians have developed a vested interest in democracy, no matter how superficial and ineffective it might have proved. In other words, the absolute interests of politicians prevent them from abandoning the façade of democracy.

In 2000, in its *Annual Survey of Freedom in the World,* Freedom House had pointed out that not a single country in the year 1900 would have qualified as a democracy by today's standards.[3] By 1950, only twenty-two of the eighty sovereign political systems in the world (about 28 per cent) were democratic. However, by January 2013, Freedom House counted 118, which is an increase of one compared to 2011. According to an unofficial assessment of the total 195 member countries of the UN, today, around 145 are those where the governments reasonably claim that they are democratic.

However, as mentioned earlier, this apparent universal acceptance of the concept of democracy need not unduly impress one. Questions about the façade of democracy once raised by former Brazilian President, Ferdinand Cardoso, cannot be ignored. He had asked, 'How many authoritarian regimes have called themselves "democratic"? How many times has the "defence of democracy"

---

[3] Freedom House is an independent New York-based non-governmental organisation, that advocates for democracy and human rights worldwide. Its annual survey on freedom in the world, which has been conducted for the past thirty years, is available on www.freedomhouse.org, as on 12 November 2004.

been used to justify repression, restrictions on freedom and even the most heinous crimes, such as torture or "forced disappearances"?'[4] It is widely accepted that the label of democracy has become so very precious that there is almost no dictatorship today that does not consider itself to be democratic.

CONSOLIDATION OF DEMOCRACY

If the nineteenth century is described as the century of the dawn of democracy and its later half the period of its development, then the twentieth century can be rightly described as the period of its consolidation. It was this century that witnessed a remarkable increase in the acceptance of democracy the world over. Nations of every hue and characteristic—communist or capitalist, developed or developing, rich or poor, theocratic or secular—all embraced democracy, accepting it as one of the most flawless systems. According to Huntington, two of his famous 'Three Waves of Democracy' occurred in the twentieth century.

The process of consolidation of democracy in this century has three aspects: First, the philosophical or theoretical; second, the practical or implementation-related and finally, the popular aspect. At the philosophical level, the century appears to be so very steadfastly supporting democracy that even diehard sceptics of this institution rarely dare to challenge its basic principles. Today even out-and-out autocratic regimes have to swear by democracy in order to seek legitimacy for their governments. Understandably, the experiences of Nazi rule in Germany, as also the blatantly autocratic tenure of the Czar in Russia, have more than convinced the entire world about the virtues of genuine democracy.

At the practical or implementation level, the twentieth century established the fact that, as a system of governance, democracy had performed in a convincing manner. Whether it was the question of the paraphernalia required or the intricacy of electoral systems and running the business of houses of representatives, it was a

[4] www.freedomhouse.org as on 12 November 2004.

reasonably smooth sailing. Nobody dared to question the advisability of democracy on these counts. At the popular level, several factors could be mentioned as indicators of public support. The remarkable amount of popular participation, not only in elections and voting but also in civil society organisations, though not always up to the mark, is an important indication. Political scientists the world over often refer to the infamous Emergency of 1975 in India to defend the relatively low ranking of democracy here. However, they overlook how aggressively people in India worked for the restoration of democracy. Examples like these can rightly be considered as pointers towards popular support for the concept of democracy.

Delivering Democracy

Even with wide theoretical acceptance, practical success and popular support, the question whether democracy has really delivered continues to haunt humanity. Democracy is, without doubt, a way of life. But, it can never be denied that it is, after all, first and foremost, a system of governance. The merits of democracy are and will have to be measured on the count of its ability to govern effectively. It cannot be eulogised merely for the sake of the lofty ideals and then popular support sought for the same. Democracy cannot be sustained if it repeatedly fails in bringing about qualitative change to the lives of the people; it has to deliver. Has democracy demonstrably succeeded or at least moved closer to achieving the real good of the people? If people under erstwhile autocratic regimes were asked as to whether today their lives were a shade better than in the past, what would be the response? Therefore, what matters most is the deliverability of democracy.

Senior American journalist and political commentator, David S Broder, once pointed out that there is a widening gap between the acceptance and effectiveness of democracy.[5] He says that death of ideology, decline of state, decline of religion, low esteem for politics

[5]David S Broder, Lecture at the Salzburg Seminar, session 384 on democracy, 13 June, 2001.

as a profession and the irresponsible role of the media in general, are the causes behind the erosion of the efficacy of democracy.

On the performance count, new and emerging democratic governments all over the world have, more often than not, met with failures. Even countries where democracy was supposed to be already well established, such as Venezuela and Columbia, became, '... destabilised and seriously threatened in the past decade by economic mismanagement, corruption, and state decay as established parties and politicians grew complacent and distant from popular concerns.'[6] Many countries in South America suffered a deep crisis of governance that inevitably resulted in a sharp erosion of the authority and capacity of the state, as also public confidence in democratic institutions. Similar is the case with some of the former Soviet countries. Even after more than a decade of democratisation here, power is wielded in the same old style that smacks of authoritarianism, elections are still less fair and rule of law continues to be fragile. One need not be surprised, then, by what Richard Rose of the University of Strathclyde in Glasgow had found in his study. According to him, 41 per cent of Russians and 51 per cent of Ukrainians favoured the restoration of communist rule.[7] Soon after the dawn of the twenty-first century, in 2003, public opinion all over the world showed an alarming decrease in the support base for democracy. The results of '*The Pew Global Attitudes Project for 2011*'[8], has brought out some interesting findings. In 1991, majority of Russians and Ukrainians clearly favoured democracy, rather than a strong leader, as the best way to address their country's problems. By 2002, the opinion had reversed, with two-thirds or more in each country saying they preferred a strong leader. In Poland and Bulgaria, views were mixed on the issue, while people in the Czech Republic and Slovakia continued to strongly support democracy. In 2007, a

[6] Larry Diamond, 'The Global State of Democracy', in *Current History,* December 2000, Vol. 99, No. 641, p. 416.
[7] *Ibid* p.417
[8] http://www.pewglobal.org/2011/?cat=commentary

report about the state of democracy in South Asia[9] revealed that only 49 per cent of Indians prefer democracy while 14 per cent believe that democracy or dictatorship makes no difference to them.

Even in established democracies there appears to be an underlying yearning for reforming the system. People who are generally satisfied with democratic governance too are looking for some improvement in the way democracy is being implemented or practised. First and foremost, poor quality of governance has become a matter of grave concern. For decades, democracies in several developing countries have failed to deal with issues like corruption, poor urban management (encroachment on public land by slum dwellers and illegal hawkers), unabated pilferage of electricity, lack of effective credit facilities to farmers, abysmal neglect of gender justice and, above all, failure in providing food, shelter and clothing to all at a reasonable cost.

LIMITATIONS OF DEMOCRACY

There are reasons to believe that there is some amount of realisation about limitations of democratic governance. One may see a discerning link between the growing scepticism about democracy and the emergence of the non-profit sector on the one hand, and the concept of good governance on the other. Especially after 1975, the non-profit organisations—popularly known as Non-Government Organisations or NGOs—have started playing a crucial role in development activities all over the world. The sheer amount of funds that are being disbursed through the NGO sector is a testimony to the fact that democracy, and leaders elected through a democratic process, cannot make bureaucracy function effectively for the welfare of the people. Hence, the importance of NGOs.

Similarly, emergence of the term good governance[10] in the

[9]SDSA team, *State of Democracy in South Asia,* p. 228-229

[10]The use of the term good governance was initially articulated in a 1989 World Bank publication. Later, the United Nations High Commissioner for Human Rights (UNCHR) identified these key attributes of good governance: i) Transparency

late 1980s could also be considered as an oblique acceptance of the fact that the practice of democracy in many countries has become divorced from its principles. In spite of the fact that there are many commonalities in the ingredients of the concept of good governance and that of democracy, the term was introduced to reinforce the real meaning of the latter.

While the reasons for the widening acceptability of democracy are not too far to seek, with regards to the reasons behind its apparent failures—quite understandably—there is no unanimity of views. The reasons are many and vary from country to country. The changing texture of international politics, the spectre of mindless globalisation and its impact on world population and the endless talk of war on terror are converting the whole world into a univocal one. All these underscore the need for giving voice to the voiceless.

There are some other reasons as well. They concern the socio-economic and cultural changes in societies all over the world. One of the most crucial is the pace of modern life and resultant absence of communicative interaction among people. Speed has become the bottom line of contemporary world. Communication and information are the watchwords today. Lure of power, whether political or economic, is the accelerating force of the present-day universe. The entire world appears to be in a great hurry, with precious little time left for people to think about themselves. They have no time to think, much less to speak and more significantly, hardly any to listen. And all this in an era that is described as one of Information and Communication Technology (ICT).

It is this particular setting that merits a health check-up of the democratic world. With failed democracies growing in number, this institution cannot really be effectively promoted. Besides, for long, people have doubted the intentions of those who claim to be promoting democracy. Thankfully, now there appears to be a greater consensus

---

ii) Responsibility iii) Accountability iv) Participation v) Responsiveness (to the needs of the people). All these principles are necessarily a part of democratic governance.

on not confusing 'democracy promotion' with 'regime change' and accepting the use of military force to remove a regime. There is a greater realisation that this approach is counter-productive.

It has been observed that countries swearing by 'democracy promotion' have failed to overcome the credibility deficit. There are several examples of countries talking of promoting democracy, yet giving friendly tyrants some amount of legitimacy. The continuance of this trend not only gives a bad name to the movement for promoting democracy, it also adds to the growing cynicism of people belonging to the socially and economically weaker sections.

For many emerging democracies, whether in sub-Saharan Africa, Latin America or South Asia and elsewhere, the biggest challenge is to institutionalise the newly-chosen multiparty democracy. The next big challenge is to help democracy deliver in terms of reducing poverty and improving the quality of life. This is certainly not easy. However, today there is greater acceptance that security and economic development need to go hand-in-hand with improving governance. Those committed to the cause of democracy need to realise that unless we ensure that democracy makes a difference, its acceptance will always remain fragile and converting it into a deep-rooted confidence in the system will become a tougher challenge.

It is a fact that strengthening institutions that facilitate the expression of democratic demands is extremely important. Introducing elections is an essential ingredient of this process, but that alone is not enough. If this process eventually fails in enhancing governance capacity in managing the delivery of basic public goods and services, it will ultimately end up promoting greater public disenchantment. If this is to be avoided, the democratic community has to come out of complacency. Mobilisations like the Arab Spring are welcome but may not be capable of evolving a robust system of democratic governance.

UNIFIED THEORY

In this context, it is worth examining what noted political scientist

Pippa Norris has presented as the 'unified theory'.[11] This theory predicts 'that the institutions of both liberal democracy and state capacity need to be strengthened parallely for the most effective progress, within the broader enduring fixed constraints posed by structural environments.' Norris's 'unified theory' underscores that regimes reflecting both these dimensions are necessary (although not sufficient) for effective development.

There is a particular pattern in the way dictators of the Middle East, whether they are called kings, presidents, or prime ministers (some of them disguising their authoritarian regime better than others) operate. This pattern involves a two-pronged approach. It involves keeping the wealthy elite in good humour on the one hand, and satisfying the lower classes through providing heavily subsidised, essential commodities on the other. However, while this pattern helps a dictator stick to power, it also makes his position vulnerable. When the country's economy is in a bad shape, the elite expect more than the leader can give. At the same time, the now educated population want jobs, prosperity and a voice in government, which has previously been denied to them. This leads to the end of the legitimacy of the leader and people gather courage to raise the banner of revolt.

The Arab Spring was a surprise for many. The general impression was that the Arab republics were generally doing well. Most of them, even today, are republics in name only. There were houses comprising representatives elected by the people and, at least ostensibly, the governments were run by them. People were fed up of this façade of democracy, as it did not deliver at all. They tolerated the autocrats who were ruling under the garb of a republic, till a point when things became absolutely intolerable.

Democracy being a holistic idea, mere elections or freedom of expression is not enough. With the advancement of information communication technologies, regimes' ability to prevent access to information and block avenues for expression of thoughts has

[11] http://www.hks.harvard.edu/fs/pnorris/Acrobat/WhyDemocraticGovernance/Chapter%201.pdf

become a lot more difficult today. Besides, universally there seems to be an acute insecurity-filled climate and hence, people want to express their pent up feelings somehow. Uprisings in the Arab world, as well as the largely extemporary character of the Anna Hazare-led Lokpal movement in India point to this state of mind of the people in this century.

PERFORMANCE OF DEMOCRACY

Developing sound institutions for facilitating a delivering democracy is fundamental to the idea of an effective one. Political parties, electoral system and parliament are, therefore, the three critical cornerstones of any democratic edifice. The absence of sound institutional development and the resultant poor quality of governance, coupled with muzzling of public opinion, has arguably proved to be the lethal cocktail for overthrowing the established regimes as seen in the Arab Spring.

Both, in the Arab countries as well as in India, young activists have been sharing ideas, tactics and moral support, but they are confronting different opponents and operating within different contexts. Now that the euphoria about the Arab Spring is over, it is high time that efforts for building strong democratic institutions in Tunisia, Egypt, and Libya are taken up by social and political leaders, with all the dexterity at their command. Much has been said about the role and impact of social media in the context of both the Arab Spring and the Lokpal movement. It does have a role, important but also limited. It allows informal association, temporarily overcomes the lack of leadership and enables free flow of information. These help greatly in organising protests, but it must also be remembered that communication can start the process of democracy but it cannot complete it.

CHALLENGES AHEAD

Preventing corruption, arresting economic decline and establishing a rule of law are the three basic challenges in all the Arab Spring countries. Corruption and economic decline have remained common obstacles in the path of successful new democracies. While these factors added to the popular scepticism about democracy in Latin America, in Russia they seriously undermined the country's democratic experiment during the Boris Yeltsin presidency.

If the challenge in the Arab world is of building institutions, in India, it is that of preventing their collapse and revitalising them.

Pippa Norris[12] presents a brilliant analysis of similar conditions which is worth understanding. She says, '...development is most effective where regimes combine the qualities of democratic responsiveness and state effectiveness'. According to her, regardless of whatever the theory suggests, in practice, liberal democracies often prove imperfect on the count of accountability and good governance related procedures, 'particularly where party competition is limited, electoral systems are manipulated, or channels of participation are skewed towards money votes over people votes'. Norris further argues that, 'The institutions in liberal democracy can limit the abuse of power, but curbing Leviathan does not ensure that leaders will necessarily have the capability to implement effective public policies addressing social needs'. Norris also points out that, 'Moreover the initial move from autocracy, and the rhetorical promises commonly made by leaders during transitional elections, often encourages rising expectations among ordinary citizens. If these cannot be met by elected officials, due to limited state capacity, this can be a recipe for frustration'.[13]

Learnings for India

What Pippa Norris has said is significant in the context of India. Venomous statements from civil society leaders like Arvind Kejriwal will always come under flak, and perhaps rightly. However, how exactly we, as a nation, are going to meet the questions that are posed by the situation, continues to be a big challenge. The ever-widening gap between the electors and the elected is an indication of how grave the situation is. When we have 78 per cent of Lok Sabha members today winning the elections, despite the fact that 50 per cent

[12] http://www.hks.harvard.edu/fs/pnorris/Acrobat/WhyDemocraticGovernance
[13] *Ibid p 15*

of the voters in their respective constituencies have voted against them, the legitimacy of representative democracy itself has come to be questioned. Should such a state of affairs continue for long, we will have neither good governance nor genuine democracy.

While describing the huge popular response to the Lokpal movement, the media had compared the Jantar Mantar in Delhi to the Tahrir Square. Comparisons like these have limited meaning. But, like those spearheading the Tahrir Square upsurge, the Lokpal movement also lost its way and failed to unveil a larger agenda for political and institutional reforms for an effective democracy. Due to this, people now have a new set of reasons to be more cynical about the system. The only conclusion that one can draw is: Strong visionary leadership with organisational skills and strategic thinking is in short supply both on the banks of the Nile and the Yamuna.

CHAPTER 2

Parties: The Forgotten *Karta* of Democracy

When was the last time you thought about political parties in India? Can you recall an occasion when you thought of parties as democratic institutions? Have political parties become whipping boys? Have we stopped thinking about them, their unabated indulgence in populism and its impact on polity, governance and society at large? Can all this be prevented? But do we really need to prevent it?

The quest for answers to all the above questions leads us to the role of political parties in a democratic system and no word other than *karta*[1] can effectively describe it. *Karta* is a Sanskrit term, underscoring the importance of a responsible leader who is also a proactive doer. On the one hand, there is abject ineptness of the political parties in providing organisational and executive leadership

[1]In Hindu law, the joint family has always been considered to be a patriarchal organisation in which the most senior male ascendant is revered as the elder of the family or *karta* or manager. According to these laws, some of the functions that are carried out by a *karta* are: Takes decisions for the welfare of the family, acts on behalf of the family regarding all important matters. (Reference: http://www.lawisgreek.com/karta-in-hindu-law).

that can demonstrably establish that it can transform this situation. On the other, there is a stark realisation about the failure of the present system of representative democracy in delivering at the ground level. Both these factors constitute the greater challenge of finding systemic solutions in order to make democracy give results.

In India, there are many who rightly believe that given the diversity of languages, socio-economic factors and belief systems, imposing dictatorship here is next to impossible. Neither can a political leader do it easily nor is a military coup possible. But then, difficulties in imposing dictatorship need not be seen as a guarantee of popular faith in democracy. Besides, when internalisation of democratic values in public affairs, and thereafter, its reflection in operational democracy is yet to be accomplished, India can ill afford the growing skepticism about democracy. The way to prevent this from happening goes via reforming democratic institutions in India. Of all these, priority needs to be accorded to reforming political parties.

Having seen almost all the available political parties forming government, Indians are now wondering about the next alternative they can look at. It was certainly not for no reason that when Shiv Sena supremo Bal Thackeray[2] used to advocate the necessity to switch over to *Thok Shahi* (dictatorship) in place of *Lok Shahi* (democracy), people would unmistakably applaud and respond very approvingly. This, undoubtedly, does not augur well for democracy in India. All this calls for an in-depth analysis of the way democracy is being practised in India while probing into the factors that have caused the degeneration of democratic institutions, mainly political parties. Exploring what kind of systemic changes can serve to reform

---

[2]Bal Thackeray was the founder-supreme leader of the Shiv Sena. The Shiv Sena is one of the main political parties in Maharashtra. Started as a party that staunchly advocated the sons-of-soil theory, the Shiv Sena is also known for its radical-sounding views and the out-of-box thinking of its leadership. The Shiv Sena had not opposed the Emergency of 1975 and Thackeray repeatedly and publicly expressed his disenchantment with democracy and preference for some kind of a benevolent dictatorship.

political parties in India, thereby further consolidating democracy, follows thereafter.

The discussion here is about systemic solutions for freeing political parties from the grip of populism and electoral compulsions. Although the state of representative democracy and the trends in party politics, as well as electoral mechanisms in established democracies is at the background, the focus necessarily is India. Sadly, the state of political parties in the country and its impact on the quality of representative democracy does not seem to be getting due attention. Even highly reputed academic journals like the *Journal of Democracy*,[3] while reviewing the achievements of and challenges before what it describes as India's 'unlikely democracy' in its sixth decade, do devote full-length essays on issues and institutions like economy, civil society and judiciary, but omit political parties.

Unfortunately, there appears to be a serious dearth of substantive work on parties in India. Besides the works of Rajni Kothari and a few others, precious little is available from established researchers and political scientists. Arun Shourie's *The Parliamentary System* successfully brings to the fore, a whole gamut of issues causing concern about our polity. However, issues like parties and their state of affairs as well as effective solutions to the multidimensional crisis are missing.

Why this Study?

The nature of this study is certainly not entirely theoretical. In a way, this is a practitioner's evaluation study. Nagging questions about the degeneration of parties, inertia on the part of party leadership to prevent this decay, the overall atmosphere of ignorance, apathy and lack of initiative for reforms are reasons serious enough to make any thinking citizen of India restless.

I must say that I was privileged to be able to observe various functional aspects of democracy in India due to the diverse opportunities that I had during the last thirty years of active public life.

---

[3] *Journal of Democracy*, April 2007 Vol. 18, No 2.

Initially as a student activist, later as a journalist and thereafter, both as an institutional head and a party functionary, I could gather enough experiential data to make some general observations.

Interaction with key functionaries and grass roots level activists of major political parties helped me cross-check my observations. I was saddened by the realisation that many in politics are aware of the perversions that have crept into India's political system but, to put it bluntly, they have apparently either chosen to ignore these threats and compromise with the situation, albeit unwillingly, or have surrendered to the circumstances helplessly. Some of them also seem to have abandoned efforts to transform the situation. The third, and the most bizarre possibility is that they have decided to make the most of this situation since changing the system, according to them, is just not possible.

However, instead of stating these observations in conclusive terms, I have considered them as an agenda for probing into certain aspects of functional democracy in India. The enquiry into some of these issues starts with a set of questions, 'Are political parties in India really in the grip of populist politics? Have they become—may be wanton—victims of electoral compulsions? Are political parties as democratic institutions in the country declining?'

It is also imperative that we look into the impact of such perceived decline of parties, on their ability to deliver as part of democratic governance. Also, has this decline affected popular faith in democracy? In the process it would also be interesting to understand as to why people in India have a peculiar kind of love-hate relationship with politicians. Is the popular mindset governing this relationship a cause, or is it a consequence of 'politics of patronage' that has given a fillip to populism?

Once we reach considerably close to the answers to these questions, it would be worthwhile to understand as to whether political parties in India could be saved from succumbing to populist pressures and electoral compulsions. And obviously, the million dollar question: Would the political class accept such solutions? Finally, the probe also should include as to why no significant efforts are being made to salvage political parties and party politics in India from its present mould. Is this lack of action a result of apathy, or helplessness, or both?

The overall inertia leading to a collective refusal to address these issues has resulted in a peculiar situation. Every Indian takes pride in describing his or her country as the world's largest democracy, and hence, rubbishes the thought of any better alternative to it. But, at the same time, s/he cannot escape from a feeling that democracy has done precious little to raise the quality of his/her day-to-day life.

True, India is the largest democracy and when several other countries disappoint the international community with their cronyism, autocracy or internal conspiracies, India continues to be appreciated for having stayed largely true to the spirit of democracy. It cannot be disputed that, 'Almost no other country that attained Independence in the post-Second World war wave of decolonisation has managed continuously to hold free and fair elections, protect and augment fundamental rights, and maintain civilian control of the military.'[4] Many, both within India and outside, are easily impressed by the fact that elections are regularly held in the country and voters turn out in large numbers and often they vote passionately to ensure a change in government. Seen in the backdrop of the fact that this is happening in a nation which is surrounded by allegedly 'failed states' like Pakistan, Afghanistan, Burma, Bangladesh and Nepal, the success of democracy in India becomes more noteworthy. However, beneath this surface, there are factors like widespread corruption, sycophancy and populism. A 2011 Transparency International[5] survey had ranked politicians and police as the two most corrupt institutions in India. Sycophancy has encouraged nepotism and criminalisation of party politics. The fact that India remains perpetually in an election mode, hence under populist pressures, leaves little room for an honest debate. All this partly explains the biggest shortcoming of

---

[4]Rob Jenkins, 'Civil Society Versus corruption', *Journal of Democracy*, April 2007, Vol. 18, No. 2.
[5]As reported in *Business Standard* of 24 December 2011.

Indian democracy, which is its failure in securing better governance, genuine and visible development and a collectivist vision of society, resulting in a highly fragmented social order.

The 'largest democracy' and 'ancient civilisation' tags have also given rise to a dichotomy of sorts where an individual appears to believe that apart from taking pride, he has almost no responsibility towards sustaining this democracy. In this situation, while a citizen relishes political gossip, generally does not mind abiding by the law or standing up when the national anthem is being played in movie halls and queuing up to vote, hardly realising that sustaining democracy demands much more. An abysmal neglect of citizenship training, right at the school level, has greatly contributed in creating an impression—deep and widespread—that democracy is only 'for the people' and not 'by the people'.

This lack of awareness about the duties of and expectations from a citizen has added to the chasm between popular expectations and the performance of India's functional democracy. While Indian stock markets are witnessing a continuous boom and an enviable growth rate has become a reality, every Indian shares the dream of becoming a superpower within a decade or two. Leaders like former President APJ Abdul Kalam have successfully shaped the national mood of 'we-can-do-it'. The moot question, however, is how to do away with the mismatch between the ground realities and the upbeat mood of 'making India a superpower'.

Democracy has offered several devices to the citizenry to use them and better the quality of their own lives. Consumer rights, human rights, and Right to Information are some of the few precious tools bestowed by democracy. However, unenlightened and unenthusiastic citizens seem to have almost negated the impact of these tools. A feudal mindset, where independent thinking is far from a habit, has added to the overall challenge. Consequently, certain notions about our democracy have taken deep roots in popular minds and unless people get rid of them, the situation cannot change. Some of these key notions are as follows:

- The present system compels a politician to be corrupt.

- If politicians are performing, their making illicit money could be condoned.
- Government, and thereby the elected representatives, are the *mai-baap* (parent-like) of the people and hence they have to do everything that is expected from them.
- Since elected representatives, and hence all politicians, are *mai-baap*, it is legitimate that they are allowed to enjoy some extra-constitutional privileges.
- Politicians can, and have to, help commoners get some illegal things regularised. There is nothing great if a politician helps in a perfectly legal work.

As observed by noted political scientist and author, Sumit Ganguly:

> ...as India approaches its sixtieth year as an independent democratic state, there is little question about the endurance of its democratic institutions and practices. The relevant questions facing both scholars and activists touch instead on the quality of India's democracy. Will the country's leaders and citizens be able to improve the efficacy of key institutions, cope with the social challenges (that) the rising inequality is generating, and sustain the secular ethos that undergirds the democratic order?[6]

While those belonging to the established leadership, both in the field as well as in academia, are also searching for answers to most of these questions, I thought that the least I could do was to try and give some impetus to the discussion about systemic solutions to this crisis. This particular background has also shaped the purpose of this study.

Attempts to bring about reforms can succeed only when there

---

[6]Sumit Ganguly, 'India's Unlikely Democracy: Six Decades of Independence' in *Journal of Democracy*, April 2007 Vol. 18, No. 2 p. 30-40.

is a yearning from within. It is a common experience that politicians, who are concerned about the quality of democracy, commit themselves to strive for it and publicly declare their intention to do so, immediately after they get elected. However, after some time, it is observed that they just forget their resolve expressed earlier for several reasons. Many of them are not serious while making promises and hence they forget. Several others, with more honest intentions, realise that the task of introducing reforms is easier said than done. This hampers their enthusiasm and later they just abandon the cause. When this happens again and again, some of the politicians also realise that continuing with the status quo, in fact, serves their own interest and hence, they refrain from even talking about reforms.

Many leaders like Lalu Prasad Yadav and others, who were at the forefront of Jayaprakash Narayan (JP)'s movement in 1974 and had declared their pledge to the cause of total reforms, seem to have no concern for political reforms. Many believe that several student leaders of those days appear to have lost any moral authority to even talk about total reforms today, let alone do anything concrete in that regard. Obviously, they have, at least apparently, developed a vested interest in the continuation of this system as it is.

Till recently, when student council elections in universities and colleges in India were regularly held all over the country, student leaders used to indulge in all kinds of electoral malpractices. 'We are doing wrong things simply to attain power and later would change this situation drastically so as to cleanse the present electoral process and make it free of malpractice', used to be the stock argument, only to be forgotten once power was attained.

Interestingly, the Supreme Court demonstrated great sensitivity towards malpractices in student council elections and had even appointed a committee[7] under the leadership of JM Lyngdoh, former Chief Election Commissioner of India, to recommend

[7]The JM Lyngdoh committee was set up by the Ministry of Human Resources Development, GoI, as per the direction of the honourable Supreme Court of India to frame guidelines on students' union elections in colleges/universities on 4 January, 2006 and the same submitted its report on 23 May, 2006.

reforms in them. Ironically, one of the recommendations of this committee was:

> All institutions must conduct a review of the student representation mechanism. The first review may be conducted after a period of two years of the implementation of the mechanism detailed above, and the second review may be conducted after the third or the fourth year of implementation. The primary objective of these reviews will be to ascertain the success of the representation and election mechanism in each individual institution, so as to decide whether or not to implement a full-fledged election structure.

While systems for university elections are being compared and their merit-demerit analysed, for general elections no such exercise has ever been seriously thought of.

The Central Government has chosen to continue to ignore several strong recommendations of the Election Commission on a number of vital issues concerning the general elections.[8]

CHANGING PROFILES OF POLITICAL PARTIES

Increasingly, people under many democratic regimes, including India, are getting more and more frustrated with democratic governance in general and political parties in particular. They believe that no party can really solve their problems and make their lives more comfortable. In response to this observation, political parties

---

[8]The Election Commission of India has been regularly addressing the government in the last six years on different subjects requiring reform. In its communication to the Prime Minister dated 5 July 2004, the Commission sent a total of twenty-two recommendations. According to the Election Commission's web site, between 2004 and 2011, it has written at least nine letters to the Central Government on this issue. However, it seems that till December 2011, the government had not formulated its opinion and moved in the direction of implementing any of these recommendations.

say that they cannot help the situation because they are the victims of the present-day system. Their political behaviour is conditioned by the system in which they are operating. Governance itself is fast becoming difficult with populist and electoral compulsions proving to be the singular most important factor responsible for repeated failures. In such a scenario, the danger of people losing faith in democracy becomes all the more pronounced. What is required, therefore, is that some systemic solutions are explored to help the political parties perform well and thereby become worthy of positive popular support.

It would be interesting to enlist the key aspects of the changing character of political parties, reflecting the overall impact of populism and electoral compulsions. Although the focus of this analysis is political parties in India, the situation in other democracies is not too different.

We often come across instances indicating a diminishing role of idealism and ideology in the functioning of political parties. This is known as the phenomenon of politics sans purpose. As a consequence, people no longer believe that politicians pursue politics for some great cause. A logical corollary of this is the widespread impression that 'all parties are the same'. With power-seeking becoming a great leveller, most parties end up giving an impression that there is little that distinguishes them from the others. Except a few non-dynastic parties, the organisational character of political parties in India is weakening fast and absolutely no significant efforts are being taken for cadre-building. Populism has also taken a toll on the leadership. It has paved way for compromises, heralding an erosion of the moral authority of the party leadership. To counter this trend, personality cults are promoted, overtly or covertly. As a consequence, charismatic leaders dominate and those working behind the scene face marginalisation.

Another important factor is the perennial electoral mode of political parties. With ideology being pushed to the periphery, unprincipled coalitions have become routine. This has contributed to the atmosphere of permanent election mode, adding to the tendency of politicising all and sundry, with a view to taking political advantage at any opportune time.

The sum total of the impact of all these factors is the diminishing popular participation in the democratic process. Political parties are increasingly losing their distinctive characteristics. This particular phenomenon is being observed in democracies all over the world. Bruno Waterfield, Brussels correspondent of *The Daily Telegraph*, completely dismisses the notion that political parties in Britain and the West offer any competing alternatives. According to him, they are all careerists, an empty cadre of more or less Left-leaning elite manager-politicians.

In one of his hard-hitting articles, Waterfield says,

> Cameron and Clegg could be interchanged, they are identikit managers for a cut-and-paste age without politics. But remember, this anti-political age does not mean the end of choices, such as the Iraq war, bank bailouts or austerity. It represents the expulsion of alternative points of view, and the public, from the arena. This new British government shows us (yet again) that the starting point for those of us with ideals, those of us who want politics to be contests between alternative ideas, must work outside unrepresentative political parties, parliaments, state institutions and, Clegg's training ground, the EU.[9]

Increasing similarities in political parties make voters realise that the emerging situation eventually denies them the element of choice. This adversely affects the level of popular participation in elections and, thereby, in the overall democratic process.

In addition to these macro-level issues concerning the quality of party competition and representative democracy, other key factors are also responsible for the degeneration of

---

[9] As quoted at the blog http://democracyreform.blogspot.no/2010/05/those-following-news-these-days-cannot.html.

political parties. Generally speaking, these factors could be described as the organisational impact of excessively election-oriented party politics in India. There are at least four major factors which are identified under this category. Firstly, it is the 'image' that has now occupied centre stage in politics. Therefore, there is now a growing tendency to always 'play to the gallery' with excessive insistence on image-building, publicity mileage and the need to remain in the limelight. As a result, political parties are not inclined to educate the masses. With no courage of conviction, parties avoid unconventional, bold/unpopular-sounding decisions.

The element of technique also plays a decisive role in electoral success. Growing dominance of money and muscle power, professionally-managed press publicity and public relations, tendency to exploit social backgrounds and mastering the art of keeping party bosses in good humour have all made electoral victories more of a matter of technique. Psephology and the minutest analysis of demographic profiles to evolve various strategies so as to deal with diverse and fragmented electorates is the most recent technique that several political parties seem to be increasingly employing.

Additionally, the nature of party-people interface has undergone drastic changes. Professionally-managed parties leave little scope for volunteers to spare some time for party work. This has adversely affected the nature of party-people interface. Professional approach in party management has also altered the nature of inter-party relationship. At certain times, it involves fierce hate-mongering whereas on other occasions, it just remains make-believe, with an element of match-fixing. Popular belief, that all politicians are hand-in-glove in reality, has added to the increasing tendency of intense dislike or hate towards the entire political class.

Lastly, erosion in the quality of governance has become omnipresent. There are two distinct aspects of this impact. Lack of ideological motivation has a cascading effect on the policy formulation processes, leading to a dearth of political will for governing with a particular set of principles. With compromises for continuing in power becoming the order of the day, marked aberration in the quality of governance seems to have become inevitable. Secondly, the quality of leadership too is deteriorating. An individual's ability to get elected (electability) is taking precedence over all other factors, leading to a quality deficit in the political leadership.

CHANGING THE MOULD OF POLITICS

The quest is primarily for a system that will ensure a greater amount of political stability, with a certainty about the schedule of elections. One also has to look for a system that will substantially reduce the element of 'technique' from the electoral exercise, thereby diluting the scope for vote bank politics. Ultimately, if populism is to be eradicated, we require a system that will help the political leadership perform without excessively bothering about the popular reaction—a set-up that would encourage parties to take courageous decisions.

Only parties and political leadership capable of looking beyond electoral successes can show the courage required for taking bold decisions. Again, if people are to be educated and enlightened, so that they can accept unpopular but right, and hence, courageous decisions, parties need to have well-oiled organisational systems, run by motivated rank and file. To that end, the system also must have an inherent mechanism to bring at least a semblance of order to the functioning of political parties, with the help of rules and regulations for their organisational affairs, ensuring intra-party democracy and transparency in financial affairs. Should a system ensuring all this be in place, the resultant climate would naturally make parties more confident about the electoral outcome. Eventually, this may restrain them from taking up emotional issues to influence the masses.

To cut the long story short, what is required is a system that is capable of limiting the influence of populism as well as electoral compulsions and eventually, lessen the dependence of political parties on them. Evolving a completely populism-free political system may sound like an unachievable objective. However, unless one aims high, even walking halfway would seem difficult. Populism is like an addiction that afflicts the health of democracy. It gives short-lived pleasure but also brings long-lasting sorrows. De-addiction is always very hard, but equally essential. Unless this is taken up urgently, it will start eating into the vitals of the democratic polity. There are instances which prove that it is not only political parties, but parliament and media too come under the undesirable influence of public opinion. In India today, the pressure of political correctness is synonymous with populism. It is so all-pervasive that one may not even realise that the executive and, at times, even the judiciary may come under its sinister influence. To try to bring reforms remains the only way for all those who consider democracy a priceless human value.

Status-quo-ism is the principal enemy of any process of reform. It offers a false sense of security. Common people may like to enjoy themselves just for today and ignore potential problems for as long as they can, but how can enlightened sections of society support the status quo and allow issues of populism, political opportunism and misgovernance to pile up until they become almost unmanageable? The responsibility of creating a strong public opinion in favour of reforms undoubtedly is on those who are aware of the perils of continuing with the established system.

When strong public opinion is created, favouring reforms, maybe a day will come when the sleeping *karta* of representative democracy—the political parties—will respond to that positive populist pressure by opening the doors for reforms. And when parties in India adopt reforms, the resurgence of this great nation will not be far behind.

CHAPTER 3

Political Culture in India

It is beyond doubt that for all those who are concerned about democracy, thinking about the state of political parties is a must. But parties do not function in isolation and the conditions in which they work have to be considered. These conditions, among others, primarily include the electoral systems. Further, it is interesting to find the discerning thread of interconnectivity between various factors. Understandably, this interconnection finds its reflection in the contemporary political culture in India.

Choice as the Core of Democracy

Democracy stands for the freedom to choose and to exert this freedom, political parties are essential. Understandably, the importance of open competition figures prominently in some of the attempts to define democracy. Eminent Finnish political scientist Tatu Vanhanen says:

> ...in modern societies, democracy means that people and groups of people are free to compete for power and that power holders are elected by the people and responsible to the people. As a consequence of free competition, political

> power is assumed to be widely distributed among various groups in democracy.[1]

Another renowned political scientist and theorist, Joseph Schumpeter, has also focussed on this competitive struggle, through his 'another theory of democracy'. According to him, democracy is an institutional arrangement to take political decisions. In this set-up, an individual gains power to decide because of a competitive struggle for people's vote.

In the procedural definition of democracy, Samuel Huntington says:

> ...a twentieth-century political system [that is] as democratic to the extent that its most powerful collective decision-makers are selected through fair, honest and periodic elections in which candidates freely compete for votes and in which virtually all adult population is eligible to vote. It also implies the existence of those civil and political freedoms to speak, publish, assemble, and organise that are necessary to political debate and the conduct of electoral campaigns.[2]

REPRESENTATIVE DEMOCRACY

With a built-in mechanism for exerting the element of choice, so very critical for democracy, representative democracy has emerged as functionally the most suitable and hence, popular form of democracy. As against this, direct democracy, which is favoured by neither politicians nor political philosophers, was considered by Schumpeter and many others as 'incompatible with responsible government'.[3] However, regardless of this fact, representation as a concept continues to be debatable. To represent means, 'to be accredited

---

[1] As quoted at http://www.nipissingu.ca/department/history/muhlberger/histdem/vanhanen.htm.

[2] Samuel P Huntington, *The Third Wave. Democratization in the Late Twentieth Century* p.7

[3] Ian McLean, (Ed.) *The Concise Oxford Dictionary of Politics* p.131

deputy or substitute for...in a legislative or deliberative assembly, to be a member of parliament for...'.[4] Different theorists have, however, interpreted this concept differently. According to John Adams, '...the legislature should be an exact portrait, in miniature, of the people at large, as it should think, feel, reason and act like them.'[5]

At the core of this particular interpretation remains the principal-agent conception, implying a situation where a particular person is authorised to act on behalf of the other/s. But here also, since the agent is acting in the overall interest of the principal, there is always some scope for the agent to apply his/her judgment.

Representatives are also looked upon as microcosms. This naturally involves a conflict because, if elected representatives decide to act as microcosms, they may not essentially be able to serve the electorate. In this entire debate about representation, it is important that a politician strikes a balance between abiding by an overwhelming popular view and going by his own judgment after reviewing the opinion of the electors.

James Madison, one of the principal architects of the American Constitution, distinguished between 'a pure democracy' which is 'a society consisting of a small number of citizens who assemble and administer the government in person'[6] and a 'republic' meaning 'a government in which a scheme of representation takes place'.[7] Since this distinction had no historic reference, it must be mainly seen as an interpretation of the Greek term 'democracy' and the Latin term 'republic'.

However, even before Madison, John Locke had analysed the limitations of representative democracy. It is in his *Second Treatise* that he has set forth his theory of natural law and natural rights. With Locke, the discussion about the strength, limitations and enormity of legislative power, as well as the concept of individual

---

[4] *ibid* p. 427-428.
[5] *ibid*
[6] Robert A Dahl. *On Democracy*'p.16
[7] *ibid* p.16

liberty and freedom graduated to a new and more serious level. To Locke, the concept of government power:

> 'is not, nor can it possibly be, absolutely arbitrary over the lives and fortunes of the people. For it being but the joint power of every member of the society given up to the legislative assembly, the power vested in the assembly can be no greater than that which the people had in a State of Nature before they entered into, and gave it up to the community. For nobody can transfer, to another, more power than he possesses himself, and nobody has an absolute arbitrary power over any other, to destroy, or take away, the life or property of another'[8].

He further argues that the power of our legislators:

> 'is limited to the public good of the society. It is a power that hath no other end but preservation, and therefore can never have a right to destroy, enslave, or designedly to impoverish the subjects. To this end it is that men give up all their natural power to the society they enter into, and the community put the legislative power into such hands as they think fit, with this trust, that they shall be governed by declared laws, or else their peace, quiet, and property will still be at the same uncertainty as it was in the state of Nature.'[9]

Although democracy is government by the people, since every individual cannot be heard, a system of representation becomes a must. This system of representation is mainly for the expression of popular will. And it is here that we come across a grey area with a long series of questions. Who are the custodians of the 'Will of the People' and why? Do people's representatives, in true sense of the term, genuinely represent popular voice? What are the factors

---

[8] *Second Treatise*, Chapter 11at http://www.blupete.com/Literature/Biographies/Philosophy/Locke.htm as on 11 January, 2006.
[9] *ibid*

that can measure the authenticity of popular opinion? The range of notions here is very wide.

On the one hand, we have Rousseau, who was averse to the notion of representation. He believed in the concept of 'election without representation'.[10] His democracy, 'elects magistrates but does not give them the chrism of representatives.'[11] According to Sartori, Rousseau had rightly envisaged the dangers inherent in the representative character of democracy, because, 'as soon as we permit the exercise of power to be transferred to representatives, the parliament becomes sovereign. And in this case, power can again slip out of the hands of its nominal holder (i.e. the people), with popular sovereignty becoming an abstract titular right that can sanction any form of slavery.'[12]

On the other, we have an equally strong argument advocating the 'independence of opinion' of a representative of people. In Edmund Burke's famous speech at Bristol, from where he was elected in 1774, while he did put 'great weight' on the wishes of his constituency and accord their opinions 'high respect'[13], he refused to be instructed by 'them', but only by reason and conscience of himself. Theorising this, he said, 'Your representative owes you, not his industry only, but his judgment and he betrays you instead of serving you, if he sacrifices it to your opinion.'[14]

Parties are Inevitable

Political parties, as institutions, provide the requisite elbow room for an individual to go by his judgment, simultaneously ensuring that the representative is accountable to his electorate. True, an individual can legitimately contest an election on his own and seek mandate. However, it is hard to imagine a government run by elected representatives, all

---

[10] Giovanni Sartori, *Democratic Theory* p.254 (Quoted from '*Politics and the English Language*' in Selected Essays p.23)

[11] *ibid* p.23

[12] *ibid*.p.90

[13] Edmund Burke, speech to the Electors of Bristol, 3 November, 1774 at http://en.wikipedia.org/wiki/Edmund_Burke as on 12 May, 2006.

[14] *ibid*

of whom have won elections as independent individuals. Democratic governance pre-supposes minimum collectivism and it is here that the role of political parties comes into play.

Recruitment of individuals in politics is one of the most essential functions that parties perform. Joining a political party still remains the best and effective option for any one deciding to play an active role at the implementation level in a democracy. With party-affiliated candidates, cultivation of a principal-agent relationship is likely to be served more effectively, making it much easier to hold the elected representative accountable. Competitive indulgence in partisan politics and its horrendous consequences prompted some Indian leaders like Jayaprakash Narayan (JP) call for promoting a party-less democracy. JP, in his 'A Plea for Reconstruction of the Indian Polity', says, 'party rivalries give birth to demagoguery, depress political ethics, put a premium on unscrupulousness and aptitude for manipulation and intrigue'. He further argues that, 'Parties often put party interests over the national interests. Because the centralisation of power prevents the citizen from participating in government, the parties, that is to say, small caucuses of politicians, rule in the name of the people and create the illusion of democracy and self-government.'[15]

If parties are considered to be responsible for the degeneration of our polity, then they also play an equally crucial role in finding solutions to the crises. The success of representative democracy mainly hinges upon political parties since they constitute its most significant vehicle. It is simply because in any democracy, where the number of electorate runs into several millions, what is always required is a 'linkage' institution that 'organises, distils and translates' public opinion.[16] Over the years it has been fairly established that the party system has become a vehicle for aggregating the preferences of the masses for political leadership and thereby converting what is diffuse to specifics, facilitating a fairly sound decision-making process.

[15] As quoted in Peter Renold deSouza and E. Sridharan, (Ed) *India's Political Parties* p.26-27.

[16] Everett Carl Ladd, *Where Have All the Voters Gone*? p. xxi

When political parties allegedly fail in doing their job properly, two significant aspects of representative democracy—popular control and responsiveness—are bound to suffer.

Not very long ago, in 1975, the British Parliament had appointed a committee headed by Lord Houghton to look into the larger question of managing political parties. The Houghton Committee observed that political parties are an essential feature of parliamentary democracy because of three important reasons, as they are:

> ...the agencies through which the electorate can express its collective will; they provide an orderly framework within which political leaders can emerge, develop and strive for political office; they provide the means whereby the members of the general public are able to participate in the formulation of policies[17]

One additional function should be added to the Houghton list, which is that parties help organise discontent and disappointment. Politics is not solely about electoral victories. It is primarily a tool for larger social participation as also a forum for the people to give voice to their discontent. It is this discontentment of the ever-aspiring people that helps parties sustain themselves.

A NEGLECTED INSTITUTION

Political parties are crucial for long-term political development in emerging democracies. In spite of this, for many years, they have been continuously neglected.

Unfortunately, the image of parties all over the world is, in several cases, worse than what they actually are. In both established as well as new and emerging democracies, they are often held in low esteem. In several democracies, party functionaries are seen as people pursuing their own interests rather than those of the people they seek to represent. This low esteem has its roots in several factors.

[17]For details, see http://www.worldcat.org/wcpa/servlet/org.oclc.lac.ui.DialABookServlet?oclcnum=473839462.

Describing the present-day scenario, American political scientist Howard Reiter (University of Connecticut), observes that political parties (today) are 'less determinative of the attitudes and behaviour of political actors on both the mass and elite levels, less highly regarded and less likely to inspire the electoral act than they once were...'[18] This scenario is common to major democracies. Declining relevance and impact of political parties has resulted in the absence of an agency mediating between citizens and the state. If parties cease to operate as an effective link, what or who can politically direct, control and moderate the ever-growing mutual involvement between the state and society?

Since ideologies do not appear to be relevant any more, ideological distinction between parties is vanishing. As a result, there appears to be a near total similarity in the policies and programmes of parties in all the major democracies, adding to the gravity of the crisis. This is mainly because parties are supposed to address the existing socio-economic cleavages and manifest their different approaches towards striving to remove them in political terms. Unfortunately, in reality, partisan politics in India as well as in other democracies today appears to be thriving on these socio-economic divisions and hence, the customary talk about removing them lacks conviction and credibility. This element of artificiality has proved to be a great leveller. Therefore, people in democratic countries more often than not see no great difference among available parties.

In India too, the scenario is similar. Post 1977, the nation has experienced regimes under practically every political formation and people in the country have realised both the difference between them or the lack of it. Understandably, for several years, the BJP, the principal opposition party today, focussed upon its once-distinct organisational and ideological profile by describing itself with the slogan 'a party with a difference'. This phrase could catch the imagination of the people until the BJP came to power at the Centre in 1998. Later, its impact remained only in certain areas like nuclear

[18] As quoted by Paul D Webb in 'Are British Political Parties in Decline?' in *Party Politics* Vol.1 No.3, July 1995, p.300.

policy, infrastructure development and creation of independent ministries like DONER (Department of North-East Region), Tribal Welfare, where the BJP-led NDA government had walked a path different from the previous governments. This distinctness still remains something of a 'unique selling proposition' (USP) in any electoral battle and BJP understandably tries to take its advantage.[19]

In any democracy, with both the political formations which are available as a choice, speaking the same language, taking up the same issues, pursuing the same policies and shaping the same kind of political culture with almost exactly the same style of functioning—whether in the government or in opposition—the electorate is bound to feel that the alternative at hand is almost negated. Option is central to the idea of democracy and in a situation like this, the electorate is effectively deprived of it. Obviously, people can have an element of choice only in a competitive situation. For competition, what is necessary is not just a reasonably even balance among contending parties, but also a feeling in the electorate that the array of political parties do provide them with a meaningful choice. It is also required that the distinctions between the parties on count of the policy positions and organisational profiles are genuine.

Terming political parties as 'empty vessels', *The Economist*[20] had pointed out in 1999 that 'it is not only voters who are turned off. Party membership is falling too and even the most strenuous attempts to reverse the decline have faltered.' Further, popular indifference, leading to non-participation, can also be partly explained by the phenomenon of 'confidence gap' between citizens and their elected representatives as observed by Lipset and Schneider.[21] Ineffective performance on the part of the elected representative, resulting in disillusion and distrust, has in many countries, led to an outright rejection of politics followed by a surge of what Sartori describes as 'anti-politics'.[22] Lately, politics has also acquired a bad name mainly

[19]*Tasks Ahead*, a discussion paper of BJP refers to this uniqueness of the party. The document can be accessed at http://www.bjp.org/Press/Tasks_Ahead.htm.
[20]'Empty Vessels' in *The Economist*, London. 24 July, 1999.
[21]Giovanni Sartori, *Comparative Constitutional Engineering* p. 145.
[22]*ibid*

due to political corruption, since greed and corruption (in politics) have reached unprecedented heights. All over the world a deep-rooted perception has set in the people's mind that politicians never keep time, much less their word. The heavy cost of electioneering makes them indulge in corrupt practices and pursue policies which are perceived as being in their party's short-term electoral interest.

There are several factors at the micro level which explain diminishing popular participation in day-to-day politics. Some of the key aspects include reluctance to take a permanently partisan view, non-conformity with all that a political party stands for, inertia for action-oriented participation and a not-so-articulated 'what will I get (if I participate)?' mindset.

There is another set of reasons concerning the way our political parties are being run. In these one can find the seeds of populist and election-oriented conceptions of party leaders. Most of these factors are both a consequence of, as also the reason for, parties preferring populist politics and buckling under electoral compulsions. The neglect of organisation weakens parties, which promotes the tendency of going populist. Since populism proves to be a shortcut to short-lived electoral success, it further weakens the parties.

Parties and Populism

Most politicians are aware of the implications of this shortcut, but apparently, they have lost the will to come out of this trap. As a consequence, there appears to be a kind of a wave of populist politics that has almost engulfed several new democracies, especially in Africa and Asia.

In societies where cleavages are sharp and of a long standing nature, emergence of a populist leader becomes easier. While in the past, populism was generally seen as a phenomenon beyond the institutional mechanism of democracy, today it is not so. Populism has become one of the hallmarks of partisan politics in several present-day democracies. Senior Canadian communication advisor and political scientist, Vladimir Torres, in one of his papers, defines populism as 'a political problem, with entrenched disregard for democratic institutions, one that leaves a legacy of deteriorated governance and deeply divided societies.'[23] While the origin of the concept of populism can be traced to economic populism, today it is no longer confined to economic policies alone. It also cannot be identified merely with the Left or the New Left. Historically, Latin America has known populist regimes that have shrouded themselves in both left and right wing rhetoric. Understandably then, populism is being practised by, as well as being attacked from, both ends of the political spectrum.

The overall socio-political climate too is responsible for the growth of populist politics across parties. There is tentativeness everywhere and the very structure of societies has become volatile. There is an atmosphere of social and even cultural homelessness. As a consequence, popular interests vary with the change in situations. It also means that people no longer find a political home in parties and hence, they prefer reacting to the situations, to vague moods, and above all, to sentiments.

Concepts like Mass Society[24] are, in fact, diametrically opposite to genuine representative democracy. Ironically however, populism has given a fillip to Mass Society-like conditions where a handful of elites easily take the voters for a ride and assume power by creating an atmosphere of popular interests being safeguarded.

Populism has also remained central to electoral strategies in India. As observed by veteran political commentator Inder Malhotra:

> From the late 1960s, when Indira Gandhi split the Congress by decisively defeating those in her party who thought they could oust her, competitive populism has been one of the baneful features of the Indian politics...consequently, a potentially contentious and perhaps explosive populist measure has already become a part of the political

[23]Vladimir Torres, '*The impact of Populism on Social, Political and Economic Development in the Hemisphere*' at www.focal.ca/pdf/VT_The_Impact_of_Populism.pdf.

[24]http://dictionary.reference.com/browse/mass+society?s=t.

> landscape thanks to the game of one-upmanship between the Congress and the BJP.[25]

Former Chief Economic Adviser to the Government of India, Shankar Acharya, endorses this, saying, 'The arch exponent of populism was Indira Gandhi (her 1966-1977 government) with her *garibi hatao* slogan, kitchen socialism and penchant for legislating government control over economic activities and agents.'[26] Acharya has, in the same article, pointed out that, 'The only effective remedy against the obvious political temptations of populism lies with the country's leadership and their motivation, courage and ability to protect long-term national interests from short-term political opportunism.'

Aggressively promoting an anti-incumbency trend forever and cashing in upon dormant anti-establishment sentiments is also an example of a different kind of populism. Voters in India have been appreciated by many for this established tendency. Promoting anti-incumbency also has its own set of implications. This disposition contributes to the technique-orientation of elections, which does injustice to a well-performing incumbent as it reduces the chances of his re-election. The more worrisome part is, it catapults even an undeserving candidate to a seat of power simply because he is available and seen as an alternative.

Populism and Electoral Compulsions

Populism and electoral compulsions are intertwined. In most cases, populism emanates from electoral compulsions. After the 2004 elections to the Maharashtra assembly, the Shiv Sena changed its strategy and instead of harping upon *Marathi manoos* (Marathi people) tried to appease north Indians in Mumbai who constitute a major chunk of the electorate in the city. Similarly, the Bahujan Samaj Party's (BSP) slogan of *sarva-jan samaj* (society inclusive of all people, all castes) just before the assembly elections of 2007 in Uttar

[25] Inder Malhotra at http://sify.com.

[26] Shankar Acharya, '*Dump populism, let India grow.*' At http://www.rediff.com.

Pradesh, had a necessary connection with the ground realities. Party strategists of both the Shiv Sena and the BSP had realised that, for electoral success, banking upon just one section of society, whether linguistic or social, may not always be enough. These are the examples of how, at times, basic populist standpoints are surrendered before electoral compulsions. Like populism, electoral compulsions also greatly influence the functioning of political parties. Compromises with basic party policies in the name of electoral compulsions dilute ideological purity, thereby disturbing the ideology-driven sections of the party members.

In India, populism makes our major political parties look and function alike. This has discredited them in the eyes of the masses towards whom, ironically, populism is directed. As a consequence, a large section of the voters understandably consider that almost all the parties are unworthy of unstinted support at the national level. With fractured verdicts, parties are forced to adopt coalition politics. In the context of both the major parties in India, the Congress and the BJP, their electoral alliance with regional parties has undoubtedly stunted their growth in the region where they have engineered alliances. Further, their electoral presence has remained limited to constituencies in which they contest since, in a coalition, a party cannot compete with its alliance partner. As a result,

> ...of these electoral compulsions in our First-Past-The Post (FPTP) system, large national parties are forced to play second fiddle in many states. If we take the seven larger states, which account for 310 Lok Sabha seats, this trend is evident. Of these states, in Uttar Pradesh (UP), Bihar, Maharashtra, West Bengal and Tamil Nadu, both Congress and BJP are forced to play second fiddle to the local partners...In fact, among states with over 20 Lok Sabha seats, only Madhya Pradesh (MP), Rajasthan and Gujarat now see BJP and Congress as the two leading political parties. This decline of large national parties is the most significant feature of our political evolution. Our FPTP system accentuates this trend and encourages growth of

> regional parties at the expense of the BJP and the Congress. Slowly, with such political fragmentation, the idea of India is in danger. (sic)[27]

In the Indian scenario, the relationship between the present electoral system and political parties indulging in populist politics for electoral gains is much more evident. With an abundance of regional, linguistic and religious diversity, parties find it convenient to identify more closely with one (or many of the same type) of the discrete groups or communities, and ensure the support of the voters belonging to them. This tendency has come to be known as indulging in vote bank politics. A populist appeal to regional and linguistic identity is the key to Dravidian politics in Tamil Nadu, the Telugu Desam in Andhra Pradesh and the Mizo National Front in Mizoram. Similarly, the capitalisation of the agony and the underdevelopment of Assam by the Asom Gana Parishad in the state, or the slogan of *Marathi manoos* given by the Shiv Sena, and the talk of *Gujarat Gaurav* (pride of Gujarat) by Narendra Modi are some of the examples of using populist regional appeal. Playing on religious identity has always remained central to the politics of the Akali Dal in Punjab and, of course, the Muslim League in Kerala and elsewhere. The Shah Bano[28]

---

[27] Jayprakash Narayan (JN), 'The Idea of India in danger', *The Economic Times*, Mumbai. 21 February, 2003.

[28] The Shah Bano case was a milestone in Muslim women's search for justice and the beginning of the political battle over personal law. A sixty-year-old woman went to court asking maintenance from her husband who had divorced her. The court ruled in her favour. Shah Bano was entitled to maintenance from her ex-husband under Section 125 of the Criminal Procedure Code—with an upper limit of Rs 500 a month—like any other Indian woman. The judgment was not the first granting a divorced Muslim woman maintenance under Section 125. But a voluble orthodoxy deemed the verdict an attack on Islam. The Congress government, panicky in an election year, caved in under the pressure of the orthodoxy. It enacted the Muslim Women (Protection of Rights on Divorce) Act, 1986. This law essentially provided for maintenance for Muslim women outside the criminal code, thus ensuring that Muslim women are not protected under the Constitutional right to equality, and that they no longer have recourse to Section 125 of the Criminal Code. *The Hindu* op-ed page, 10 August 2003.

case of 1987 was a classic example of populist religious politics indulged in by the Congress. The BJP responded to this by making political *Hindutva*[29] its ideological mascot. The BJP and its earlier incarnation, the Jan Sangh, were always known for Hindu-oriented politics but it was only after the Shah Bano case that political *Hindutva* started yielding results. No wonder then, BJP leaders like LK Advani and others could popularise *Hindutva* only after 1987 and terms such as 'minorityism', 'pseudo-secularism', 'minority appeasement' became a part of the BJP lexicon.

ELECTORAL SYSTEMS

Electoral compulsions are closely related to the electoral system. Also, as underscored by the famous Duverger's law,[30] the number of parties in a country and consequently the nature of the electoral competition, depend on the electoral system a country adopts. With the Westminster system of parliamentary democracy being practised in India, including a First Past The Post (FPTP) voting system, many have observed that political parties here perpetually remain in an election mode. At any given point of time, in one part of the nation or the other, parties are always preparing for elections and this greatly impacts upon their style of functioning. Also, the stability of a government depends on the electoral system and if

[29] This is a term used by many, including political commentator Swapan Dasgupta, with a view to describing the politicisation of aggrieved feelings of the majority of Hindus in India. Although, *Hindutva* literally means Hindu-ness, the political connotations of the term vary from person to person. Swapan Dasgupta refers to Advani's description of Hindutva as BJP's 'ideological mascot' in his article 'Whatever happened to Hindutva?' in *The Seminar*, issue 533, January 2004.

[30] Duverger's law is a principle which asserts that a plurality-rule election system tends to favour a stable two-party system. The discovery of this tendency is attributed to Maurice Duverger, a French sociologist who observed the effect and recorded it in several papers published in the 1950 and 1960s. In the course of further research, other political scientists began calling the effect a 'law' or principle. Duverger's law suggests a nexus or synthesis between a party system and an electoral system: a proportional representation (PR) system creates the electoral conditions necessary to foster party development while a plurality system marginalises many smaller political parties.

voters realise that in spite of their participation, elections have been resulting in fractured verdicts, it affects their enthusiasm for voting. Generally speaking, the behaviour of political parties is governed by the electoral system and both these factors have an impact on the quality of democracy.

To sum up, the decline of political parties in major democracies, including India, has resulted in competitive indulgence in populism on the part of parties. Since this has adversely affected the quality of governance, as a consequence it has also made people a lot more sceptical about the effectiveness of democracy. That this scepticism about its efficacy should erupt when it is being seen as the most acceptable form of government, is bound to jeopardise the onward march of democracy.

In India, democracy is considered as fairly deepened. The point is, has it delivered? And the success of democracy not only in India but everywhere hinges upon how effectively it has delivered. It is against this background that one has to diagnose the ailments which are bothering Indian democracy. In this context, it is important to find ways and means of rescuing Indian democracy from the grip of populism and electoral compulsions.

Democracy in India

After over sixty years of India becoming a republic, some new trends are clearly discernible. Following the breakdown of the Congress system, one can see a perceptible shift—the Indian party system has now moved from hegemonic to a competitive multi-party system at the national level. Broadly, three alternatives are emerging, although the durability of these alliances is always uncertain. In the states, an independent party system is emerging and at times and in certain states it is totally different from the national system. In a large number of states, it is Congress+ versus Regional Party+. In some others, it is Congress+ versus BJP+ and in the remaining, it is between two largely regional alternatives.[31] In other words, while the popularity

[31] Jammu and Kashmir, Haryana, Andhra Pradesh, Kerala, West Bengal, Meghalaya, Odisha, Sikkim and Mizoram come in the first category where the polarisation is

of the Congress is declining in some key states like Bihar, Uttar Pradesh and Tamil Nadu, the BJP is still to find an effective foothold in Kerala, and many states in the North East. The absence of the BJP consequently leads to a vacuum which regional parties are able to fill. This has added to the fertility of political ground, resulting in greater political fragmentation. Obviously, this does not augur well for the evolution of a sound two-party system. Another notable trend is that of anti-incumbency, mentioned earlier. While this particular element has reinforced the process of polarisation of the polity, it has also posed an altogether different kind of challenge for representative democracy. With anti-incumbency becoming an established trend, the element of deterrence of the voters' power, which is inherent to electoral politics, is getting weakened for obvious reasons. Those in power indulge in corruption for a huge collection of ill-gotten funds since they believe that any way 'they have to forgo power'. Similarly, those in opposition can afford to remain docile since 'anyway the next turn is theirs'. In the emerging scenario, it is democratic governance that gets a raw deal.

If Congress has to maintain its pan-India supremacy, it has to institutionalise itself in a sound way. The BJP has to emerge as a pan-national alternative while creating a national consensus by removing misgivings and reservations about some of its policies from the minds of the people. All other parties, mainly the Communists, have to concentrate upon expanding their base and appear as a credible third alternative.

In the absence of any serious efforts to meet these challenges, for a large section of the people, democracy has been reduced to just a partisan competition to win formal popular support. As elsewhere in the world, even in India, people have started feeling that democracy has failed to live up to expectations. Several blogs and internet

between Congress and regional alternatives. In Himachal Pradesh, Punjab, Uttarakhand, Rajasthan, Madhya Pradesh, Delhi, Gujarat, Chhattisgarh, Maharashtra, Bihar, Jharkhand and Karnataka it is Congress+ versus BJP+. In states like Tamil Nadu and Uttar Pradesh, it is a fight primarily between two regional party conglomerations.

debates are a testimony to this.[32] The indefinite fast undertaken by veteran social activist Anna Hazare in April 2011 and the response that he could elicit is a pointer to this growing dissatisfaction about the state of democracy in the country. Citizens also feel that, in a way, they are trapped. They can neither abandon democracy nor can they endlessly tolerate whatever is happening in the name of democracy. With constitutional guarantee of fundamental freedoms and rights, so many political parties competing for power through regularly held elections and elected representatives attending legislatures and hitting the headlines whenever politics of pandemonium is religiously played, how can one deny that democracy in India is vibrant and deep-rooted? And yet, to many it appears that democracy in India is lost in technicality and the real spirit has been allowed to evaporate. This has certainly resulted in some kind of frustration on the part of thinkers and opinion-makers.

This disappointment about democracy will, as compared to any other developed nation, cost India more heavily and hence a quest for solutions is all the more important in the nation's context. While this discontentment has partly contributed to shaping the contemporary political culture in India, the political culture itself adds to the dissatisfaction. Hence, it is necessary to look into the salient features of political culture in India.

Democracy and Changing Political Culture in India

It can be reasonably argued that a democratic spirit was always a part of the Indian ethos. The theoretical foundations of this spirit could be traced in our long history of sustainable pluralism and spiritual democracy. A theocratic state was never a part of this ethos. On several occasions, Hindu kings large-heartedly welcomed visitors and traders from across the seas and ensured that they enjoy freedom of worship. With notions such as *Ekam sat vipra bahuda vadanti* (The truth is one, but knowledgeable and wise persons interpret the

[32] An example could be a blog created by Public Affairs Centre at http://www.pacindia.org/blogs/whats-wrong-with-democracy-in-india.

same differently) firmly rooted in the essentially Hindu ethos, ideally, practices like proselytisation could never be a part of it.

However, the basic tenets of this spiritual democracy and sustainable pluralism could not stop evils like caste-based discrimination and the practice of untouchability from entering our social structure. In order to keep their stranglehold on political, economic and religious power centres intact, members of the upper castes promoted these inhuman practices. Over the centuries, the caste system has resulted in social fragmentation leading to a brazen politics of identity. Here, it is obviously relevant to probe as to how all this has affected our political culture.

There is a necessary interrelationship between the fundamentals of the political system in a country and its political culture. If, arguably, India's present political system is plagued by populism, electoral compulsions and their grave impact on political parties and thereby on the quality of representative democracy, political culture in the country is bound to reflect the same. The definition of political culture given in *The Concise Oxford Dictionary of Politics* underscores this point. According to this dictionary, political culture refers to 'The attitude, beliefs and values, which underpin the operation of a particular political system.'[33]

Democracy, with a spirit of accommodation as its central pillar, has remained a part of popular and hence, also the political culture in India. Renowned political scientist, Robert A Dahl, in fact, has said that democracy is the 'National ideology of India'.[34] It is a well-known and widely accepted fact that the people of ancient India not only knew about democracy but they also practised it in one way or the other. Ancient Indian scriptures such as *Aiteraeya Brahmana* are replete with references suggesting that apart from monarchy, republics too existed in India in the fourth century BC. Although the fundamentals of democracy were recognised in these systems, its

[33]Ian McLean, (Ed). *The Concise Oxford Dictionary of Politics* p.379.

[34]Robert A Dahl, *On Democracy*, p.159.

form was certainly far more different from what we have today as representative democracy.[35]

'There was a time when India was studded with republics and even where there were monarchies, they were either elected or limited. They were never absolute,'[36] says BR Ambedkar. In the Indian republics, as in the Greek *poleis* or the European cities of the High Middle Ages, economic expansion enabled new groups to take up arms and eventually demand a share in sovereignty. For the numerous members of a sovereign *gana* or *sangha* to interact with each other, there existed a well-laid-down procedure. Buddhist literature is replete with details of the functioning of such assemblies. Historian and scholar Steve Muhlberger has pointed out that:

> By the time of Panini (fifth century BC), there was a terminology for the process of corporate decision-making. Panini gives us the terms for vote, decisions reached by voting, and the completion of a quorum. Another cluster of words indicates that the division of assemblies into political parties was well known. Further, Panini and his commentators show that sometimes a smaller select group within a sangha had special functions—acting as an executive or perhaps as a committee for defined purposes.[37]

The first chapter of the *Maha Parinibbana Suttanta* gives rules for conducting the Buddhist *sangha*. In the case of the Buddhist *sangha*, the key organisational virtue was the full participation of all

---

[35] Even in the absence of voter lists, or regularly held elections or universal franchise, there is evidence suggesting that several ancient systems of governance in India ensured a reasonable amount of scope for people's participation through elected representatives. It can also be described as some form of limited government. Lichchhavi, Videha, Youdheya, Vaishali and Malav were some of the well-known republics in India.

[36] BR Ambedkar, 'Constituent Assembly of India', at http://lawmin.nic.in/ncrwc/finalreport/v2b1-2ch3.htm.

[37] Steve Muhlberger's essay *Democracy in Ancient India* at http://www.infinityfoundation.com/mandala/h_es/h_es_muhlb_democra_frameset.htm.

the monks in the ritual and disciplinary acts of their group. Again, as mentioned by Muhlberger:[38]

> To assure that this would be remembered, detailed rules concerning the voting in monastic assemblies, their membership, and their quorums, were set down in the *Mahavagga* and the *Kullavagga*. Business could only be transacted legitimately in a full assembly, by a vote of all the members. If, for example, a candidate wanted the *upasampada* ordination, the question (*ñatti*) was put to the *sangha* by a learned and competent member, and the other members asked three times to indicate dissent. If there was none, the *sangha* was taken to be in agreement with the *ñatti*. The decision was finalised by the proclamation of the decision of the *sangha*.

Panchayati Raj

A discussion about democratic traditions in India will be incomplete without any reference to the Panchayati Raj system. India's Panchayati Raj traditions constitute one of the main reasons behind the success in making people adopt parliamentary democracy with ease. On several occasions during the freedom struggle, Mahatma Gandhi referred to this rich heritage. Gandhi was also strongly influenced by his reading of Sir Henry James Sumner Maine. Using Maine's *Indian Village Communities*—from the book *Village Communities in the East and West*—as one of the principal pieces of evidence in a petition to the Natal Assembly (South Africa) in 1894, he argued that franchise should be extended to the members of the Indian community. A key passage in the petition reads as follows:

> The Indian nation has known, and has exercised, the power of election from times prior to the time when the Anglo-Saxon races first became acquainted with the principles of

[38] *Ibid*

> representation...in support of the above, your Petitioners beg to draw the attention of your Honourable Assembly to Sir Henry Sumner Maine's *Village Communities*, where he has clearly pointed out that the Indian races have been familiar with representative institutions almost from time immemorial. That eminent lawyer and writer has shown that the Teutonic Mark was hardly so well organised or so essentially representative as an Indian Village community until the precise technical Roman form was grafted upon it.[39]

Gandhi wanted to drive home two fundamental points while arguing for representation to be given to the Indian community in South Africa. Firstly, that the Indian people were as civilised as any other and therefore entitled to vote and secondly that they were long accustomed to the concept of representative democracy and indeed enjoyed the powers of voting (at least some of them) for members of municipal councils and provincial assemblies in India.[40]

Functional autonomy and self-reliance through a process of consensual decision-making are the hallmarks of Panchayati Raj. Describing the fortified villages, which had sprung up around Delhi in the years after the collapse of Mughal power in 1761, Charles Metcalfe, in 1832, wrote to the Select Parliamentary Committee on the East India Company's charter in brilliantly evocative terms:

> The village communities are little republics, having nearly everything they can want within themselves and almost independent of any foreign relations. They seem to last where nothing else lasts. Dynasty after dynasty tumbles down; revolution succeeds revolution; Hindoo, Pathan, Mogul, Mahratta, Sikh, English, are all masters in turn; but the village community remains the same...This union of the village communities, each one forming a separate state in itself, has, I conceive, contributed more than any other cause to the preservation of the people of India through

---

[39] MK Gandhi. *Collected Writings*, Vol. 1, p. 256-272.
[40] *ibid*

> all the revolutions and changes which they have suffered, and is in a high degree conducive to their happiness, and to the enjoyment of a great portion of freedom and independence.[41]

Beyond the structures and systems that existed in India, what is more important is India's cultural unity in the midst of apparent diversities. According to political scientist and analyst Rajni Kothari, India is perhaps:

> 'the only great historical civilisation that has maintained its cultural unity without identifying itself with a particular centre. The essential identity of India has not been political but cultural...it was through a constant interplay between the political and the cultural, the secular and the spiritual, that the system was able to adapt itself to changing situations'.[42]

One can infer that this culture of accommodation in India paved the way for the smooth functioning of political democracy. Unlike in China, where the state is also considered as being the moral custodian, such a monopolistic stance of the rulers was never acceptable in India, thanks mainly to its tradition of 'society's autonomy.'[43]

This makes it clear that India's inherent cultural unity, with an essential spirit of accommodation at its core, was a strong foundation on which representative democracy should have easily flourished in the country. Even in the absence of social democracy, since Hindu ethos had a strong current of spiritual democracy, it was not wrong to expect an effortless and effective institutionalisation of modern representative democracy. Unfortunately, that has not been the case. Researchers in democratic governance do not rate democracy in India any higher than democracy elsewhere and this calls for analysing the role of systems in strengthening democracy.

---

[41]Dewey CJ, "Images of the Village Community (1972):a study in Anglo-Indian ideology", '*Modern Asian Studies*', Vol. 6, No. 3 (1972).
[42]Rajni Kothari, *Politics in India*, p.251.
[43]*ibid*.p.264

Institutionalisation

It is on this setting that one has to view the organic relationship between democracy, parties, populism and elections in the Indian context. If elections, parties, electoral campaigns and peaceful transfer of power are the instruments of democracy, India certainly can boast about them being properly in place for over six decades. The question, however, is whether these instruments have effectively contributed in developing a culture of democratic functionality or not. If the overall quality of functioning of political parties, voluntary organisations and institutions, legislatures, and media organisations in the present day is any indication, institutionalisation of the intrinsic democratic spirit is yet to come about. True democratic spirit requires to be further deepened while internalising democratic values. All the stakeholders too need to resolutely work and demonstrate that the core values of democracy are reflected in the functionality of its institutions in India.

As commented upon by economist and thinker LC Jain, in the context of any democracy, and particularly India, '...the electoral framework adopted is recognised as necessary but not sufficient. It affords equality (arithmetical equality) in the electoral sphere. But that equality faces threats from gross disparities which plague the life of the citizens in other crucial spheres, economic and social.'[44]

In this context, the findings of a survey carried out by the UK-based Overseas Development Institute are noteworthy. The summary of this report says, 'Policy-making is rather divorced from the people—especially the poorest members of society. Democracy in India is more impressive in form than substance.'[45]

Democracy and Well-being

The answer to the question 'Has democracy delivered in India?' will

[44]LC Jain in his article "We have to pay for our democracy" at http://www.humanscape.org/Humanscape/2004/Nov/wehave.php.

[45]Julius Court in his report 'Assessing and Analysing Governance in India: Evidence from a New Survey'at http://www.odi.org.uk/wga_governance/Abstracts/Governance_in_India_abs.htm.

vary from the perspective of the questioner. To many, the fact that democracy has survived for so long is in itself an achievement. However, how and why democracy has survived is of more importance. Noted political scientist Prof Kanchan Chandra has tried to explain this while saying, '...over time, politicians in India have developed a stake not only in democracy, but in patronage, and the two cannot now be disentangled easily without depriving a whole political class of power. Thus, we have the problem of a highly competitive democracy, in which there have been fundamental changes in the identity of those who take power, but no change in the style according to which this power is used.'[46]

This explains partly as to why and how, in spite of regularly held elections and people voting against those in power almost like an established trend, no real transformation is achieved. Thus, if a culture of patronage is adversely affecting polity in India and as a consequence the quality of democracy in the country, the key to transformation also lies in changes in the country's state structure. The relationship between governance and polity is interdependent. Good governance is a product of good polity and vice versa.

PRINCIPAL FEATURES OF INDIAN POLITICAL CULTURE

After the seminal work of Gabriel Almond and Sidney Verba's *Civic Culture* (1963), a long series of studies have emphasised that, besides resources facilitating civic engagement, a strong motivational attitude to become active in public life is a prerequisite for a citizen's political participation. Social scientists also suggest that the psychological orientation towards political systems and participatory habits are learnt at an early age. In India, there is an utter lack of systems imparting any such training in schools, localities or social institutions. A subject called Civics is a part of school curricula in the country, but its teaching and learning normally remain confined to general knowledge. Hardly any serious efforts are made for developing a deeper understanding of the democratic process and the role of a

[46]Kanchan Chandra 'Elections as Auctions' *Seminar* 539, July 2004, p.28

citizen in it. This has caused a great handicap. Urban dwellers in India normally do not rush to help a road-accident victim mainly because they are afraid of entanglements that their noble act may invite.

On the whole, a total of five major aspects could be identified as principal features of political culture in India. These features are classified on the basis of factors like political parties, populism, electoral systems, and above all, a citizen's orientation to democratic values in general.

Leader-centric Organisations

In the absence of any legal provision making internal democracy mandatory, most of the political parties in India today have become leader-dependent and hence leader-centric. Dynastic rule within the party is the logical corollary of this situation.

Of the forty-nine recognised parties, both at the national as well as state level, barring the Congress, the BJP and the Left parties such as the Communist Party of India (M) and the Communist Party of India, almost all other parties are single-leader-centric and/or family-controlled.[47] In the case of the Congress, the craving for and dependence on leadership of the Nehru-Gandhi family has converted this grand old party of India into a party of dynastic leadership. The way Rahul Gandhi, son of Rajiv Gandhi, is being projected as the future prime minister, speaks volumes about the dynastic character of party leadership in the Congress. Similarly, in the Shiv Sena, Uddhav Thackeray was nominated as a natural successor to Bal Thackeray and in the Samajwadi Party, Akhilesh Yadav became

[47]This has been endorsed by P Chidambaram, in his article in *India Today* (18 September, 2000) where he says, 'Another sorry consequence of the devaluation of politics is the person-centric party. The party is cast, or recast, in the image of the leader. Often, the leader includes his family. There are only three political parties which are exceptions to this rule: CPI, CPI (M) and the BJP (of today). Historically, the Congress had set the benchmarks for inner party democracy, but in recent years it has chosen to follow the rule rather than be an exception. The DMK, AIADMK, PMK, and MDMK in Tamil Nadu are person, or family-controlled parties. So are the Shiv Sena, TDP, Trinamool Congress, Samajwadi Party, RJD, AGP and HVP.' http://www.india-today.com/itoday/20000918/chidambaram.shtml.

the successor to Mulayam Singh Yadav. An example from the South to join this bandwagon of heir-apparents is Kanimozhi, daughter of the Chief Minister of Tamil Nadu, M Karunanidhi. This trend indicates that many consider the party as a personal or family property. (See Appendix A for a table giving details of the dynastic parties in India). Writer and commentator Patrick French has also analysed the phenomenon of family politics in great detail. Pointing out that at least 28.6 per cent of MPs elected to the 15th Lok Sabha had significant hereditary connection, he has lamented that in the case of the Congress, 37.5 per cent of its MPs had reached the Lok Sabha through a family connection. In the case of the BJP, this figure comes to 19 per cent, whereas in that of the CPI (M), it is 25 per cent. 'The Indian republic was founded on the truth that power should not be handed over by the colonial rulers to the princes, (but still) India's next general election was likely to return not a Lok Sabha, a house of people but a Vansh Sabha, a house of dynasty,' rues Patrick French.[48]

Dynastic rule is becoming an accepted trend in several regional parties, mainly because the existing leadership deliberately wants to promote this orientation. Another reason is that the leader-centric parties do not allow any parallel centre of authority to emerge. This brings in an element of invited solitude and leaders become friendless. These 'lonely at the top' leaders then start depending upon their children heavily.[49] By giving their children the reins of their own fiefdom, these leaders try to compensate for their acts of omission in the past.

The roots of this leader-centric character of India's political parties could be found in the traditional social structure with feudal

---

[48] Patrick French, *India: A Portrait,* page 123.

[49] As explained by Dr Harish Shetty, a psychiatrist from Mumbai, at a session on 'Psychological health and stress management' at a Workshop for Ministers held at Rambhau Mhalgi Prabodhini (RMP) on 5 May, 2005. According to him promoting their progeny, '...also satisfies the politicians', yet another psychological need. Since hectic political activity does not allow them to spend quality time with their children when the latter requires it the most, leaders often carry a sense of guilt.'

features and the resultant mindset. In the traditional joint family system that survived in India for a very long time, perverse-collectivism thrived, leaving an extremely narrow space for individual aspirations. Abject surrender, initially to the family-head and later to the head of the organisation—the leader—to prove one's loyalty, many a time becomes a prerequisite if one is expecting rewards. A case in point is that of India's former Minister for Communications, Dayanidhi Maran—his loyalty to the party and its chief. Maran is the owner of a popular TV channel in Tamil Nadu and it had conducted a survey about 'whom Tamil Nadu people accept as the political heir of DMK Chief and state Chief Minister M Karunanidhi'. This inadvertently triggered a war of succession between two of M Karunanidhi's sons, MK Stalin and MK Azhagiri. Subsequently, Maran resigned 'simply because his political mentor and grand-uncle was annoyed with him.'[50]

In the past too, party politics in India has witnessed several instances of this 'total surrender to party leadership' phenomenon. In the late Seventies, Dev Kant Baruah, the then Congress president, proclaimed that 'Indira is India' and famously defended all the actions of Indira Gandhi, who was then Prime Minister of India. Scores of examples of how otherwise powerful individual leaders have compromised with their self-respect simply to be in the good books of the party patriarch could be found in the history of political parties in India. Leaders like M Karunanidhi of the DMK, J Jayalalitha of the AIADMK, Bal Thackeray of the Shiv Sena, Mayawati of the BSP, Chandrababu Naidu of the TDP and Lalu Prasad Yadav of the RJD have always demanded total surrender of fellow leaders to the party, even at the cost of their self-confidence. To expect that these parties will genuinely cultivate any internal democracy in their respective organisations on their own is absolutely unrealistic.

In the Congress, during the time of Indira Gandhi, 'Party High Command' became extremely pre-dominant. Since then, the practice of the state legislature party 'giving the authority of

[50]As commented in *The Economic Times*, Mumbai, May 16, 2007

selecting the leader of the legislative party and deciding who would become the Chief Minister' to the supreme leader of the party, started. This practice was at its height in Andhra Pradesh in the early Eighties. The fact that the Congress changed state chief ministers four times within a span of five years was exploited to the hilt by the Telugu Desam's Founder-President NT Rama Rao in 1983. In fact, the political vocabulary in India also underwent a significant change around this time. 'Strengthening the hands of the leader', became one of the often-used terms to connote total surrender. Unfortunately, later this trend did not remain confined to the Congress alone.

When party patriarchs behave in a crass feudal manner and expect abject surrender to them even from their senior colleagues, this chain of expectations continues with leaders at various levels following the same footsteps. In parties like the Congress, the NCP and the Shiv Sena, some kind of a *subedari*[51] system has thrived, under which, apex level party leadership gives a total free hand to the sub-regional leader and refrains from meddling in the party affairs at a regional level. These sub-regional leaders enjoy total autonomy at the cost of their complete submission. Consequently, a similar leadership pattern evolves even at the grass roots. Party leaders and elected representatives wield their political power more for the purpose of either obliging an individual or a group or creating nuisance for them. It is an established practice in India that when elected leaders meet their voters en masse, these events are named as *janata darbars*. From Indira Gandhi of the Congress to IK Gujral of the Janata Dal and NT Ramarao of the Telugu Desam Party to Manohar Joshi of the Shiv Sena, leaders at various levels have indulged in this trend, which has a necessary feudal character. Events like these are also used to give a clear message to their electorate that the leadership can make or mar their lives. Understandably, all these traits have hugely contributed to the cultivation of a sycophantic culture in the organisation of parties in India.

What APJ Abdul Kalam,[52] former president of India, had

---

[51] *Subedar* is an Urdu/ Hindi term meaning *satrap* or regional head.

[52] As quoted at http://www.indianexpress.com/story/204383.html.

once mentioned as 'shortage of leadership with nobility' has not only afflicted the government but also parties. Both nobility and courage are also lacking and the moral bankruptcy of the leaders across the political parties has confounded the crisis. They appear to be wary of questioning others, let alone correcting them. Young leaders seem to be confused and do not want to endanger their own political career by asking uncomfortable questions to their seniors. Whereas seniors, otherwise known for their uprightness and high ethical standards, see little point in raising any issues and inviting the wrath of the incumbent leadership at the very end of their careers.

EMERGENCE OF A CULTURE OF SYCOPHANCY

Lack of internal democracy in most of the political parties in India has suppressed dissent. Political party leaders at the top are no longer known for tolerating any difference of opinion. With leader-centric organisations, party forums like executive committee or parliamentary boards have become ornamental. Provisions in their respective constitutions apart, in most of the leader-centric parties, these bodies rarely meet and even when they meet, deliberations there are more or less a formality. As compared to most of the existing political parties, it is only in the BJP and the CPI (M) that the apex level bodies meet relatively more regularly and engage in serious deliberations. In the case of the Congress, the once powerful Congress Working Committee is today facing an erosion of its authority.[53]

With party forums losing their relevance, middle-rung leaders have also lost their importance. In most of the leader-centric parties, the party supremo enjoys a direct rapport with the so-called rank and file. Firmly believing that his party organisation needs him more than he needs the organisation, a leader weaves the whole organisation around himself. Party workers also realise that, to have a direct connectivity with the apex level leadership, will eventually pay. Hence, they wantonly indulge in every tactic

[53] As observed by veteran Congress leader Vasant Sathe, in an interview with the author at Gurgaon, Haryana on 9 Feb, 2004.

that may keep their leaders in good humour. This trend has now acquired the dimension of an established practice and paved a culture of sycophancy. Instances such as composing a *Lalu Chalisa*, eulogising Lalu Prasad Yadav on the lines of the *Hanuman Chalisa* (a composition of couplets in praise of the Hindu deity, Hanuman) in Bihar; reported attempts of self-immolation by the followers of leaders like Jayalalitha or M Karunanidhi after either electoral defeat or imprisonment; appealing to Sonia Gandhi to accept prime ministership through a letter signed in blood; constructing a statue of Mayawati and having it inaugurated in her presence—are only a few examples of this culture of hero worship. Adulation and overstatement has almost become a trend. Two episodes in the recent past in this regard could be cited. First, the then Rajasthan's Chief Minister Vasundhara Raje was depicted as a goddess in a calendar published by one of her over-enthusiastic fans in 2007. Secondly, Sonia Gandhi was portrayed as the goddess, Durga, by a Congress worker a few years ago. It may also be noted here, that in 2009, when the Chief Minister of Andhra Pradesh, YSR Reddy died in a plane crash, at least sixty people reportedly committed suicide as the grief became unbearable.

For many, sycophancy has become the most 'result-oriented' way of entering the close circles of the powers that be. This craving is understandable since the process of decision-making has remained largely confined to the topmost leader only, and the best way of influencing his/her thinking is by being around him/her. With ideology pushed to the periphery, personal ambition has remained almost the sole motivating factor for a majority of party workers. 'If sycophancy is the only way of moving upward, we have to adapt ourselves to that and we are doing the same,' is the primary sentiment shared by several middle-rung political leaders. Sycophancy could also be described as a product of a personality cult coupled with the erosion of internal democracy.

When the mechanism for collective decision-making is sidetracked and a dominating leader is allowed to usurp all power by going beyond the constitutional brief, a personalised authority is bound to emerge. Except the communist parties and the BJP, since most of the parties in India are personality-centric, the decision-making processes followed by the party organisations are through the respective personalised authorities. When the party rank-and-file realises this, they take a short route and just keep the personalised authority in good humour, thus promoting sycophancy.

Give-and-take in its most crude form has now become the basis of the mutual relationship between a political party worker and the party leader. The characteristic of Indian culture of showing respect to the elderly is being routinely abused in India's contemporary political culture. Several party workers have made it a habit to touch the feet of their leaders and the latter, regardless of their age, take pleasure in this. Besides, this has also made the relationship dry, purely artificial and formal. The overall picture is that of leaders without friends and party workers sans a mentor.

One of the key factors behind the flourishing of the culture of sycophancy is a deep-seated sense of insecurity. With day-to-day politics claiming all energy and enthusiasm at their command, low and middle-rung leaders are fast becoming uni-dimensional in their thinking. Their mind is always preoccupied with the singular objective of retaining political power. Bereft of any courage of conviction and moral authority, these leaders always feel deeply insecure. Since most political leaders cannot and do not build their professional career alongside their political career, especially in the case of elected representatives, they realise that they can do precious little outside politics. This explains the sense of uncertainty about the future and resultant feeling of insecurity, either real or imagined.

To sum up, party leadership, especially in leader-centric parties, normally takes a shortsighted approach and neglects even basic organisational matters. It is often seen that leaders wantonly belittle their own organisation to give a clear signal that beyond them, the party organisation has no meaning. In the near total absence of any serious party forums to take up one's case, aspiring party workers take to sycophancy and end up as cheerleaders rather than party activists.

LACK OF AN INSTITUTION-BUILDING APPROACH TO PARTY AFFAIRS

As is being examined in this study, parties in India appear to have long forgotten their theoretical role. Organisational structures in the parties have become almost lifeless. There is a reason to believe that a strong point for a party, and that too for a particular phase, may prove to be a weakness for other parties or even for the same party later. What Rajni Kothari[54] describes as the 'Congress System', meaning a party set-up organised loosely with the accommodation of different views, was not always effective for the Congress. During the heyday of identity politics, after the collapse of a disputed structure in Ayodhya, the Congress continuously faced reversals as it could not identify with a particular social segment.

While several meetings and conferences are organised, party functionaries rarely find time to look back and discuss what the party was formed for. What exactly has the party achieved? And if it has not achieved anything, what was it supposed to, what are the reasons behind the failure? Senior party leaders seem to be disinclined to discuss these questions as answering these might prove to be inconvenient. A sense of having given up is visible across the political spectrum. Even those senior leaders, who have passed the stage of having a vested interest in this undesirable state of the party organisation choose to keep quiet as if they are convinced that nothing will and nothing can happen, at least in their lifetime. This, according to Govindacharya, is mainly because senior party leaders have no moral courage to talk about these issues as they themselves carry a feeling of moral hollowness from within.

In India, populism appears to have pushed constitutionalism within the party organisation to the periphery. If breaking rules to accommodate the wrongdoings, either on humanitarian grounds or for any other reason, is an indication of low levels of constitutionalism,

---

[54]On Sardar Patel's efforts to build the Congress's organisation, Rajni Kothari comments: 'Patel's idea of transforming the Congress into strictly a political party with a single ideology and tight discipline showed an equal lack of understanding of the eclectic code that the Congress, as a government, was to be called upon to perform in the decades to follow.' (*Politics in India*, p.156)

then, in India, it is omnipresent. This attitude, too, is both a reason for and an impact of promoting what can be described as organisational populism.

A near total lack of institution-building has contributed to the present political culture in India. This myopic attitude is reflected in the manner in which parties are being administered. The absence of any serious attempts at cultivating a genuine internal democracy has encouraged several well-meaning party leaders to succumb to group dynamics and get affiliated to one section within the party or the other. This has brought in an element of perennial instability and tentativeness in party affairs, resulting in a sense of insecurity enveloping the whole functional set-up of a party. When party leaders themselves are engrossed in warding off threats, either genuine or hypothetical, to their own survival, serious efforts towards building the party as an institution are hard to come about.

Growing Domination of Market-friendliness

Whether it can be considered as the impact of socio-cultural life on politics or vice versa, markets are playing a key role in determining the contours of our popular culture. In the literary world, if classics are not being produced, it is mainly because they are not in demand. This trend is also impacting the theatre and the film world. With growing urbanisation, fast pace of life and decreasing peace of mind, people are more inclined to go for whatever is easy to digest. Naturally, we come across literary works, films and plays that are simple and with a high entertainment value. It is because of this that the television-entertainment industry comes out only with run-of-the-mill type of soap operas, strategically designed to attract high a Television Rating Point (TRP). Arguably, this particular trend has adversely affected the overall standard of creative talent in our society. From commodities to ideas, issues and policies—whatever is easily, if not guaranteedly, marketable alone is being introduced. Ready-made markets are in demand everywhere. It is of little wonder then, that public policy and issues in competitive electoral politics should succumb to market pressures. A case in point is the euphoria created for FDI (Foreign Direct Investment) in retail or the enthusiasm on the part of the government to allow foreign universities to function in India.

EMOTIONAL ISSUE-DRIVEN ELECTORAL POLITICS

General elections held in India from 1950 to 1970 witnessed the domination of a single party with almost no challenge. Later, in almost every election barring a few, emotional issues have dominated and influenced the electoral verdict and even negated the impact of a strong current of anti-incumbency. A glance at the list of decisive issues that dominated the electoral campaign in some of the past elections to the Lok Sabha in India brings forth the impact of emotional issues. In 1984, sympathy for the Congress after the assassination of Indira Gandhi resulted in a more than two-thirds majority for the party under Rajiv Gandhi. History was repeated in 1991, especially after the assassination of Rajiv Gandhi and the Congress was able to emerge as the single largest party. In 1999, the post-Kargil emotional surge helped the NDA emerge victorious under the leadership of Atal Bihari Vajpayee.

Having realised that secular issues that concern the day-to-day lives of the people make only marginal impact, matters related to identity have dominated electoral strategies of parties in India. There are three basic issues concerning identity—regional, caste-oriented and religious.

At the micro level too, there is a history of elections to legislative assemblies in the states that had been fought and won on an emotional plank, with the domination of regional identity issues. In Jammu and Kashmir, the subject of *Kashmiriyat* has always figured prominently in election campaigns. As has been referred to earlier, in Maharashtra, the Shiv Sena has appealed to the Maharashtrian voters in the name of *Marathi manoos* (Marathi people). Narendra Modi, in 2002, successfully orchestrated his campaign in the state on the theme of *Gujarat Gaurav* (the pride of Gujarat). At times, personalities and leaders are projected more on a regional basis in order to make an emotional appeal. In 1975, Indira Gandhi went before the Gujarati electorate in traditional Gujarati attire, describing herself as *Gujarat ki bahu* (daughter-in-law of Gujarat). PV Narsimha Rao, in 1996, sought popular mandate from his home state, Andhra Pradesh, in the name of being a *Telugu bidda* (Telugu son). In 1998, in Rajasthan, the BJP eulogised its chief ministerial candidate as a regional hero through the slogan *Rajasthan ka ek hi sin(g)h, Bhairo Singh, Bhairo Singh* (The only lion in Rajasthan). Similarly, in West Bengal in 2011, Mamata Banerjee rode to power with the slogan of *Maa, maati, manush*.

Caste and community too have a significant emotional appeal, and these have been exploited to the hilt by politicians in India. Although this has happened more at the micro and constituency levels, it remains a fact that the rise of leaders like Lalu Prasad Yadav, Mayawati and M Karunanidhi has given a sense of self-respect to the respective marginalised communities that they represent. Thanks to this sense of self-confidence, castes and communities support their leaders collectively. Mayawati was more straightforward in indulging in an anti-upper caste campaign in her earlier elections (again, it was under electoral compulsions that she tried to broaden her appeal in 2007 and succeeded). Several recent instances of changing the names of cities, districts and railway stations or airports are a testimony to how identity issues continue to dominate. For instance, Mumbai VT station was renamed as Chhatrapati Shivaji Terminus whereas Chhatrapati Shahu Maharaj Terminus is the new name for Kolhapur railway station. Similarly, several cities/districts in Uttar Pradesh have been renamed. (Akbarpur as Ambedkar Nagar, Greater Noida as Gautam Buddha Nagar etc.)

The use of religious symbols to create an emotionally charged atmosphere for electoral gains is also an established practice in Indian politics. Under Rajiv Gandhi, the decision of the government in the Shah Bano case—mainly based on the 'fear of losing the Muslim vote'[55]—was a clear case of religious populism. Similarly, many critics argue that the BJP's official resolution at its National Executive in

[55]RD Pradhan, *Working with Rajiv Gandhi*, as quoted by Ramachandra Guha in *India after Gandhi* p.582.

Palampur (Himachal Pradesh), in 1989, on the Ram Janmabhoomi Temple at Ayodhya was an instance of religious populism. However, one cannot deny that this argument holds little water, as in a highly fragmented Hindu society, there is hardly any Hindu vote bank, per se.

GREATER ROLE OF MEDIA IN SHAPING POLITICAL CULTURE

An indirect effect of the growing prominence of emotional issues in electoral politics is the disproportionate importance given to image. Since the media has the power to make or mar one's image, its role is increasingly becoming more important. Many senior and experienced political leaders admit that today, instead of politics influencing media, it is the other way round.

On several occasions in the past, people have witnessed how headlines of morning newspapers or major news items telecast by news channels the previous night have influenced and altered the business in state legislatures and even the Parliament in India. This is a global phenomena and India is certainly not an exception. A study about how Belgian parties, parliament and government react to what appears in the media has come out with similar conclusions. Researchers Stefaan Walgrave and Michiel Nuytemans have observed, 'We may consequently expect mass media in Belgium to affect the activities of the Belgian Parliament more than the decisions of government'.[56]

No wonder then, that the role of the media in shaping the present-day political culture is growing disproportionately.

COMMERCIALISATION OF ELECTORAL POLITICS

With black-money regimes continuing unabated, moneyed sections of society require clandestine avenues to park their wealth. Politics has emerged as an attractive destination for them. The elections,

---

[56]Stefaan Walgrave and Michiel Nuytemans in their essay specifying the media's political agenda-setting power. 'Media, civil society, parliament and government in a small consolation democracy' (Belgium, 1991-2000) at http://www.snsoroka.com/fi les/2008WalgraveSorokaNuytemans(CPS).pdf.

particularly, have become an industry for investing ill-gotten money for illegitimate purposes, capturing power, and finally employing public offices for generating manifold returns on these investments. This has converted transfers in government offices into money-minting devices. A percentage in public contracts and tenders, 'cuts' in constituency development funds, cash-for-questions in Parliament and using diplomatic passports to facilitate illegal migration of individuals have become all too common. What Jayprakash Narayan (JN) describes as 'legal plunder'[57] of government resources, is now too deep-rooted to check with ordinary measures. Corruption, criminalisation and cronyism have become the three pillars of politics today. Unfortunately, the word 'politics' now prompts grave distaste and revulsion in those with integrity and self-respect.

That politics has now become a domain reserved only for those who have money or who can generate financial resources has been proved through several factors and on various occasions. Way back in 1989, when a state-level ideological training camp for the BJP was conducted in Maharashtra, of the 143 participants, only three were salary earners. All the others were from the self-employed category, like farmers and traders, besides party full-timers and elected representatives. Today, one may not find even a single individual from a salary-earning category reaching high in politics.

UNSUSTAINABILITY OF SUITABLE AND WELL-MEANING PEOPLE IN POWER POLITICS

With changing organisational characteristics and patterns of fighting and winning elections, unscrupulous elements are bound to thrive at the middle level of party organisations. As a consequence, well intentioned and sincere activists are either opting out of politics or being pushed to the periphery, if not thrown out. Many senior political leaders in mainstream parties feel out-of-place and, at times, even frustrated. Besides, for conscientious persons, stressing on righteousness and values has become so difficult that any attempt

---

[57] Jayprakash Narayan (JN), *India Together* at http://www.indiatogether.org/2007/nov/med-mediaind.htm.

on their part would be considered as being unaccommodating or stubborn. They may even face a crisis of survival. To accept the situation as it is and to try to remain as scrupulous as possible in the given situation is the only thing they can do. While this satisfies them personally, it just fails in making any substantial impact on party affairs.

GENERAL APATHY OF CITIZENS AND LACK OF CIVIC INITIATIVES

Although democracy in India has survived a number of challenges, the challenge of changing the popular mindset of overdependence on the government continues to be difficult. Fatalism has always remained a dominant force governing Indian minds. Earlier, if it was god who was responsible for everything, now it is the government. When representative democracy was first experimented with in India, way back in the 1930s, much before Independence, even elected representatives would relish blaming the government for everything that had gone wrong. But we continue with the same mindset even after so many years of Independence. Citizens continue to look at the members of governing bodies at every level as all-powerful agencies who have to shoulder responsibility for all and sundry. From municipal to national, participative government has remained confined to the conceptual level.

At the municipal level, the 74th Constitutional Amendment has provided for ward committees as vehicles for active participation of the citizens. A study report of the National Institute of Urban Affairs says:

> It is learnt that in the southern states, they are functional in Tamil Nadu and in Kerala. In Andhra Pradesh and Karnataka, they are practically not functional except in Hyderabad and in Bangalore, which have municipal corporations. In the case of Bangalore, it is further learnt that they are neither meeting regularly, nor working effectively. It may be stated that Kerala is a unique example, where ward committees have been constituted in every ward and in towns with a population of more than a lakh.

> In the case of Chhattisgarh, it is learnt that although ward committees have been constituted in Raipur Municipal Corporation, no responsibilities have been assigned to them and no budgetary allocation is being given. In fact, they are completely non-functional.[58]

Another report reveals, 'None of the cities in Uttar Pradesh has ward committees even though it is a mandatory constitutional provision.'[59]

Also, wherever such committees are set up, in majority of them, the level of citizens' participation is dismal. Despite the 74th Amendment, in a number of municipal corporations in most of the states, no ward committees have been established at all. Neither citizens' groups nor any political party has taken up this issue even after over a decade and a half.

Dealing with the Changes

Besides the features discussed here, Rajni Kothari has pointed out certain central themes forming the core of political culture in India.[60] These include tolerance of ambiguity, notion of authority as dispersed and a high degree of tolerance for the gap between what is said and what is done.

In the evolving world, culture too has undergone fundamental changes with all the central themes—mentioned earlier—losing their strength, developing into grave weaknesses and threatening the fundamentals of democratic governance. Unless the Indian political class takes the basics of India's traditional political culture in its stride and makes a renewed and concerted bid to bring reforms, the political culture cannot change suitably to make democracy deliver.

---

[58] A study of the National Institute of Urban Affairs about the impact of the 74th Amendment has thrown some light on how this amendment has been implemented shoddily in many states. This study could be accessed at www.niua.org/.../74caa_v1/Impact%20of%20the%2074th%20CAA-consolidated%20Report%20Vol%20-%20I_summary.pdf.

[59] www.ids.ac.uk/logolink/resources/downloads/Recite_Confpapers/PRIAPolicy_Paper_Urban1.pdf.

[60] Rajni Kothari, *Politics in India* p. 257

Parties are supposed to govern ably, perform and thereby bring more quality to the life of the commoners. The changing contours of democratic politics in India demand that the ruling elite play their role effectively. Kothari has rightly pointed out that, '(political elites in India are) still not the most important element in the ordering of community lifestyles. It has achieved its importance not through its authority, but by dispersing its goods and mediating in other spheres through its resources and persuasive capabilities, thus taking on the roles that were hitherto performed by the non-political elites.'[61]

How do we transform this situation and evolve a new political culture? If democracy in India remains confined only to regularly held elections, reasonably satisfactory voter turnout and peaceful transfers of power, and has only little to report about the delivery aspect of democratic governance, there is a danger of democracy being reduced to an untrustworthy set-up. Samuel Huntington has observed that the subject of democratic culture focuses attention on the relation between the performance or effectiveness of (new) democratic governments and their legitimacy. What he has further said about new democracies is applicable to India as well. According to him, '...[new democracies] lacking legitimacy cannot become effective; lacking effectiveness, they cannot develop legitimacy.'[62]

Public discourse in India has still not paid due attention to the question of reforming the systems to ensure good governance. Not enough literature is available on political parties—their organisational functioning and performance as the government, besides their success or failure in institutionalising their functioning. For any analyst, this handicap puts some limitations while gathering evidence and making a point. The absolute lack of credible records of party functioning, including membership records, minutes of party meetings and documentation on important policy issues, is yet another significant handicap.

To conclude, it must be mentioned that people are looking for

[61] *ibid.*p.292

[62] Samuel P. Huntington, *The Third Wave: Democratization in the late twentieth century* p. 258

an alternative, a more real and meaningful, political system. Cosmetic changes will not help, since what is required is a kind of an overhaul. Transforming political culture and creating a new landscape for politics is the only solution. Genuine democratic politics is expected to be all encompassing, aiming at harmonising individual interests with collective advancement. If India is to move towards that, the process of this overhaul will have to start with reforming political parties. But before talking of reforms, it is required that one puts political parties, as institutions, under the scanner and diagnose the ailment.

APPENDIX A

DYNASTIC PARTIES IN INDIA

State	Dynastic Parties
Andhra Pradesh	Telugu Desam (the NTR-Chandrababu Naidu dynasty)
Bihar	Rashtriya Janata Dal (Lalu Prasad Yadav dynasty)
Haryana	Indian National Lok Dal (Devi Lal, OP Chautala dynasty)
Jammu and Kashmir	National Conference (Abdullah dynasty)
Karnataka	Janata Dal (Secular) (HD Devegowda dynasty)
Maharashtra	National Congress Party (Pawar dynasty) Shiv Sena (Thackeray dynasty)
Odisha	Biju Janata Dal (Patnaik dynasty)
Punjab	Akali Dal (Badal dynasty)
Tamil Nadu	DMK (Karunanidhi dynasty)
Uttar Pradesh	Samajwadi Party (Mulayam Singh Yadav dynasty)
Uttar Pradesh	Rashtriya Lok Dal (Charan Singh dynasty)

CHAPTER 4

Political Parties: From People's Voice to Empty Vessels

If the idea of democracy has elements which are central to its core concept, like freedom of choice and resultant competition amongst the alternatives (choices), then political parties become principal players in this competition. Obviously, the centrality of political parties in any democracy, especially representative democracy, is simply undisputed. It is, therefore, critical to take an overview of the role played by parties. In the course of the discussion, the changing character of political parties also merits some attention. While discussing these issues, a review of the role of parties in shaping public opinion, its relationship with the ideological clarity and organisational health of a party and the changing nature of party-public interface in general is also necessary. While examining the phenomenon of party decline, it is also required to analyse the reasons for this.

Definition of a Political Party

Definitions of organisational entities like political parties have evolved over a period of time. They present us a graph of conceptual development and, thereby, an insight into the changing perspectives about political parties. (Since this discussion is basically about populism and its impact on party-people relationship, the review is confined only to those definitions where this relationship is duly recognised.) Some of the notable attempts at defining a party include those of Sigmund Neumann, Maurice Duverger and Samuel J Eldersveld. While defining a political party, Neumann observes:

> As the articulate organisation of society's active political agents, those who are concerned with the control of governmental power and who compete for popular support with another group or groups holding divergent views. As such, it is the great intermediary which links social forces and ideologies to official governmental institutions and relates them to political action within the larger political community.[1]

Duverger tried to define a party strictly from an organisational point of view. He felt that 'a party is not a community but a collection of communities, a union of small groups dispersed throughout the country (branches, caucuses, local associations etc.) and linked by coordinating institutions.'[2]

Joseph La Palombara and Myron Weiner also offered their own definition of a party. They perceived that for any organisation to be called a political party, four key characteristics are essential. A continuity of organisation—an organisation whose expected life span is not dependent on the life span of current leaders—is the first requirement. It is also important to have a visible and presumably permanent organisation at the local level with regulated communications and other relationships between local and national units. Another crucial factor is the self-conscious determination of leaders at national and local levels to capture and to hold decision-making power alone or in coalition with others, not simply to influence the exercise of power. Lastly, a concern on the part of the

[1] Sigmund Neumann, (Ed) *Modern Political Parties*, p.396

[2] Maurice Duverger, *Political Parties*, p.17.

organisation for seeking followers at the polls or, in some manner, striving for popular support.[3]

A general analysis of key attempts to define a 'political party' shows that emphasis on organisation, leader-follower relationship, consideration for power and concern for popular support are some of the vital characteristics of a political party. It needs to be mentioned here that ideology, which is a 'comprehensive and mutually consistent set of ideas by which a social group makes sense of the world'[4], has been neglected by most theorists. This apathy towards the fundamental rationale behind the existence of a party is apparently inexplicable. Due to this neglect of ideology, analysis of the motivational aspect of party organisation also stands ignored.

THEORIES OF EVOLUTION OF PARTIES

Parties as organisations emerged earlier in the USA than in Britain. The emergence of the Democratic Party in the USA dates back to 1828, whereas around the same time, opponents of what was earlier known as the Democratic-Republican coalition took the label of the Republicans and emerged as an independent bloc. In Britain, the 1832 Reforms Act proved to be an impetus to the process of the emergence of formal party structures. With the decline in the Crown's ability to mount support in the House of Commons for its chosen ministers, party leaders had to try and create their own support. The complex property qualifications introduced by the Act required intervention from the Centre to control the nominations of candidates and to create some organisation at the constituency level to monitor the registration of voters on the electoral rolls. The 1867 Reform Act gave a further fillip to the process of party formation. Ostrogarski,[5]

---

[3] Joseph La Palombara and Myron Weiner, *'Political Parties and Political Development'* 1966, p.12 (Footnotes 1, 2 and 3 are as quoted by AG Kulkarni in his unpublished thesis, "A study of Political Parties in Maharashtra with special reference to the period 1947-62-67."1968. p.26).

[4] Ian McLean (Ed.) *The Concise Oxford Dictionary of Politics*, p.233.

[5] Moisei Yakovelvic Ostrogorski was a political thinker, whose book *Democracy and Organisation of Political Parties,* originally written in French, was influential in Britain and the United States in the early twentieth century. He has been quoted by Jack and Adam Lively, in *Democracy in Britain: A Reader*.p.154.

influential French observer, had very rightly noted at the turn of the century, that the breakdown of old hierarchies and social ties had been countered, at least in the political sphere, by the creation of extra-parliamentary, mass-membership parties incorporating and organising the newly-enfranchised electoral masses.

The sustained political party culture in American democracy has its origin in serious disagreements between the major political leaders. Differences of opinion between principal politicians like Alexander Hamilton, Thomas Jefferson and James Madison on several key issues paved way for the emergence of two different groups. The differences ranged from financial planning to the starting of a political newspaper. In 1792, Jefferson and Madison went so far as to call themselves the Republican Party. The others remained Federalists although, initially and technically, they could not become a full-fledged political party.

The fact that the emergence of parties has always been a subject of intense debate amongst political theorists, underscores their centrality in a democratic polity. The basic issue of the origin of political parties caught the imagination of theorists and eventually several theories were advocated, explaining the same.

It is noteworthy that only a few of the various theories mentioned earlier consider ideological basis as something crucial for the existence of parties; something like their raison d'être. For example, Lord Macaulay believed that 'there would always exist political parties of different, rather opposing temperaments; a party of order, authority and status quo, the Conservative, opposed by a party of liberty and progress, the Liberal.'[6] Edmund Burke cited political principles as the main cause of the origin of a party. In 1770, he[7] wrote a pamphlet titled 'Thoughts on the cause of the present discontent' and provided a classic defence of parties. His defence is based on three propositions. He felt that the House

[6]Lord Macaulay. 1913. *History of England*, pp.82-83, as quoted by AG Kulkarni. *op.cit.*

[7]As quoted by Jack and Adam Lively (Ed.) in *Democracy in Britain: A Reader*, p.141.

of Commons existed as a control over the administration and that it could exercise such control only if it had, within it, political groups actively opposing the administration with criticism and alternative policies. Burke also mentioned that the serious politician will realise the need for a combination with like-minded persons if he is to play any kind of effective political role.

In today's context, Burke's defense of political parties may sound simplistic because it takes the existence of the fundamentals of parliamentary democracy for granted. It is noteworthy that in the changing circumstances, not all the opposition parties are seen as 'actively opposing administration' and the question of 'criticism and alternative policies' also does not always arise. Also, the notion of 'effective political role' on the part of a politician is questionable since the ideas of an effective role differ from person to person. It means that for some, the essence of the phrase lies in pursuing all those policies and programmes that are in the interest of the people even at the cost of votes. For some others, indulging in all necessary compromises and remaining in power may be at the core of Burke's concept.

On the other hand, theorists like Henry Sumner Maine, while putting forward the 'brokerage theory', suggests that mainly in the expectations of the fair sharing of political economy—the distribution of the spoils—lay the origins of a political party.[8]

While it is obvious that principles and philosophies should ideally explain the eternal process of the evolution of parties, changing ground realities make the gap between theoretical and factual, more obvious. In the context of India today, parties declare that they are established on certain principles and try to conceal the real cause of their origin, such as the furtherance of group interests or the fulfilment of the material aspirations of the leadership. In India, the emergence of breakaway factions—such as the Indian National Congress-I in 1969, the Charan Singh-led faction of the Janata Party in 1979, which later came to be known as the Lok Dal, and the

[8]As referred to by AG Kulkarni, *op.cit.*

Chandra Shekhar-led faction of the undivided Janata Dal (Secular) of the early Nineties—are cases in point. All in all, the fact remains that most of the classical theories of the origin of a political party lack universal validity, much less an eternal relevance, as they are absolutely relative.

INDIAN VIEW OF PARTIES

Similar to the parties in several other countries that were fighting against colonial rule, the emergence of the Indian National Congress was closely linked with the Independence movement. Due to this, unlike in other countries, expectations from politicians and political activists in India are always charged with elements like selflessness, sacrifice and integrity. As opposed to Americans, Indians are hardly comfortable with the concept of a 'professional politician'. In fact, during the pre-Independence era, leaders like Gopal Krishna Gokhale had sought 'spiritualisation of politics'[9] in their bid to take political activism to a high moral ground. Understandably, the traditional approach of Indians towards political activism is different and they have distinctive expectations from political activists.

It is also pertinent to understand the thought process of Indian leaders and political philosophers in the context of political parties as institutions. Since the birth and growth of the Congress was almost parallel to the freedom movement, thinking about parties as institutions was never a priority during the pre-Independence era. Even after Independence, since Congress hegemony continued almost unchallenged for over two decades, there was apparently no need to build a political party as an institution. Besides, except for the Communists, almost all political formulations originated from the Congress and hence, whatever the Congress leadership had thought of or had not thought of as a party, reflected in their thinking and functioning.

Mahatma Gandhi and the entire Gandhian thought-leadership were always sceptical about political parties. In fact, there are several

[9]NR Phatak, *Adarsha Bharat Sevak: Gopal Krishna Gokhale yanche charitra (Marathi)* p.74.

instances show Gandhi had some reservations about the democratic process itself. He had observed, 'Democracy can only represent the average, if not less than the average.'[10] About the Congress, he had several lofty ideas. Once, he wrote: 'I have always conceived Congress to be the greatest school of political education for the whole nation.'[11] However, he was also aware of the ground realities. He had lamented, 'The Congress is far from the realisation of the ideal. One hears of manipulation of Congress registers and bogus names being put in for the purpose of showing numbers. When the registers have been honestly prepared, there is no attempt to keep in close touch with the voters.'[12] Although on several occasions he bluntly commented on the state of the Congress, there were hardly any practical suggestions coming from him to salvage the situation. In the draft Constitution for the Indian National Congress prepared by him, he had clearly observed that, 'Congress, in its present shape and form, i.e., a propaganda vehicle and parliamentary machine, has outlived its use[13] and it must be disbanded and converted into a Lok Sevak Sangha.' Perhaps, this was the stark realisation on Gandhi's part that a party contesting elections and seeking power cannot serve the people in a selfless manner.

Jayaprakash Narayan (JP) who waged a struggle against the infamous Emergency imposed by Indira Gandhi in 1975, was once an ardent supporter of well-organised parties. In June 1948, as leader of the Socialist Party, he had observed, '...the primary essential is Party organisation and active work to organise and educate the masses and to bring them under the Party's political leadership.'[14] While this reaction on his part after his party's debacle in the by-elections of Uttar Pradesh in 1948 was understandable, there is no evidence to suggest that he had given any serious thought to the nuances of building

[10]As quoted in Prabhu and Rao (Ed.). *Mind of Mahatma Gandhi*' (3rd edn), p.343.
[11]Compiled by HM Vyas, MK Gandhi, *Gandhiji Expects*, p.154.
[12]*Ibid*.
[13]MK Gandhi, *India of My Dreams*, p.290.
[14]Bimala Prasad (Ed.). *Socialism, Sarvodaya and Democracy, Selected Works of Jayaprakash Narayan*, p.42.

the party organisation, at any point of time earlier. In one of his books, he has severely criticised the partisan aspect of parliamentary democracy. According to him, when unanimity is required, parties are keen on harping upon their differences. Many a times, parties prefer their interest to the interests of the nation. JP has also observed that it is ironic that members of the public, whose fate, is in a way in the hands of political parties, have no control whatsoever on parties and their functioning.[15] Yet another Gandhian, Vinoba Bhave, also had strong reservations about party politics. He 'made a distinction between *raj-niti,* the politics of power and *lok-niti*, the politics of self-governing people. Vinoba's *lok-niti* rejected parliament, parties and elections and believed in decision-making through consensus, where people transcended all business.'[16] Vinoba had appealed to the people to 'give up the party spirit' because, 'Party divides what should be undivided and the country's strength is dissipated. Freedom from Party is as necessary as freedom from caste.'[17] Gandhian thinker, Acharya Dada Dharmadhikari, too was critical of parties. According to him, '...a political party is a conspiracy against the common man'.[18] He had also strongly recommended complete internal democracy within the parties and a strict code of conduct for their members.

Ram Manohar Lohia believed that '...the Socialist Party worked as an instrument to bring about a socialist society.'[19] He was also of the opinion that in the name of representative democracy, the common man was left '...merely with the choice of persons whom he might prefer over others to think and act for him'.[20] Like Lohia, BR Ambedkar too had no aversion to parties, although both of them were aware of their limitations. What is most noteworthy

[15]Jayaprakash Narayan, *Bharatiya Rajya Vyavastha Ki Punar Rachana: Ek Sujhav*, (Hindi) p.68, 70

[16]Rajendra Vora and Suhas Palshikar (Ed.) *Indian Democracy: Meanings and Practices*, p.12.

[17]Vinoba, *Democratic Values*, p.65.

[18]As told by Justice Chandrashekhar Dharmadhikari and his son in an interview with the author on 27 June 2007.

[19]Rajendra Vora and Suhas Palshikar (Ed.) *op.cit*, p.13.

[20]*Ibid.*

about Lohia is his unambiguous, pro-organisation approach. In *Marx, Gandhi and Socialism*[21], he says, 'PSP (Praja Socialist Party) must devote its attention to organisation as much as to policy. Those days are gone when the universal hunger for freedom from foreign rule could make up for the lack of organisation by the fervour of mass spontaneity.' Further, he also emphasises that, 'The PSP must attempt to build up a strong, well-knit, vital organisation. While it must encourage initiative at even the lowest unit of organisation, the need for disciplined functioning of the party must not be lost sight of.'

Almost parallel to those who were sceptical about parties, were the views of leaders of the Rashtriya Swayamsevak Sangha (RSS), the parent organisation of the BJP. MS Golwalkar, RSS chief for over a quarter of a century, was always critical of the party system as well as the political system in India. A staunch nationalist, he had observed, 'For, a party without persons of good character and selfless devotion to the total national cause is like a body with paralysed limbs, useless and even harmful...'[22] He wanted a political group to be 'an organised homogenous party'. He was apprehensive that in the absence of a well-knit national life, 'political parties (would) degenerate into mutual hostility and ruin the national fabric,'[23] since democratic institutions will come into play only when the people are firmly rooted in the consciousness of 'nation above party'.[24] Understandably, Deendayal Upadhyay, ideologue and one of the founding fathers of the Jan Sangh, had similar views. He had stressed that parties should be giving importance to qualities like devotion and discipline, besides being 'wedded to certain ideals', with all their policies 'framed with a view to realising these ideals.' He was of the firm view that democracy is not just about elections but also well-organised people, well-built parties and well-established conventions of political conduct.[25]

---

[21] Ram Manohar Lohia *Marx, Gandhi and Socialism,* p.416.

[22] MS Golwalkar, *Bunch of Thoughts,* p.680.

[23] *Ibid.*p.523

[24] *Ibid.* p.524.

[25] From a compilation of his writings published in *Manthan,* New Delhi, April-June, 2004. p. 32-36.

The history of political parties and party system in India appears to have validated most of the doubts and apprehensions voiced by the likes of Vinoba Bhave, Jayprakash Narayan (JP) or MS Golwalkar. In fact, the seeds of degeneration are sown in the way parties emerge. The manner in which political parties have been coming into existence, have a bearing upon the way their affairs are conducted later. As is very obvious, when a party comes into existence purely to fulfil the aspirations of its ambitious leader/s, it is but natural that such an organisation will unabashedly pursue populist politics simply for the sake of attaining power. In India, out of a total of six national and forty-three state parties recognised by the Election Commission of India,[26] at least twenty-five have come into existence to serve the cause of a leader, at best a social group. (For details, see Appendix A)

The present-day scenario in India is far from reassuring. While overambitious politicians have consumed their parties, power-centred politics dominated by these parties has subsumed the state. Sociologist DN Dhanagare points out that this primacy of political power compels the ruling elite 'to take recourse to populist measures to ensure that they remain in power...'.[27] It may be noted here that in India, establishing a political party is easier and more beneficial than establishing a Non-government Organisation (NGO). Besides, the level of control over the parties by the controlling authority—the Election Commission of India[28]—is far too less when compared to the control of the Charity Commissioner over the NGOs, or the Registrar of Societies over the cooperative institutions.

---

[26] According to a booklet, *Political Parties and Election Symbols,* published by the Election Commission of India in 2009, there are six national and fifty-four recognised state parties. Considering that some state parties are counted more than once, the total number of parties comes to forty-three. Besides this, there are some parties known as Registered Parties and not all of them are duly recognised by the Election Commission of India.

[27] DN Dhanagare, 'Civil society, state and democracy: Contextualising a discourse,' *Sociological Bulletin,* 50(2) September 2001, p.183.

[28] For details, please see http://www.eci.gov.in/ElectoralLaws/OrdersNotifications/Registration_of_Political_Party.pdf.

PARTIES AS INDISPENSABLE INSTITUTIONS

Democracy cannot be just a concept. The real test of democracy is in its practice. Theoretical correctness and conceptual clarity are undoubtedly very important, but equally crucial are its practical aspects. And here comes the question of the practitioners of democracy, mainly the political parties. Especially under any kind of representative democracy, parties become the voice of the people. Although parties appear to have become inevitable today, their evolution as an institution is intertwined with the evolution of functional, representative democracy. As is the fact, before the nineteenth century, no country had a formally organised political party. Quite understandably, the evolution of the concept of a political party and its gradual institutionalisation is commensurate with the extension of suffrage.

Parties may not be as old as democracy itself, but they certainly are the very foundation of modern representative democracy. For the aggregation of popular interests, articulation of the grievances of the people, as also for providing a vehicle of participation in the democratic process, parties as institutions are a must. By institution, it is meant that parties have a legitimate, definite and permanent role. Their general functional set-up is well laid down, and their existence is universally recognised. There are several other public institutions and organisations in a democratic polity, but the role of political parties is unparalleled.

British Prime Minister of the early nineteenth century, Benjamin Disraeli, had described parties as an 'organised opinion'[29]. In the form of an organised opinion, parties are a basic requirement of modern democratic system. On the one hand, in practical terms, parties are a '...twentieth century mechanism designated to solve the problem of how to bring the people, the new mass voters into the political community'[30], on the other, it is also meant 'to give to the

---

[29] DW Borger's *Foreword* to Maurice Duverger's *Political Parties: Their Organisation and Activity in the Modern State,* p.5.
[30] *Ibid.*

man in the street, a voice in politics that he (otherwise) cannot have'.[31] The contest between different political parties to win the allegiance of the electorate and form a government is central to the very concept of representative democracy. Obviously then, in any democratic set-up, as compared to any other institution, the role of political parties acquires focus. In the absence of political parties, it would be hard for voters to judge as to what individual candidates stood for or intended to do, once elected. One just cannot deny that, if political parties fail in gathering public interest, society will disintegrate, with the promotion of self-interest dominating.

The more one applies the democratic principle, the more important becomes the role of parties. Understandably then, Sartori is tempted to call democracy, a 'party-cracy', meaning that the 'locus of power is actually shifted from government and parliament to party directorates.'[32] Notwithstanding the fact that in several democracies, including India, the state of political parties is far from desirable, the pre-eminence of parties has never been theoretically challenged.

Collection of Communities

Since democratic way of life springs from the voluntary emergence of free communities, parties also need to be seen as voluntary associations aimed at political expression in a democratic system. In the context of India, the present state of most of the political parties substantiates Duverger's definition of parties as 'a collection of communities'. The BJP, too, over the years, has developed an understanding of the importance of having at least one Muslim as its office bearer at various levels. Similarly, once famous for its anti-upper caste rhetoric, BSP today talks about *sarvajan samaj* (society comprising all the people) and tries to embrace all sections of society. Shiv Sena too abandons its anti-north Indians approach sporadically. It can safely be concluded that as parties grow and attain power even once, they realise that as institutions they are expected to aggregate and express political demands. Further, they do apprehend that they

[31] *Ibid.*
[32] Giovanni Sartori, *Democratic Theory*, p. 254.

have an important role to play in the management of conflict in societies divided along cultural, linguistic, religious or regional lines.

Although a voluntary character is the basis of any genuine activism, it never can be effective unless it is organised. This is because of the fact that to mobilise the populace at large into the system, a suitable apparatus is required and parties fulfil this requirement. Mobilisation of the populace and organising a party are interlinked. As is the case with India, both tend to fuse in a developing polity. Due to this, a show of strength by way of organising mammoth public meetings and rallies has become a fashion in present-day politics.

It is not for no reason that the first step taken towards full democracy in Central and Eastern Europe was the formation of new political parties. One of the greatest social inventions of the modern age, at par with electricity and computers on the technological side, are political parties. Undoubtedly, mass democracies cannot do without them. While reviewing the relationship between what parties preach and what they practise, through an extensive research, renowned political scientist Hans-Dieter Klingemann and his colleagues concluded that:

> ...political parties are the major actors in the process that connects the citizenry and the governmental process... political parties aggregate demands into loosely coherent policy packages...thus, they are crucial to decision-making and implementation. From this perspective, political parties must choose policies. They have to rule and they have to take responsibility for their decisions. They are the major actors in the representative democratic systems when it comes to solving societal problems.[33]

PARTIES HAVE NO ALTERNATIVE

The omnipresent contempt for the political class and thereby parties

---

[33] HD Klingemann, RI Hofferbert and I Budge. 1994. 'Parties, policies and democracy', Boulder, CO: Westview. As quoted by Paul D Webb, 'Are British political parties in decline?' in the July 1995 issue of *Party Politics*, (Vol. 1, No. 3).

in major democracies notwithstanding, it is hard to imagine a genuine representative democracy without a political party. No matter how fast is the growth of lobbies, interest groups and voluntary organisations, none of these are seen as alternatives to political parties. According to Kay Lawson, political scientist and professor at the San Francisco State University, 'The need for political organisations is greater today than ever before, thanks to the changes that have made us both less and more capable of ruling ourselves without them.'[34]

There are several examples of how non-political groups in India realise sooner than later that the limitations to their NGO-like efforts could be overcome only through the formation of a political party. The latest example is that of Arvind Kejriwal. Earlier, in 2004, Medha Patkar of the Narmada Bachao Andolan and her colleagues had decided to take their battle to the electoral arena and fight elections as an independent political party.[35] Similarly, in 2006, Jayprakash Narayan (JN) converted his NGO, *Lok Satta*, into a political party. Earlier in the mid-Seventies, the *Navnirman Samiti*, which had spearheaded a popular drive to oust Chimanbhai Patel's government in Gujarat, as well as the *Sampurna Kranti* movement led by Jayprakash Narayan (JP), also ended in the formation of political parties to fight elections. In the Eighties in Assam, the All-Assam Students Union (AASU) led the anti-infiltration (of Bangladeshis) movement in the state. Later they established the Asom Gana Parishad (AGP) to contest elections. Organisations like the *Samyukta Maharashtra Samiti* (SMS) and the *Shetkari Sanghatana*, both from Maharashtra, were not established as political parties, but later they thought it wise to contest elections and become a political party. It is noteworthy that in 1957 the SMS fought in the elections through the formation of a front, while in 1994, the *Shetkari Sanghatana* established the *Samarth Bharat Paksh*. All these examples clearly bring forth the fact that voluntary organisations and

[34]Kay Lawson in Kay Lawson and Peter H Merkl (Ed.) *When Parties fail*, p.36-37.
[35]Medha Patkar's interview in *The Hindu* at http://www.hinduonnet.com/2004/03/28/stories/2004032800971300.htm.

popular movements ultimately have to think of establishing a party when the ultimate objective is to effect a change in the government. This further underscores the element of indispensability of political parties.

Modern democracy is all about party democracy. With only a few notable exceptions such as Herbert Croly,[36] MN Roy[37] and Jayprakash Narayan (JP),[38] most thinkers and political scientists have accepted the inevitability of the existence of parties in a modern state. Noted Indian thinker and liberalist, MN Roy, was a strong advocate of the concept of a party-less democracy. Known for his radical humanist approach, Roy, in 1944, prepared a draft Constitution for India. Apart from proposing a system of political economy emphasising the decentralisation and devolution of power, he also suggested rejection of political parties themselves as legitimate instruments for the spread of democratic values, and in 1948, dissolved his own Radical Democratic Party, which he had founded in 1940.

In the mid-Seventies, JP had mooted the same idea. He was known for his strong reservations about the party system. While rejecting Nehru's offer to join his cabinet, JP explained, 'The party system, so it appeared to me, was seeking to reduce the people to the position of sheep whose only function was to choose periodically, the shepherds who would look after their welfare.'[39] He had further pointed out that parties promote undesirable traits such as demagoguery, unethical practices, unscrupulousness, manipulation and intrigue, where 'small caucuses of politicians rule in the name of the people and create the illusion of democracy and self government.'[40] JP was all in favour of what he has described as 'Communitarian

[36]Herbert Croly, *Progressive Democracy,*p.311.

[37]MN Roy, *Politics, Power and Parties*, p.94.

[38]Bimala Prasad (Ed.). 1964. *Socialism, Sarvodaya and Democracy. Selected Works of Jaya Prakash Narayan.* p.218 from AG Kulkarni's unpublished doctoral thesis "A Study of Political Parties in Maharashtra with Special Reference to the Period 1947-62-67". 1968.p.1.

[39]As observed by *Time* Magazine as on 5 June, 2007.

[40]Jayaprakash Narayan, 'A Plea for Reconstruction of the Indian Polity' (1959) as reproduced in *Manthan,* New Delhi, April-June 2004, New Delhi. p.38-44.

Democracy', where 'there may conceivably be parties, but they are likely to be local factions, and, in any case, their role in the state will not be as commanding as that of the parties in the parliamentary system.'[41]

In a different sense, the concept of a party-less democracy has also been referred to by political scientists in the context of Tony Blair's premiership.[42] According to them, a dominant leader like Blair can eventually do away with the party by setting up his own professionally managed organisational-functional structure. However, notwithstanding the growing trend of projecting a prime ministerial candidate, (just like a presidential candidate, in a presidential democracy) being set in a parliamentary democracy, it is true that even a rebellious prime ministerial candidate can hardly do without a party tag.

In 2004, the New Delhi-based Lokniti: Centre for the Study of Developing Societies (CSDS),[43]conducted a National Election Study. It clearly indicated that the idea of a party-less political system was absolutely unacceptable to a whopping 72 per cent of the respondents. The same study also showed how the percentage of votes gained by independents had considerably gone down from 15 per cent in 1952 to just 4.25 per cent in 2004 and 5.19 per cent in 2009 in the Lok Sabha elections held in India (see Appendix B), indicating a greater number of voters preferring party candidates over non-party aspirants.

---

[41]*Ibid.*

[42]British political scientist Dennis Kavanagh has argued that although Tony Blair and Margaret Thatcher reinvented their parties (they) 'also presided over their decline', in the emerging scenario, 'one where populist leaders seek inclusive or target audiences and communicate with them directly via web sites, Question Time, media interviews, and such television shows as *Richard and Judy*. Perhaps there is less need for mass parties in the age of communication via focus groups, direct mail and call centres, finance from a mix of wealthy donors and State funding, and policies from think tanks. Parties as electoral organisations can operate as partnership franchises, contracting out key tasks to private and voluntary agencies.' (From Dennis Kavanagh, 'The Blair Premiership' in *Blair Effect- 2001-2005* Cambridge University Press 2005, p.7).

[43]For details, see www.lokniti.org/WPS-1.pdf.

The most distinguishing aspect of political parties is the institutional mechanism for their accountability, by way of fighting elections. Unlike voluntary organisations and interest groups or even think tanks, parties have to face the electorate at least once in the stipulated tenure of the respective houses of elected representatives. Naturally then, the parties have to be more responsible while playing different designated roles. Unlike lobbies, interest groups and voluntary organisations, parties have to be far more responsible while deciding on major policy issues, selecting candidates, managing party organisation and running a government as a ruling party or organising popular discontent as an opposition party. Again, unlike all other organisations, parties also have to take both credit and discredit for successes and failures.

Role of Political Parties

Parties have a particular role and this very role makes them indispensable institutions. The institutional role of political parties involves serving as intermediaries between a mass public and the formal structures of the government. Parties are the vehicles of people's participation which democracy presupposes.

Political parties, at least in theory, are expected to work for structuring of the ballot, integrating and mobilising the mass public, recruiting political leaders, organising government, forming public policy and aggregating interests.

The participation of people in party affairs is central to all these functions. This can be achieved effectively only with the activism of party workers. For parties to have a sustained participation of volunteers and activists, an enduring organisational structure is essential. It is here that the question of the mutuality of expectations of the party and its rank and file comes into the play. Party workers, motivated ideologically or otherwise, have multiple expectations from the party. They expect that parties will give an impetus to their (party workers') social mobility and give them some identity and status, besides satisfaction. However, this is hard to come by in an organisation which is heterogeneous in membership, eclectic in ideology, and voluntaristic in motivational orientation.

A vivid description of the role parties are ideally expected to play is given by Derek Holroyde, a representative of the BBC in India in 1954. In a symposium on Parliamentary Democracy, he observed:

> The chief link between those who formulate policy in the Centre and State and the man whose vote supports them is the politician. By this I mean, both the elected member and the party worker. It is the men and women who are in contact both with the villager on the one hand and the Government on the other who bear the main responsibility for seeing that the voter is informed on the topics that concern him and equally that government is made aware through the member, of voter's feeling. Theirs is the supremely important task of keeping both sides informed, and educated, about the trends of thinking and action.[44]

There appears a near total unanimity amongst theorists about the significance of the role parties are expected to play. Parties are duly recognised as agencies helping the processes of formation and expression of public opinion. Earnest Barker has aptly described the role of parties: '[as] a conduit or sluice by which waters of social thought and discussion are brought to the wheels of political machinery and set to turn those wheels.'[45] Political parties could also be described as agencies translating public opinion into public policies.

Nature of Political Parties

Whether parties can play the role that is expected of them is closely related to their nature. The nature of parties varies from system to system. The historical background of a country, people, and socio-political and cultural environment in general affect the character of a

---

[44] The text of the speech by Derek Holroyed, then BBC Representative in India, at the symposium on Parliamentary Democracy in India, organised by the Harold Laski Institute Of Political Science, Ahmedabad in 1956.

[45] Earnest Barker. 1948., *Reflections on Government*, p.39.

political party. Nonetheless, attempts have been made to distinguish parties on the basis of their character. If one follows the evolution of parties as traced by researchers, the 'elite party' was popular in the political arena in the first stage (1800-1850), followed by the 'mass-party' (1880-1960) and later, the 'catch-all party' (mainly after 1945).

Renowned political scientists Richard S Katz and Peter Mair have added yet another category to the existing list. They call it 'cartel party'. One of the most important characteristics of a cartel party is a greater degree of professionalism in party work and campaigning. Here, politics is looked at as a purely professional responsibility. Obviously then, more than commitment, managerial abilities and efficiency come into play.

CADRE PARTY AND IDEOLOGY

Organisationally speaking, the two established categories of parties—cadre and catch-all—are well known and, as their names suggest, their characteristics are markedly different.

Cadre, although primarily from the military lexicon, in the political context means 'a disciplined, hierarchically organised, and swiftly responsive'[46] organisation. The concept of a cadre party presupposes the existence of a systemic arrangement of recruitment, nurturing and development of the members of the party organisation. The term 'cadre' originally means 'the permanent skeleton of military knit, the commissioned and non-commissioned officers etc. around whom the rank and file may be quickly grouped.'[47] The origins of the practice of using this military term in party politics can be traced to Russia under Lenin. In practical terms, cadre connotes something much more than hired personnel or storm troopers. As is obvious, storm troopers have very little to do with the objective and the impact of their being active. As against this, it is expected that the cadre is committed to an ideology, which means, 'any comprehensive

[46]Ian McLean (Ed). *The Concise Oxford Dictionary of Politics*, p.52.
[47]*Ibid.*

and mutually consistent set of ideas by which a social group makes sense of the world.'[48] Ideology not only motivates the cadre but also serves as a driving force. Ideology, above all, instils a deep sense of purpose in the minds of party workers. A majority of party workers are miles away from the seat of power and many of them hardly get any benefit from the party's ascendancy. And still, they continue to work for the party. For them, ideology alone continues to be the driving force.

Yet, when several senior political leaders observe that initiation of a political worker is not necessarily linked to ideology or ideology alone, it is not far from the fact. Senior party functionaries from the BJP and the Congress feel that in the case of a considerably large section of committed party workers, family background, peer pressure or neighbourhood connections or an intense desire to work for a temporary cause or a short-lived issue (taken up by the respective political group) brings young individuals to the doorstep of a party. Many senior party functionaries from both the BJP as well as the Communist Party of India agree that at least in India, in the changing circumstances, the percentage of individuals joining a political party purely for ideological reasons is comparatively marginal, although it remains a very important factor at the subconscious level. It is also undeniable that in most cases, differences in ideologies mean very little if they only rarely reflect in the style of functioning of the party leaders and workers.

According to many senior political leaders, the cultivation of inter-personal relationships, the resultant sense of security and creation of comfort zones, and later almost non-erasable identification with an ideological group, normally keeps an individual connected with a political party. Besides, it is also a fact that liberalisation, globalisation and privatisation have pushed the ideological aspects of political activism to the back burner.

As compared to cadre parties, catch-all parties are more open, less structured and hence, cadre driven to a lesser extent. In the

[48] *Ibid.*

Indian context, parties such as the CPI (M) and the BJP could also be described as cadre or semi-cadre parties, with their hold-all and 'everything for everybody' character, while the Congress can be cited as the classic example of a catch-all party.[49] The emergence of the cartel-party is a recent phenomenon. With the diminishing importance of ideologies and a structured party organisation, appearance of cartel parties is on the rise in India. Most of the personality-driven parties, such as Rashtriya Lok Dal (RLD) of Ajit Singh or Biju Janata Dal (BJD) of Naveen Patnaik, are the best examples of cartel parties where professional party managers run the affairs of the party, just as professional event managers conduct events. Naturally, ideology as such has almost no or at best a very marginal role in a cartel party.

This classical way of categorising holds good only to a limited extent. Populism and electoral compulsions are influencing the functioning of parties belonging to all the categories. The way in which serious and primarily organisation-based political parties in India are coping with the changing situation and in the process undergoing a transformation in their character has been discussed in detail, later in this chapter. But there is no doubt that parties can play their particular role effectively, only if they have sustainable organisational structures.

Party Models in India

Traditionally, two different models of party organisation are almost universally recognised. They are rational efficient or cadre, and party democracy or mass membership. While this classical distinction between parties is fast losing relevance the world over, in India, there is an entirely different and confusing scenario. The Indian National

---

[49]This is endorsed by Prof KC Suri, in his essay 'Parties under pressure: Political Parties in India since Independence'. He says, 'In India, except the communist parties, and the recently emerged Dalit parties, all other parties appear to be, using Kirchheimer's term, catch-all parties. The Congress party, Swatantra, Socialists, Janata Party, Janata Dal and most of the regional parties cannot be simply termed as parties of this or that interest or alliance of specific interests'. http://www.lokniti.org/WPS-1.pdf.

Congress is the classic example of a rational efficient party and yet it hardly cultivates any cadre, and on the singular issue of secularism, it has always tried to appear as an ideological party. On the other hand, the BJP is known for its strong—if not always very clear and articulate—ideological position, but post-NDA rule, it is trying to become a catch-all party and embracing different shades of the ideological spectrum. Besides, it has also tried to become a cadre-based party with a mass following.

Power-driven parties are more likely to succumb to populist pressures. Wary of media criticism and its consequences, parties try to camouflage their succumbing to populist pressures in one way or the other. In the process of adopting populist measures to win support from new sections of society, parties try to take their traditional voters for granted and face failures. As several elections in Uttar Pradesh held in the recent past have shown, Muslims and upper caste Hindus appear to have deserted the Congress and the BJP, respectively, thanks mainly to their alleged populist tactics.[50]

In India, while family-centric party organisations are common, not all ruling families prefer taking the reins of power into their hands. In parties like the NCP, Janata Dal (Secular), INLD and BJD, the members belonging to the families of Pawars, Devegowdas, Chautalas and Patnaiks wield 'Direct Power' while the Congress and the Shiv Sena have adopted an 'Indirect Power' model. Under the Congress system, 'everything for everybody' as the winning formula and the almost uninterrupted rule of a supreme dynasty are two strong features. Earlier, members belonging to the First Family in the Congress used to take the reins of power in their own hands. But now, perhaps having learnt from the Shiv Sena, the First Family has adopted a strategy of enjoying all the benefits of power without occupying any position in the government. To a great extent, this is 'seeking power without responsibility'. This is the indirect power model. Here, one also has to note that while the Gandhis have been

[50]Many political observers have commented that upper caste Hindus alone do not necessarily favour BJP any more and Muslims have also deserted Congress after 1992.

contesting elections and testing the electoral waters, the Thackerays have steadfastly remained away from even that.

While in the Congress and the Shiv Sena, the indirect power is with a family, in the case of the BJP as well as the CPI (M), it vests with the party organisation. Albeit, there is a significant difference in the models adopted by the RSS-BJP and the CPI (M). In the RSS-BJP model, the RSS is at the centre and the BJP and other RSS-inspired organisations are all around it. In the CPI (M), unlike the RSS, the party itself is at the centre and other front organisations are around it. However, both are examples of organisation-centric models.

The third model—if any—could be that of the Janata Dal (United) and smaller regional parties like the Asom Gana Parishad (AGP) etc. where, although a particular leader is at the helm of affairs, his family is not wielding any power, directly or otherwise.

MODELS OF PARTIES

Which of the models discussed here is perhaps the most suited for democracy in India? Since there are hardly any attempts to study these models in depth and come to a conclusion, it is difficult to say anything with certitude. However, if institution-building with professionalism at its core is the key to the success of any organisation, then the non-family-centric models stand a better chance of being successful. On the count of strong organisation, the absence of which may lead to a split in the party, non-family-centric parties have fared far too well. While India has witnessed the emergence of varieties of Congresses and Janata Dals, no significant leader of the BJP and the CPI (M) could ever think of splitting the party organisation at the national level successfully. To that extent, non-family centric parties are more capable of avoiding splits and inviting instability.

This is also important in the context of the greater institutionalisation of political parties. Considering the high mortality[51] of political parties in India, it is important to examine

[51] In India, each election has been witnessing the emergence of some new parties. Only the INC and the CPI have fought every national election since 1951. Parties like the

as to how many leaders or founding fathers of these parties were/are serious about building their respective party organisation as an enduring institution. Parties that have a well-defined, distinct and articulated ideology, a structured organisation (where leadership is not always inherited) and an administrative establishment, can well be considered a serious political party. As mentioned on the website of the Election Commission of India, out of a total of 1,366 registered (including both recognised and unrecognised) political parties in 2011, only 58 fit into this category.

CHANGING CHARACTER OF PARTIES

What exactly is the worldwide party scenario today? The volumes of *Political Parties of the World* (fifth edition published in 2001 and seventh edition, 2011)[52] have clearly brought into focus certain interesting features of the contemporary political party scenario. Identity issues seem to be dominating everywhere in the first decade of this century.

In the preface of the fifth edition, it has been observed that:

> The growing importance of racial and/or religious identity as a determinant of political affiliation and the often related rise of regional political movements demanding greater autonomy and in some cases outright separation.

Whereas the editors, in the preface of the seventh edition, observe:

> Furthermore, the conventional shorthand that placed most parties in the 1980s on a well-understood left-

---

Janata Party exist today, but only in name. Major political players that have faded into oblivion during the last fifty years include Ramrajya Parishad, Bharatiya Jan Sangh, Swatantra Party, Praja Socialist Party (PSP), Samyukta Socialist Party (SSP), Bharatiya Kranti Dal (BKD) and several other regional parties like Scheduled Caste Federation mainly in Maharashtra, Utkal Congress, mainly in Orissa. These parties have either vanished or merged themselves into a different party in the course of time.

[52] Alan J Day, (Ed.) *Political Parties of the World*-5th edition 2001, p.4.

> right continuum increasingly fails to characterise large numbers of parties. Issues of national, regional, ethnic and religious identity are seemingly to the fore, while even well-established party systems are being strained by the emergence of parties around issues, such as integration in the European Union or cultural identity in the face of in-flows of different population groups, that have moved from the fringe to the main-stream"[53]

These observations show how identity issues are increasingly affecting politics. Also, this is the reaction to the all-pervading influence of the forces of free markets since no other alternative is in sight. Both these points also indirectly refer to a multi-dimensional crisis that has plagued primary parties in major democracies of the world. This is a three-fold crisis: A crisis of ideology, of organisation and almost as a result, crisis of the ability to deliver the goods.

Here, it would be enlightening to understand some critical analyses of political parties and political culture in India in general. Rajni Kothari, in *Politics in India*, presents an overview of political thinking as well as approaches to political activism in the country. In a brilliant analysis of the strong points as well as weaknesses of the Indian polity, Kothari almost concludes that failure in effectively dealing with the problems of equality, pluralism and mass participation will give rise to an apprehension, and there he sounds prophetic. He has also warned that if democratic governance lags in performance, it may lead to spurt in cynicism and cause the withdrawal of the masses. He has also rightly stressed upon the study of the relationship between penetration of institutional and political forms, response of society to such penetration and the performance of the political system in meeting the needs and resolving the problems generated at different levels of society. Published in 1972, this book is, perhaps, the first enquiry into the relationship between institutional development and governmental output with a focus on the ability of the system

[53] DJ Sagar, (Ed.) *Political Parties of the World*, 7th Edition 2011, p vii

to perform. Kothari has dwelt at length on issues like political culture, political institutionalisation and the peculiarity of the Indian model of democracy. He has also touched upon issues like authority and leadership very effectively. The author has raised pertinent questions, the answers to which, even after several years have passed since the book was written, are still to emerge. Outlining a whole range of issues which need attention and amicable resolution, Kothari asks: '...is the present Indian leadership capable of delivering the goods?' He has also tried to find an answer and, in doing so, expressed his apprehensions, saying, '...as to whether a consensus leader is not, by the very nature of being a consensus leader, too much of a compromiser and a drifter.'[54] The patterns of leadership that one can discern through a minute analysis of decisions taken or avoided by successive prime ministers from Rajiv Gandhi, VP Singh, Narsimha Rao and AB Vajpayee to Manmohan Singh validate what Kothari had apprehended. And here, one is reminded of what Harold Laski is said to have once pointed out, that a leader is expected not only to lead but also refuse to be led by the masses.

Another book, *Context of Electoral Change in India,* edited by Rajni Kothari, is a collection of essays dealing with party politics, electoral participation and analysis of political scenarios in different states. It has not covered issues like populism and electoral compulsions since these factors were not all that prominent when the book was first published in 1969. Yet, the observations are noteworthy. Notwithstanding the informal character of the party organisation, which is an inherent part of the 'Congress System', and perhaps its strength as well, Kothari has emphatically called for greater institutionalisation of the organisational functioning of the party, especially that of the process of selection of candidates for different types of elections. One wonders, whether the lack of systemisation of party affairs in the Congress, proved to be the fountainhead of excessively unprofessional, unorganised and equally ineffective in real terms, party politics in India.

---

[54]Rajni Kothari, *Politics in India*. p. 449, 450

Contemporary Scene of Parties in India

Commenting on the state of parties in India and their performance, noted political scientist and researcher, KC Suri, has said:

> While the success of parties gives us some satisfaction, their shortcomings cause disquiet. The very success of parties in establishing and working out democracy in the spirit of nationalism, secularism, and socialism gave birth to tensions that parties find difficult to manage or resolve. For some desire more democracy, more power and more benefits from the state. Others feel that Indian democracy has gone awry and they tend to blame it on the populism, paternalism, corruption, and criminality indulged in by party leaders. The latter argument became more strident, as the principles and practice of libertarian democracy became dominant in the changed international environment of globalisation.[55]

While analysing the party scenario the world over, even in an otherwise confusing situation, certain factors, responsible for the dilution of ideology and weakening of organisation as well as leadership, emerge very clearly. The first, and perhaps the most important, is the steady but unchecked dilution of ideology.

The last century saw that politics across the world was dominated by ideology. On the extreme Left, it was communism while on the extreme Right, fascism. Even in the countries where neither of these extremes has ever seriously taken hold, political parties have largely been defined by where they claim they are, and are perceived to be, on this scale. In most parts of the world today, these arguments between Left and Right have ceased to be the defining feature of the political system. With the end of the Cold War and in an increasingly globalised capitalist economy, left-wing parties have

---

[55] KC Suri,'Parties under pressure: Political Parties in India since independence', at http://www.lokniti.org/WPS-1.pdf as on 2 January, 2006.

struggled to retain electoral support for a socialist agenda. A new consensus has emerged in India, as well as the world over, on the role of free markets in delivering efficiency and value, previously the preserve of the Centre-Right. Earlier in India, parties like the Jan Sangh and the Swatantra Party had taken firm positions against the expansion of the public sector. On the other hand, Congress and Left-leaning secular parties had always criticised the privatisation and dis-investment measures of the then NDA government. Today, a Right-leaning Shiv Sena is found opposing the revocation of the Urban Land Ceiling Act while the UPA government was seen pursuing the privatisation of airport management and the Left Front (while ruling in West Bengal) stoutly supporting Special Economic Zones. It is not simply the Left parties who have adopted the rhetoric and beliefs of the Right. In the context of social services and welfare, the so-called Centre-Right parties too have accepted that while private enterprise and markets have a key role to play, government intervention is essential in the overall scheme of things.

Generally speaking, parties are formed on the basis of some ideology, which in practical terms means a set of fundamental philosophical tenets of a group of persons who are competing for popular support in a democratic polity. Parties are expected to serve this particular ideological cause. Political parties and the process of attaining power through them are both means and not the end. Ideally, parties just like voluntary organisations, are expected to be vehicles for repaying the social debt, leaving practically no scope for pure selfish motive.

Such fundamental approaches to party activism and pursuit of power are expected to inspire political leaders to shape policy perspectives. If lofty conceptions are idealism, doctrinal positions could be considered as ideology. Policy perspectives are expected to reflect both. In practice, since the ideological fault lines have become blurred, ideology has been reduced to only the applied aspect. During the BJP-led NDA regime, since the BJP was handling the affairs of the country for the first time, this question of ideology and its relationship with or reflection in governance had become an important issue of debates and discussions internally, within the party, as also in the ideological movement.

On the overall scenario, political commentator Vandana Mishra comments:

> Opportunism has overtaken ideology in politics. It is hard pragmatism that matters. The parties are governed not by adherence to the norms of democracy, nationalism, secularism and socialism—they are all dispensable. When it comes to vote politics, compromise and surrender of ideals is a common behaviour pattern of the political leadership. Populist slogans, media management, Bollywood charisma and personalised electioneering are considered as election winning techniques. Consequently and unfortunately, ideology and idealism have lost not only their relevance but also their mass appeal.[56]

Why the Ideological Drift?

The reasons behind this trend of drifting away from ideologies, as observed in many political parties, are not far to seek. The fundamental reasons behind this phenomenon can be summarised as a growing and perhaps apparent irrelevance of doctrinal positions. As a result, ideology has become an impediment in the path and not a ladder to climb on to the seat of power.

Seymour Martin Lipset[57] has not only recognised the irrelevance of ideologies, but in a way, has also welcomed it. Commenting on the end of ideology, he says, '...the ideological issues dividing left and right (have) been reduced to a little more or little less government ownership and economic planning' and that it really makes little difference 'which political party controls the domestic policies of

[56] Vandana Mishra, 'Crises of Indian Parties' in *Mainstream*,Vol. XLVII, No. 13, 14 March, 2009.

[57] As quoted extensively by Stephen W Rousseas and James Farganis, in *American Politics and the End of Ideology* at http://www.writing.upenn.edu/~afilreis/50s/end-of-I-farganis.html.

individual nations'. All this, according to Lipset, '...reflects the fact that the fundamental political problems of the industrial revolution have been solved, the workers have achieved industrial and political citizenship; the conservatives have accepted the welfare state and the democratic left has recognised that an increase in overall state power carries with it more dangers to freedom than solutions for economic problem.' Howsoever simplistic at the first instance this may sound, it also has its own set of implications for representative and participatory democracy and they will be discussed later.

Changes in ground realities also affect ideological positions. The most fitting case is that of socialist parties in India in the mid-Sixties. Immediately after the official adoption of socialistic pattern of society by the ruling Congress in 1956, at its National Convention at Avadi, the relevance of socialist groupings itself became questionable. As a logical corollary, later, the ruling Congress successfully lured many socialists of that time, on the grounds of ideological proximity. Similarly, in the tiny state of Goa, initially the ruling Maharashtravadi Gomantak Party had a unique doctrinal position in its demand for the merger of Goa with Maharashtra. Later, when the issue did not remain relevant due to several factors, the party dropped the demand (although, it continues to call itself 'pro-Maharashtra').

Besides the irrelevance of ideologies, the crisis of motivation also has precipitated the predicament. With the waning influence of ideological motivation, politics of patronage started showing its magic. It is widely accepted that much of the success of the Congress in the Sixties was due to its ability to forge widespread patronage networks, providing critical linkages between local demands and central response. Once a monopoly of the Congress, politics of patronage has now become almost a success mantra for almost all political parties.

The origins of this politics of patronage could be traced to India's feudal past, where regional satraps used to work for the emperor even for the crumbs thrown at them. Government job quotas for sections eager to declare themselves as weaker, plum positions in the government offered to community leaders, establishing an independent development corporation especially for one or many communities, erecting statues and memorials for community icons or renaming buildings after them, are some of the ways and means of indulging in politics of patronage. Commenting upon the Congress' love affair with the state, journalist Edward Luce said that attaining power: 'is also about preferential access to a wide range of public goods', including, 'opportunity to jump queues, the ability to pull strings and the provision of free services for which the poor have to pay.'[58]

During the times of Indira Gandhi, this politics of patronage was reduced to a scheme of personal obligations and from there on, the role of ideology diminished further. As a result, post the Seventies, unlike its previous incarnation, the Congress became a centralised organisation insisting on loyalty to a single leader. Consequently, it lost touch with real issues and was interested in government till such time as the flow of patronage continued. Many believe that this 'loyalty' to a leader was also based on the ability to ensure this flow. The result was that the Congress 'fell prey to internal bickering and factional fights that were more personal than policy related.'[59] There are many who believe that it was during this phase that the process of degeneration of democratic institutions like the party and parliament got underway. This is also obliquely endorsed by many. Shivraj V Patil, senior Congress leader, says that more than other factors such as the erosion of ideology or weakening of organisation, 'the mistakes committed by rulers and the personalities of the leaders'[60] need to be held responsible for the electoral reverses faced by his party. The state of the Congress in India is a vivid example of how politics of patronage and personal equations have pushed ideology to the periphery.

In the last decade of the twentieth century, thinker and

---

[58]Edward Luce, *In spite of Gods* p.204.

[59]Kuldeep Mathur, *Decline of a centralised state: Changing Nature of Political Power in India* at http://planningcommission.nic.in/reports/sereport/ser/vision2025/polipowr.pdf.

[60]Shivraj V Patil, *Emerging Vision of India*, p.13.

renowned littérateur, Vijay Tendulkar, known for his Left leanings, had once candidly admitted that under the present circumstances there is nothing like Left (ideology) and Right (ideology).[61] Amidst this debate, there is also some talk about the attempts of finding a third way, but it has hardly led to any meaningful, comprehensive theorisation. As noted by EJ Dionne Jr, '...the third way is primarily a reaction to the old left and the new right' and seen 'more as a captive of past debates than as guide to the future.'[62] Obviously then, ideological confusion persists.

In India, the contours of coalition politics, a phenomenon discussed more elaborately later, clearly bring about both limitations as well as strengths due to the ideological grouping of political parties. Nobody can dispute the observation that, as things stand today, theoretically, any party could fit into the UPA, except the BJP. The Third Front, born, dead and struggling to take shape again, can accommodate any party except the BJP and the Congress; and the NDA can take any party except the Congress and the Communists. These exclusions and preferences are more due to party competition and electoral considerations, rather than ideological warfare.[63]

The limitations of ideology are very obvious in both the major ideological groups in India. Both the far Left and far Right have not been able to find solutions to the issues arising out of globalisation. On the one hand, there are hardly any buyers when some of them argue for blanket opposition to Foreign Direct Investment. On the other hand, the pro-globalisation groups have not been able to find convincing answers to the problems emerging out of mindless consumerism, vesting of veto power with the market forces and increasing insecurity of jobs with 'hire and fire' replacing archaic and over-protective labour laws. The CPI (M) in West Bengal had effectively reconciled the apparently conflicting trends of movement and government with a view to

---

[61] From Vijay Tendulkar's speech at the inauguration of the personal book collections of SG Majgaonkar in Rambhau Mhalgi Prabodhini, near Mumbai on 1 August 2001

[62] EJ Dionne, Jr., 'The third way is vogue on both sides of the Atlantic', *The International Herald Tribune*, London, 11 August,1998

[63] KC Suri, *op.cit*

developing itself as a unique practical political outfit that depends on organisation, entrenchment, networks, patron-client relationships and a down-to-earth, pro-people/pro-poor image. All this has helped the party to declass itself as and when required. But, after the Nandigram episode,[64] the CPI (M) too seems to have erred on several fronts. Noted political analyst Yogendra Yadav has pointed out this gap in what CPI (M) preaches and has actually practised while Nandigram was burning. In November 2007, he commented that while the proportion of upper caste MLAs have gone down elsewhere in the country, in West Bengal it is continuously on the rise and about two-third of the ministers of the state cabinet are coming from upper castes like Brahmins, Boddis and Kayasthas.[65]

This all-pervading crisis of ideology is more vivid in the post-communist landscape. Some of the key features of this landscape can be mentioned as 'tribal collectivism, clericalism and ethno-centric populisms',[66] along with cynicism and contempt for intellectual inputs.

In spite of this, it is true that even today, parties come into existence under the pretext of ideological differences, if not on the basis of some ideological positions. Parties sustain their identity, which is anchored in the cleavages and issues that give rise to their birth. In other words, regardless of the fact that ideology is taking a back seat, parties cannot make voters, in general, forget their background for seeking short-term advantages.

---

[64]Nandigram Special Economic Zone (SEZ) controversy, which caused the Nandigram massacre, started when the West Bengal government decided that the Salim Group of Indonesia would set up a chemical hub under the SEZ policy at Nandigram, a rural area in the district of Purba Medinipur. The villagers took over the administration of the area and all the roads to the villages were cut off. The administration was directed to break the Bhumi Ucched Protirodh Committee's (BUPC) resistance at Nandigram and a massive operation with at least 3,000 policemen along with cadre of the Marxist ruling party was launched, first on 14 March 2007 and later in November 2007. Over fifty persons died in this agitation, some of them allegedly at the hands of CPI(M) party cadres and others, the state police.

[65]Yogendra Yadav, 'Party Games', *Indian Express*, Ahmedabad, 21March 2007.

[66]Vladimir Tismaneanu,'The First Post-Communist Decade', published in *Romanian Journal of Society and Politics*. Vol. 1, No. 1. p 6.

Another important reason for ideology losing its prominence is the fact that, increasingly, continuing in power is being preferred to adherence to ideology. There are many reasons for this growing tendency to compromise with basic ideological positions. On the one hand, compromises are made for the sake of power, while on the other, they are seen as a mark of pragmatism. As against the popular impression, the tendency to compromise with the basics of ideology may not always be for the sake of power. Factors such as compulsions of coalition politics, a genuinely larger interest of the people and an understandable give and take approach, or a strategic adjustment also prompt political parties to compromise with ideology. Problems arise when cadres feel that they have not been taken into confidence about the reasons for such adjustments.

For parties which are not cadre-based, and hence, less ideology driven, such compromises are convenient and easy. They may not exactly invite allegations of opportunism, at least from within. But for other parties, they have to pay the price for such compromises and face an erosion of their credibility. In the Indian context, a large section of supporters of the BJP and the Asom Gana Parsihad (AGP) drifted away from them because of what was perceived by many as compromises with avowed ideological positions on the part of these parties. The same was true with the Nationalist Congress Party (NCP) of Sharad Pawar. One of his lieutenants, Ratnakar Mahajan had, in fact, sought the merger of the NCP with the Congress when the relevance of its independent politics was lost, after it practically withdrew its opposition to the idea of Sonia Gandhi taking over Premiership.

Apparently, the bases of these compromises are the compulsions of remaining in power. Parties come into existence for power and hence, they have to ensure that they continue in the government and prove that they can govern, and govern for the entire term of office. As explained by a senior BJP leader, the driving force behind BJP's coalition politics and the resultant compromises was the urge to establish that parties other than the Congress are also capable of giving a government that lasts a full term. As principal partner of the coalition, the BJP had to accommodate several such things, which were otherwise clearly unacceptable to the party.

Coalition politics also has some positive aspects. In India, it has helped dilute ideological stubbornness and the resultant practice of 'untouchability' to a certain extent. Besides, with concepts like 'coalition dharma'—Atal Bihari Vajpayee's significant contribution to the democratic lexicon—national politics as a whole matured further, (as compared to national politics in the Nineties) to accommodate divergent views with an urge to offer a stable government given top priority. Pratap Bhanu Mehta, in a telling comment, observes, 'The BJP [had] also discovered that there is a disjunction between technical policy competence and the themes that animate masses.'[67] Issues like *Swadeshi* and removing Article 370 from the Constitution could be pointed out as examples of this disjunction. However, this disconnection is not confined to the BJP alone. Parties like the Congress too had to backtrack from their declared plans for providing free electricity for agriculture after attaining power in Maharashtra in 2004.

With mutually agreeable give-and-take on ideological issues for the sake of continuing a coalition, certain examples of a brazen craving for power also need to be noted. Instances of otherwise avowedly opposing political parties joining hands at the state level or municipal level clearly bring out the potential of the lure of power. Early in the last decade, the NCP had no hesitation in joining hands with the BJP in Meghalaya. Instances of the BJP occassionally supporting the Congress or the CPI (M) in Kerala are also not unheard of.

Besides, alliance politics, more often than not, also exerts limitless pressure on the process of governance. The ruling combine—as seen in the recent past in India—invariably includes parties with not just varying, but at times, even conflicting, ideologies. As a consequence, political parties in the country are becoming 'coalitional rather than consensual, segmental rather than holistic, pragmatic

[67]Pratap Bhanu Mehta, 'Where is the party?' *Indian Express*, Mumbai, 29 June, 2005.

rather than ideological.'[68] Pratap Bhanu Mehta[69] has pointed out this mixed bag of the good and bad effects of coalition politics. He observes that 'because of coalition politics, regional parties and leaders now exercise more power at the Centre'. India has a large number of political parties. While these parties give voice to many sections of the population in the political system, they impede the process of democratic negotiation in three ways. First—as witnessed in the announcement of the Railway Budget in 2012, when the Trinamool Congress chief Mamata Banerjee insisted on a roll back of the fare hike—in coalition politics small parties can come to exercise veto power over policy. Also, the proliferation of parties makes preference aggregation more difficult. Most of the parties have undemocratic structures, and hence only a small coterie of individuals controls the party finances, agenda and selection of candidates. This, beyond doubt, amounts to playing with the vital task of policy making.

The fact that ideology is now increasingly taking a back seat has some kind of a cascading effect on the institutional character of political parties. With ideology becoming secondary in every respect, the core group of ideologically motivated and committed political workers is driven to the periphery. This afflicts the quality of party organisations, leading to a fractured electoral verdict. Consequently, coalitional politics, where even ideological compromises are indulged in, becomes almost mandatory. This apparent compulsion of coalition also impacts upon governance. When ideologically driven political workers, who stick to some basic principles at any cost become a rarity, the requisite zeal for making a difference in the lives of the people while in power, also diminishes fast. How can this not have any effect on the quality of governance?

As pointed out by political scientist Everett Carl Ladd Jr., 'Successful governance is simply harder to achieve in the absence

---

[68] Prakash Sarangi, 'The Party System in India' at http://www.mssu.edu/projectsouthasia/tsa/VINI/SarangiPFVhtm.

[69] Pratap Bhanu Mehta at http://www.carnegieendowment.org/files/Mehta.pdf.

of strong parties and stable supportive coalitions. To ignore the implications of electoral de-alignment and party decay would be foolish indeed.'[70] A case in point is that of the parties in Central Europe. Coalition politics has become the hallmark of the post-Communist era. But, due to the incompatible coalition partners, personalities matter more than ideologies. As a consequence, the distribution of benefits has become a central issue.

The unabated weakening of internal party organisation has given a fillip to the institutional decline of parties. Party decline is a direct result of the absence of, or weakening of, the institutionalisation of the party system. There are two crucial aspects of the process of institutionalisation of the party that are closely linked to its organisational health. They are, the extent to which a party has stable roots in society and the manner in which it is organised internally. The increasing trend of indulging in what could be described as community-politics-appeals as short cuts to electoral success, has given rise to the phenomenon of social-group or community parties. At least this particular category of parties is little known for any organisational health. On the contrary, these parties normally have low levels of ideological coherence and programmatic commitment, lack a well-developed organisational structure and recruitment base, depend on clientelistic mobilisation for their electoral success and tend to be organised around a single charismatic leader. Several parties in India, from Lalu Prasad Yadav's Rashtriya Janata Dal, Om Prakash Chautala's Indian National Lok Dal, to Bal Thackeray's Shiv Sena, or Chandrababu Naidu's Telugu Desam are cases in point. They may not be ethnic parties in the strict sense of the term, but having a largely sectarian appeal and personality-oriented organisation, are more than a match for the above description.

Party organisations are also political communities, and in that sense, a constantly decreasing level of community life also afflicts these. Becky Cain,[71] former president of the League of Women

[70] Everett Carl Ladd Jr. *Where have all the voters gone?*, p. 127.

[71] 'Leadership for a new century: A blueprint for a more participatory democracy', JMB Academy of Leadership, University of Maryland, 1998, p.12.

Voters (USA) once noted,'...nomadic lifestyle of industrial nations has led to a loss of permanence, of rooted-ness in a single community and thus plummeting the numbers in voter participation. Besides, technological advancement also has had some impact upon party organisatons.' Unlike in the past, today, electoral success doesn't depend solely on local party organisers. Now that television has come into almost every home, party leaders can directly communicate with the voters even without local organisers. This has also helped a spurt in what could be described as visibility-populism. Leaders rush to the sites of calamities mainly to ensure that they are seen and thereby an image is built. Besides, this visibility-populism is easy to indulge in. If an individual has excellent relations with persons in the electronic media, he can easily create an illusion about his strength, even without any ground support. In an era where people believe that whatever does not appear on the small screen may not be true at all, this visibility-populism has become essential. However, this may be harmful as it may promote distortions and illusions. Now that the impact of social networking through the Internet has increased manifold, visibility-populism is gaining further momentum.

However, these developments are not confined to India only. A comment on the scenario of the presidential election in 2004 in the Philippines is extremely revealing. It underscores the fact that parties are not performing even traditional and rudimentary roles supporting their claim of being a political party. A political commentator, Randy David, has said that political parties in the Philippines have become totally irrelevant because their role in choosing candidates has been reduced to zero. Almost everywhere, individuals carrying the banner of the same party are running against one another. To local politicians, the whole country has become a 'free zone'. Their link to national politics is not a programme of action, but the presidential candidate, to whom they turn, not for leadership or guidance, but for campaign funds.[72]

One finds a parallel to this in India too. Especially during the

[72] http://www.inq7.net/opi/2004/may/02/text/opi_rsdavid-1-p.htm.

municipal and village level elections, parties like the Congress very often allow several individuals to describe themselves as the official candidates and adopt the one who ultimately wins. This phenomenon of clandestine candidacy has an element of deceit in it. Obviously, it not only undermines the fundamentals of party organisation but also weakens the democratic process.

In India, the process of the decline of party organisation in the Congress started way back in the Seventies. The election to the Lok Sabha in 1989 was a watershed, as the defeat of the Congress vividly reflected the decline of the party's organisation. The entire organisational structure that had once effectively linked villages with the highest decision-making bodies, during all these years, lost its salience as no democratic elections were held and all power was usurped by the central leadership. Even today, things have not changed. Even at the local level, the rein remains in the hands of individuals who have more access to the top echelons of the party than knowledge about voters.

With ideological distinctness on the wane, accommodating equally ambitious leaders and managing their personal aspirations is emerging as a serious challenge even in cadre or semi-cadre parties in India. Besides, with the first post-Independence generation of politicians, who had built the party organisation at the grass-roots level without expecting any returns, almost disappearing from the scene, towering personalities with requisite moral authority are also missing. This has made the task of containing ultra-ambitious elements all the more difficult. The BJP has been trying hard to apply the Rashtriya Swayamsevak Sangha–Akhil Bharatiya Vidyarthi Parishad (RSS–ABVP)[73] model of organisation, based

---

[73]The RSS-ABVP model of organisation is more or less based on principles of pure selflessness, moral authority of the seniors, total loyalty to ideology, and complete surrender to the organisation. One of the reasons behind the success of this eighty-year-old model is the fact that youngsters in their impressionistic age are contacted and influenced by the senior RSS cadre mainly through their personal conduct. While the RSS style of functioning laid down the foundation of this unique organisational model, it was the late Prof. YV Kelkar of the ABVP who not only championed the cause of this model, but also philosophised it and presented it with greater articulation.

on team-building. It includes rejection of excessive self-projection, emphasises collectivism, ideological integrity and moral authority of the seniors, but that has succeeded only marginally. 'In ABVP, I used to consider all our colleagues as my friends and well-wishers but here I realise that they are also my competitors,' observes a senior BJP functionary who is also a former ABVP full-timer. According to Swapan Dasgupta,[74] an RSS watcher, it is high time the BJP evolves its own distinct ideology and inter-personal relationship-based model of organisational management.

The CPI (M) also faced internal differences of opinion in 2007. But in spite of the ideological drift, it has been able to keep its organisational base and structure fairly intact. CPI (M) watchers argue that this is so mainly due to the supremacy of the party organisation that it maintained steadfastly. As observed by researcher and Communist Party watcher Dr Ashok Modak in a study report, in West Bengal during the Left-front rule, the government programmes were conducted under the party's control. The Marxists also gave more importance to their cadres than to their ministers, MLAs or MPs.[75] Obviously, it is not for no reason that the CPI (M) ruled the state uninterruptedly for over thirty years.

Another important factor contributing to the decline of parties is the crisis of leadership. There appears to be a severe lack of leadership at the organisational as well as governmental level. On both the fundamental counts of leadership—ability to actually govern a party or run an administration and that of the moral authority emerging from mutual confidence—leaders of political parties appear to be failing. Again, both these aspects of leadership are in a way inter-dependent. Leaders with a low level of credibility generally lack the requisite moral courage to take tough decisions and unless a leader takes tough decisions, he or she cannot sustain moral authority.

In so far as governance is concerned, while people's

---

[74] Interview with Swapan Dasgupta on 2 December 2004.

[75] Ashok Modak, et al (Ed.). 1997. *Left Front Rule in West Bengal: Genesis, Growth and Decay*.p. 31.

expectations are always on the rise, the quality of leadership is continuously on the wane. As is the situation today, expectations placed on the government have grown dramatically within the century and have become somewhat unreasonable. The government's inability to fulfil these has resulted in a loss of faith. Further, the ability of the government to actually act is of considerable importance to our citizens, and the perception that it does not execute the plans as is claimed, is one of the obstacles to a real sense of faith in our political system. the erosion of mutual trust between the governed and the governing has almost reached its nadir. Analysing this collapse of trust, former US senator Bill Bradley once observed:

> Citizens are expressing deep misgivings about a political process that has lost sight of moral commitments we have towards each other. They believe that politicians are controlled by special interests that give them money, by parties that crush their independence, by ambitions for higher office that make them hedge their position, and by pollsters who convince them that focus group phrases will guarantee them victory. They often don't trust their legislators to act fairly or independently or even, in some cases, democratically. They doubt that facts or honest conviction play much of a role.[76]

When political leadership displays ineptitude and lacks the ability to grasp the situation, looming threats to democracy start raising their ugly head, for instance the military coup in Thailand in 2006, or in Venezuela in 2002. In both the cases the moral authority of the governing politicians was questioned. Due to corruption and political favouritism, the political elite has often failed miserably to control and manage core institutions such as the military. This makes governance highly vulnerable. Very often, it is realised

---

[76]Bill Bradley's (ex-Member of US Senate) keynote address in James McGregor Burns, *Leadership for a New Century: A Blueprint for a More Participatory Democracy*, JMB Academy of Leadership, University of Maryland. 1998, p.34.

that the leadership of a particular nation just does not have any moral authority to expect that citizens accept the rule of law when the leadership itself is widely seen as a lawbreaker.

The situation in several established democracies, whether in India, Indonesia or Sweden, appears almost the same in its entirety. The events that caused the Arab Spring in several countries of the Middle East were not very different. In order to understand the striking similarities in the ground situations, both in Egypt and India, it would be enlightening to read what an article in *Foreign Affairs* has said about the former:

> Everything in Egypt—from obtaining a driver's license to getting an education—is formally very cheap but in practice very expensive, since most transactions, official and unofficial, are accompanied by off-the-books payments. The government pays schoolteachers a pittance, so public education is poor and teachers supplement their salaries by providing private lessons that are essential preparation for school exams. The national police were widely reviled long before their brutal crackdowns at the inception of the January 25 revolt because they represented, in essence, a nationwide protection racket. Ordinary citizens had to bribe police officers all too ready to confiscate licenses and invent violations.[77]

The dearth of leadership also is a critical issue. Leadership is crucial in several ways. Without a capable and visionary leadership, neither is the renewal of the system of government and democracy possible, nor can political parties conduct themselves purposefully. In present-day politics, political party leadership has become extremely demanding. A leader has to be an organiser, a mobiliser of public opinion, a master of the art of winning elections, a person who can take care of the aspirations of the cadre and simultaneously

[77] Demystifying the Arab Spring, *Foreign Affairs*, May/June 2011.

intertwine them with the larger good of the people. An ability to visualise ahead of the times, as also to think out of the box, are the basic qualities required for a political leader.

Understandably, to lead a political party from the front is no easier. Ground realities, of the compulsions of winning elections and the competitive indulgence in compromises, make a visionary leader lose his sight and focus only on electoral politics. No wonder then, charismatic leaders who are self-centred to the core, encourage emotional regression in their followers in periods of overall instability. Using fierce and one-sided rhetoric, they make people think sentimentally and put reason aside. This has not only dwarfed democratic political leadership, but has also hampered the cause of people's education in general.

In India, an overall decline in the credibility of political leadership has also contributed to this crisis. Scores of political leaders in contemporary India who were once respected across the party line for their vision, forthright thinking and ability to rise above petty partisan considerations have today almost lost their credibility. The predicament of Prafulla Kumar Mahanta, former chief minister of Assam and the founding father of the Asom Gana Parishad, or the contemptible condition of Shibu Soren, once the inspiring leader of the Jharkhand Mukti Morcha in Jharkhand, are cases in point.[78]

All these crises pose a dire threat to democratic development. This makes it important to understand the process of the institutional decline of political parties. The changing nature of the party-people interface is one of the crucial aspects of this process of deterioration.

---

[78]Prafulla Kumar Mahanta became the Chief Minister of Assam for the first time in 1985, mainly due to the groundswell of support to the anti-foreigners (Bangladeshis) agitation in Assam. But he could do precious little to solve the problem. In spite of becoming the chief minister again in 1995, he could do nothing and eventually lost both, elections as also credibility. For some years he was expelled from the Asom Gana Parishad. Shibu Soren is one of the main architects of the Jharkhand movement. His party became infamous during the PV Narsimha Rao government rule for having 'sold' its votes to save the incumbent government.

Parties and the Process of Shaping Public Opinion

When it comes to the role of political parties and its significance, it is obvious that the way they play their part and the internal mechanism they adopt have a bearing on the citizen's perception of political parties. This very approach also decides the measure of acceptance the parties receive. It is a two-way process: The strengths and weaknesses of political parties influence the citizens and civil society, in turn civil society affects the polity in general and the parties in particular.

The modern-day political parties are voluntary associations and their declared aim is to be represented in the government and to lead it in a given state or political community. This is achieved by way of fulfilling these critical functions:

- Nominating candidates for public offices.
- Reviewing public policy issues and taking positions.
- Mobilising public support by influencing popular minds for each of the above.

There is an inherent link between these three functions which a party ought to perform. While the first is undoubtedly very crucial, it is futile if a party has very little to talk about the second aspect. The responsibility of taking positions will become just a formality, unless a party has the ability to perform on the last count—influencing popular minds and garnering support. In this sense, the third function is the fundamental characteristic of any party's operations. It is in this way that the function of reviewing public policy issues acquires a pivotal role. The positions adopted by the party decide their ability to make inroads amongst the masses and only through that, party candidates who opt for public offices can win. In order to execute this, political parties aggregate public interests and in the process also develop a consciousness about their own idea of the genuine good of the people. Here comes the question of influencing the popular mindset. Political parties are expected to educate the masses. Thomas Jefferson underscored this need by describing people as the most effective 'repository of the ultimate powers of the society'.[79]

[79] As quoted at http://spot.colorado.edu/~mcguire/rptheo.html.

He had further said that, '...if we think them not enlightened enough to exercise control with a wholesome discretion, the remedy is not to take it from them, but to inform their discretion by education.'[80]

With sound bite journalism taking centre stage in the twenty-first century, people's education appears to be further neglected. Influencing the thinking of the common man by way of deafening noise and slogan-mongering is one thing and educating him to understand and have his own judgment is quite another. For democracy to develop roots, along with propaganda, parties also must undertake, at least in a non-formal way, some steps to enlighten the citizens. Public education is also important because democracy is all about people's involvement, and undoubtedly it has to be an informed participation. Since this engagement is going to have a great impact upon the quality of the decision-making processes, parties have to ensure that they shape an enlightened public opinion. In this context, it is noteworthy that traditional means of reaching out to the masses, including door-to-door campaigning involving a dialogue, are no longer used by parties in a meaningful way. In Maharashtra, once the Shiv Sena used to communicate with the masses through hand-written messages on publicly displayed blackboards. Today, writing on these 'community blackboards' is not being pursued with the requisite zeal.

Political parties do not appear to be taking any serious steps to create awareness amongst the voters and the people in general. There are multiple causes for this inertia. The first and foremost reason is the lack of courage of conviction. In fact, when it comes to taking sides and if there is an electoral cost attached to doing so, parties refuse to take positions. The tussle over the issue of a quota, between the Gujjar and Meena communities in Rajasthan in May 2007, is an example of parties avoiding taking any position. When parties realise that they lack organisational strength and a force of knowledgeable party workers, they opt for an easy way, of not taking positions, especially on issues concerning the environment, education, social or economic reforms.

[80] *Ibid.*

Commenting on both these processes of propaganda as well as public education, Harold Laski rightly observed that, 'much of what has been achieved by the art of education in the nineteenth century has been frustrated by the art of propaganda in the twentieth century.'[81] In the contemporary scenario, parties have almost lost their inclination as well as the ability to educate the voters. Wolfgang Weeg, a senior national level functionary of the Socialist Democratic Party (SPD) in Germany, in an interview with me, frankly admitted that parties in Germany are not performing their pedagogical function. Citing an example, he further said that even while Germany is facing a severe crisis of unemployment, more than one-third of the unemployed youth prefer taking shelter under the social security cover, than working as an apprentice. 'We have failed in motivating the youth on this front,'[82] he admitted.

Similarly, even the electoral education of voters is dealt with very casually in several countries. According to the results of the studies conducted under the Election Process Information Collection (EPIC) project of the International Institute for Democracy and Electoral Assistance (IIDEA) and International Foundation for Electoral Systems (IFES), in 53 per cent of the democratic countries, voter education programmes are conducted only at the time of elections. It is only in 36 per cent of the countries, that political parties play some role in the process of voter education.[83]

Of the three main aforementioned functions a political party is expected to perform, two are directly concerned with the process of shaping public opinion. Political parties, and more particularly the leaders, require ground level support from key factors to structure the general conception. These include the dexterity to gather authentic inputs through credible sources, an ability to analyse such inputs without any pre-conceived notions and lastly but more importantly, the strength to show courage to arrive at some conclusion and take

---

[81] Harold Laski, *A Grammar of Politics*, p.147.

[82] Interview with SPD representative Wolfgang Weeg at the party's Bonn headquarters on 8 August 1998.

[83] http://epicproject.org/ace/compepic/en/VE02.

decisions that may not always be palatable to certain sections of society.

It would be interesting to review as to where our political parties stand on these counts. Of the three points mentioned here, the first concerns the organisational network in general and the process of a continuous dialogue between leaders and the rank and file and their mutual trust. The other two aspects are more to do with the quality of leadership as also its motives. Since all these have a necessary connection with the organisational health of a party, they are dealt with separately in the ensuing discussion about party decline.

Decline of Parties

The decline of political parties in a representative democracy is a cause of concern. Political scientists across the world have been discussing this phenomenon for more than two decades. While there may be differences about the degree of the deterioration or the reasons behind it, there is near unanimity about the onset of this downfall.

In India, party decline is more than obvious. Leaving aside a few honourable exceptions, most of the parties are personality driven. With a clannish character, there are hardly any efforts undertaken to build a philosophy-based, truly nationwide, and long-lasting organisational foundation for such parties. An indication of the fact that these are fast losing credibility is found in two different research projects carried out by the teams of Lokniti-CSDS, New Delhi and Public Affairs Centre, Bengaluru. The findings of both these studies confirm that more than 50 per cent of the persons interviewed have indicated that factors other than party—candidate, caste—decide their voting preferences.[84]

In the US, however, there are two distinct schools amongst the political scientists, the 'Declinists' and the 'Revivalists'. Those who believe that parties are on the decline among other things, mainly refer to the waning partisan identification, the increase in voter

---

[84] http://www.pacindia.org/citizenaction/Election2004/index_html/view, www.lokniti.org/WPS-1.pdf.

volatility, rising levels of expressed public distrust of parties, and emerging alternative organisations and groups.

Those who believe that parties in the US are, in fact, reviving organisationally, base their conclusion mainly on increasing professionalisation of party functioning and their enhanced money power. The main contention of the revivalist argument is that, '... parties are unwilling victims, attempting to adjust their organisational patterns to the vagaries of an undisciplined electorate.'[85]

The decline of party thesis means that the parties have become less important than what they were. This diminishing importance of parties has several facets. They include their shrinking space, deteriorating performance and the leader's ability to deliver. Well known American political scientist Everett Carl Ladd Jr's comments about parties in the US are universally applicable. He has said:

> [Of the two major US parties] neither party commands anything approaching a secure majority. Neither can achieve sustained coherence in the development and implementation of public policy. Neither possesses a public philosophy or pragmatic approach that rallies the populace to its standard...the partisan and electoral drift continues.[86]

This has taken the spirit of representative democracy away, leaving only a lifeless skeleton of formal structures. Naturally, the discussion also leads to the organisational revival of parties through, among others, party reforms.

The decline of parties as an institution is a universal phenomenon. In established democracies, several factors of the changing public life are threatening the very institutional existence of parties. In new democracies, for example in post-Communist

[85] Andrew M Appleton and Daniel S Ward, 'Measuring Party Organisation in the United States', *Party Politics*, Vol. 1. Issue 1, January 1995.
[86] Everett Carl Ladd Jr., *op.cit*, p.126-27.

countries, political parties are plagued with small memberships, as 'personalities matter more than ideologies and the division of spoils looms large.'[87]

A recent study on political parties in Central America, Panama and Dominican Republic also reflects this overall trend towards decline. This study has underscored the contrast between the rise of democracy and the decline of parties. Two political scientists from Uruguay, after scanning through the institutional self-portraits which they had asked thirty-seven political parties to prepare, concluded that '...parties need to reform themselves to cease being simply electoral machines as well as to overcome vices such as corruption, patronage and an aversion to renovating their leadership...They are seen as part of the problem, not the solution.'[88]

INDICATORS OF PARTY DECLINE

This phenomenon of party decline is multi-faceted and complex. Political scientist Howard Reiter has summarised this process aptly while saying that parties in general are 'less determinative of attitudes, and the behaviour of political actors on both the mass and elite levels, less highly regarded, and less likely to inspire the electoral act than they once were.'[89]

As suggested by an authority on the party system, Paul D Webb,[90] there are two principal dimensions of party life which largely determine the rise or downfall of a party: Legitimacy of the parties in public perception and organisational vitality.

Examining the ground realities of party politics, especially the functionality of parties in India, on the basis of these factors may help in determining the level of party decline. The functionality of a

[87]From 'Party games', in *The Economist*, 28 January, 2006, p. 46.

[88]Inter American Development Bank Press Release at http://www.idea.int/news/inthenews/2006_mar.cfm.

[89]As cited by Paul D Webb, 'Are British political parties in Decline?', *Party Politics*, Vol. 1, No. 3 (July 1995), p.300.

[90]*Ibid.*

party is an enormous concept. Here, this discussion covers only four fundamental concerns:

- Ability of the political parties to offer policy alternatives and their relevance as well as uniqueness.
- Human resources of political parties, their cadre base and their mass following.
- Functional infrastructure developed by parties and their ability to mobilise financial resources legitimately.
- Overall image of political parties in the opinion-making classes, primarily in the media.

Even a cursory glance at the state of affairs of the six national parties—the BSP, BJP, CPI, CPI (M), Congress and NCP—recognised by the Election Commission of India brings about several interesting aspects. While the Congress and the BJP can reasonably claim sound functionality, the other four parties are strong on some points while weak on others. On the count of legitimate financial resources, it is an open secret that no party is able to contest elections without mobilising funds, most of them collected unofficially, through a not-so-transparent system.

Erosion in party legitimacy can largely be described as a precursor to party decline. There are several prominent and largely acceptable indicators of abrasion in party legitimacy the world over. In the Indian context, some of the key pointers could be listed as conflicting trends in voter turnout and party affiliation, waning membership of parties and an overall drop in the respectability of party work.

From Jean Jacques Rousseau[91] to Robert Dahl, all major theorists agree that mass participation is the lifeblood of representative democracy. Theorists like Joseph Schumpeter have stressed a limited role for citizens. Yet, all share the perception that voters' participation is one of the essential features of representative government.

---

[91]Jean Jacques Rousseau and some theorists saw politics as a matter of judgment rather than opinion. According to them, other things being equal, the more people who are involved in arriving at a decision the more likely the decision is to be correct.

Since voting figures could also be considered as directly linked to the availability of options and party affiliation to the voters, a decline in these figures is certainly a significant indicator. A slump in voter turnout has been observed all over the world. From established economic powers such as the UK, USA and Germany to developing and under-developed countries such as Sri Lanka and Kenya, people are becoming more and more disinterested in exercising their voting right.

Besides, in India, whenever the voter turnout is satisfactory or even above average, it is not necessarily an indication of their strong partisan nature and growing strength of parties. According to two prominent leaders of the Congress and the BJP, over the years, there appears to have developed a disconnect between the organisational strength of parties and their ability to induce voters to vote. Generally speaking, there are four categories of voters. A majority of the voters are casual voters who vote, but not very thoughtfully. Then there are enthusiastic voters among which a large section of first-time young voters are included. Thirdly, there are duty-conscious voters who vote religiously. Lastly, there is a miniscule minority of party-loyal voters. This categorisation itself is indicative of a certain disconnect that has developed in voting figures and the organisational strength of parties. This, perhaps, explains as to why several exit polls in India have proved to be incorrect recently. It is also a fact that persons who associate themselves with a particular party for professional reasons do respond affirmatively to routine questions in surveys about their party affiliation, but that hardly means that they have a sense of belonging towards the respective political party. Although the Election Commission of India has become stricter, in notorious constituencies, the number of cases of booth capturing, organising mass impersonation and proxy voting has not reduced considerably.[92] Many have written extensively on how money power and muscle power are becoming effective. This is mainly thanks to parties finding themselves bereft of committed manpower. It can

[92]Interview with Vasant Sathe and Dr Mahesh Chandra Sharma, in New Delhi in February, 2004.

also be stated that to appear to be close to all parties has become a fashion. In the overall atmosphere of political correctness and safe play, even at the level of an individual, people shy away from taking sides and take a partisan approach.

A falling voter turnout is closely linked to the overall reluctance of the people to take sides in partisan politics. Where a particular party is strong, the turnout also remains strong since it is boosted by, among other things, the strength of party group alignments. Pippa Norris, concurring with this, observes:

> ...relationship between turnout and party competition is actually rounded. Both the extreme factors such as intense fragmentation (where the leading party wins less than 30% of the vote) and absolute one-party predominance (where the leading party gains more than 60% of the vote) make a negative impact on voter turnout. This is because in both cases, the ability of the voters to generate a decisive result most of the times aiming at 'throwing the rascals out' is adversely affected (sic).[93]

Though the reasons for this particular phenomenon are varied, it remains a fact that voters turn hesitant to become partisan mainly because they find hardly anything to distinguish between the available choices. Also true is the fact that when significant differences do exist between the available parties, these are not clearly communicated to the public. This ignorance also contributes to the erosion of partisanship. As the figures of voter turnout in India suggest,[94] voter turnout has been decreasing almost consistently since 1962, with the exceptions of 1977, 1984 and 1998. These three important instances were driven by largely emotional issues like the

---

[93] As told by Pippa Norris of the Kennedy School of Government in an interview with the author on 29 January,1999.

[94] Compiled by the International Foundation for Electoral Systems and presented by IDEA at their website: http://www.idea.int/vt/country_view.cfm.

urge for re-establishing democracy in the post-Emergency scenario in 1977, a sentimental upsurge due to Indira Gandhi's assassination in 1984, and the intensity of the realisation that a stable government is the need of the hour in 1999—after three short-lived governments lasting from thirteen days to about a year.

The idea of the availability of genuine and distinct options is most central to the overall concept of electoral representation, but unfortunately, of late, this is facing severe threats. As a result, with people not perceiving options as being such, partisanship is fast eroding. In the changing circumstances, this can be attributed to ideological convergence. In major democracies of the post-globalisation era, where a bi-polar polity (if not a clear two-party system) is fairly established, this 'ideological convergence' is more evident. Besides the UK, the scenario is the same in Germany, Israel, Turkey, Sweden, and to some extent, in India too. In established democracies like Germany and Israel, principal political parties opposing each other have already experimented with forming a joint front to run the government. In India too, there are many who sincerely believe that the Congress and BJP should be joining hands in the larger interest of the country.

It must be noted that this ideological convergence may eventually endanger the very foundation of democracy. Paul D Webb, who succinctly brings forward the underlying threats to democracy in such situations, comments, 'Deciding between the alternatives on offer becomes a more difficult task, and partisan loyalty and even turning out to vote simply do not matter so much when the differences between parties are not so great.'[95] Not very long ago, a British election survey indicated that between 1964 and 1992, the number of persons with a strong partisan identity fell from 48 per cent to just 19 per cent. Several BJP watchers believe that the party could succeed only marginally in establishing that it is genuinely different and hence, a meaningful alternative to the Congress (the dominant and Grand Old

---

[95] Paul D Webb, 'Are British political parties in Decline?', *Party Politics*, Vol. 1, No. 3, (July 1995).

Party of India). The case is the same with two political formulations in major democracies, from the US to Australia.

All these have taken away the positive aspects of being partisan. While theoretically the majority of the people prefer democracy, they fail to realise that democracy sans popular participation has no great future. Thanks to the lack of this understanding, many honestly believe that neither their casting a vote nor their abstaining from voting matters.

To many, casting a vote is like giving vent to agony. In the pre-voting-machine era in India, several instances were observed when agitated voters expressed their anguish about the entire system by inserting small satirical hand-written notes into the ballot box. This explains why the demand for providing for negative voting, raised by some NGOs, merits serious consideration.[96]

There are also some very practical reasons for people abstaining from voting. Too many elections, too, is an important factor. A voter in India has to cast his vote at least three times within a span of five years and, at times, even more.

The decline of party membership in democracies the world over is one of the most significant indicators of a growing popular alienation from political parties. In India, membership of political parties remains a vague idea. Although the dictionary meanings of terms such as a member, supporter and a follower differ greatly, 'in practice there is hardly any distinction between a follower, supporter and member,' feels KC Suri.[97] He further observes:

> [In India] membership [of political parties] is not very important. The rival leaders in a party at the local level enroll members more as a demonstration of their strength,

[96]'Negative voting provides the option of exercising one's vote to none of the candidates, by providing an extra button in the Electronic Voting Machines that says "none of the above". This exercising of negative voting can be interpreted as an expression of discontent by the common man/voters' http://www.sentinelassam.com/editorial/story.php?sec=3&subsec=0&id=73567&dtP=2011-05-03&ppr=1.

[97]KC Suri, *op.cit.*

> and often the leader who takes up the 'membership drive', or someone on his behalf, pays the subscription amount for the 'enrolled'. Most parties do not maintain membership registers and even where they are kept very few bother about them. The registers when maintained, and whatever maintained, find little use.[98]

In such a scenario, there are obvious limitations to drawing any inferences on the basis of the record, whatsoever, available with political parties.

The British experience in this regard is worth noting. In 1964, a total of 9.4 per cent of all registered electors were the members of the three main parties in the UK with nationwide organisation. By 1992, these figures saw a 79 per cent decline, reducing the figure to just 2 per cent.[99] Having said that, it must also be noted that there is enough evidence to suggest that a declining party membership may or may not have an impact on the way a political party is organised. This is mainly because of the growing trend of professionally managed parties who can hire the required manpower and even in the absence of party volunteers, can present a façade of organisational strength. Party organisations have shown a relatively weak capacity to conduct campaigns. This has led to the emergence of professional campaign managers, signaling a kind of privatisation in this field as well. These campaign management agencies are an arsenal, replete with all the skills and weapons of modern political combat—speech-writers, pollsters, public relations specialists, media consultants and fundraisers. No wonder then, that party leaders have started undermining the importance of ideology driven, committed and emotionally attached volunteers in the entire process of electioneering.

The recent Lokpal movement led by Anna Hazare has clearly brought to the fore, the declining respect for work associated with a political party. The image of a politician has never been so bad

---

[98] *ibid*

[99] Paul D Webb, in 'Are British political parties in Decline?', *Party Politics*, Vol.1, No.3, (July 1995).

in India. Today, people take it for granted that if one is a politician, and that too an elected representative, he must be quite resourceful. That politicians normally cheat, they never keep time, much less a word given and are normally inaccessible, are some of the set notions about a person in politics. None of the active politicians are found to be discussing this image crisis haunting the entire political establishment. There appears to be an unspoken acceptance of the fact that a politician has to mobilise monetary resources and therefore, corruption—the magnitude notwithstanding—is quite natural. Due to this, after the Bofors[100] scam in 1989, corruption was never made a central election plank either nationally or at the state level.

About five decades ago, while delivering the first GD Mavlankar Lecture, YN Sukhtankar, the then Governor of Odisha, had said, 'The most popular picture of a politician is of one who lives in deceit, thrives in the midst of squabbles and is at home in the atmosphere of pettiness.'[101] Since then, little has been done to arrest this slide in the image of a politician. Today, well-meaning and public-spirited persons do not dare to join politics. This may explain why only a small section, just 13.7 per cent of the respondents, at a National Election Study conducted by the Lokniti-CSDS, New Delhi, was found to be official members of any political party (*see* Appendix C).

Today, even after a communication revolution, a deep-rooted feeling of disjointedness has gripped the whole world. This disjointedness between the people and the political class is extremely acute. The political world that leaders are forced to inhabit has fallen into disrepute. This diminishing respectability and declining trustworthiness of a politician has become a

[100]The Bofors scandal was a major corruption scam in India in the Eighties; the then Prime Minister Rajiv Gandhi and several others were accused of receiving kickbacks from Bofors AB for winning a bid to supply India's 155 mm field howitzer guns. The scale of the corruption was far worse than any that India had seen before, and directly led to the defeat of the Congress party in the November 1989 General Elections.

[101]YN Sukathankar, *Human Nature and Politics*, p. 6.

universal phenomenon. The results of a survey conducted in 2011, by GFK Ad Hoc Research Worldwide,[102] is a testimony. According to this survey, although politicians have been able to improve their image somewhat over the last year, they remain at the bottom of the rankings, with an overall trust of 17 per cent. Esteem for politicians is the highest in Sweden (39 per cent), which still puts them third from the bottom of the rankings in this country. In the Czech Republic and Romania (8 per cent in each case), as well as Germany and Italy (9 per cent respectively), politicians have a serious image problem. The situation is the same in countries like Canada.

The public conduct of party leaders and their acts of commissions and omissions always influence popular perspective about the entire political class in general. Since this perspective is the product of existing systems and institutions in a democratic polity, it also brings about the fact that democratic contestation, on its own, provides an insufficient check on the exercise of power without responsibility.

Major Reasons for Party Decline

There are several reasons for the decline of parties. This phenomenon is necessarily institutional in nature since it has encompassed several parties in a number of democracies and the process seems to be largely unabated. The key reasons for this also pertain to the metamorphosis of democratic politics, especially the electoral mechanism. At the macro level, the reasons could also be found in the changing character of our social interactions. The poor quality of institutional life in many of our public institutions, crass commercialism afflicting several NGOs in the voluntary sector and continued erosion of trade union movements are some of the indicators of the overall decline in the quality of contemporary public life. At the same time, a spurt in individualism and an onslaught of overall disjointedness are also responsible for the changes in the texture of our social fabric. The principal reasons for party decline

[102] http://www.gfk.com/group/press_information/press_releases/008190/index.en.html.

could be found in the twin trends of personalised party-politics and the emergence of resources-oriented administrative functioning of parties.

Personalised Politics and Lack of Internal Democracy

Since the number of parties as an outcome of any political movement with a particular cause is fast declining, personalised politics is very much on the rise. Famous personalities with charisma as their strong point are often tempted to establish a new political party. Some key examples of personified parties in India are Telugu Desam, founded by NT Rama Rao, All-India Anna Dravida Munnetra Kazhagam (AIADMK) by MG Ramachandran and Shiv Sena by Bal Thackeray. Except the BJP and the Left parties, most of the parties in the country today are leader-centric and personality-based. As commented on by *The Economic Times*:

> How personality-oriented have political parties become? To a ridiculous extent, if you go by the behaviour of elected MPs. So many MPs owe so much to their leader that they feel obliged to do his bidding even before he so much as lifts a finger. If the leader of one of the small parties leaves the House for a visit to the loo, all members of his party present in the House also troop out, pronto.[103]

A group of grass-roots level workers around a leader at the local level, followed by several such clusters around a regional satrap and a similar set of leaders around a so-called national leader—such is the organisational structure of many political parties in contemporary India. The protection of mutual interests is important to this organisational pyramid (*as illustrated in* Appendix D).

Naturally, these parties just do not require any scientific organisational apparatus to run their organisation. In a situation

[103] Appeared in '"Through the Third Eye"', '*The Economic Times*', Mumbai, dated 31 January 2006.p.12

like this, any form of internal democracy becomes irrelevant. In the absence of any genuine internal democracy, most political parties in India have failed in growing as long-lasting institutions. This has greatly contributed to the process of their overall decline.

As explained, it is a direct result of charismatic leadership occupying the position of an indispensable crowd-puller and by that, also a vote-catcher. Within the party, these leaders are often projected as larger than life and that helps them to acquire power without authority. In a situation like this, very often, motives and the yearnings for 'personal gain' override or disregard the interests of the people leading to 'adoption of unscrupulous means'[104] by the parties for gaining power. The crisis gets confounded when the motives and designs of politicians become suspicious. In countries like India and many others, joining a particular party is almost no longer the acceptance of a political programme much less an ideology and hence, when someone leaves that party to join another, more often than not, there is no question of a change in political ideals, but merely a change in overall mentoring, mainly involving patronage and protection.

Some years back, Lok Satta carried out a study of the internal organisation of major parties in Andhra Pradesh. According to the conclusions drawn by Lok Satta, none of the major existing parties in the state are truly democratic as per the criteria of Lok Satta.[105] The only difference between them is in the degree and kind of authoritarianism practised. In order to sustain the top-down style of functioning, euphemisms like consensus, ideology or loyalty to the leadership are used.

Turning Parties into Election-contesting or Winning Machines

Ideology is no more a principal motivating force for the cadre of parties. Organisational activities, if any, between two elections

---

[104]HD Shourie 'The Basic Functioning of Political Parties in India' *Liberal Times*, Vol. IX/No.1, 2001, published by Freidrich-Naumann Stiftung, Regional Office South Asia.

[105]Lok Satta website, www.loksatta.org.

too are reduced in both numbers as well as the level of impact. This has changed the character of party organisations. In several cases parties are reduced to simple administrative units. A majority of parties have ceased to be live wire organisations. Naturally then, to sustain the façade of their active existence, an uninterrupted supply of resources becomes all the more important. This ushers in rampant and unchecked corruption, subsequently leading to further decline of the party. Here, populism plays an extremely important role since it seems to be the easiest shortcut for gaining instant political power. Later, it becomes a vicious circle, extremely hard to break and come out of, for most of the parties that have already tasted power in one way or the other. As KC Suri rightly commented, 'Most parties have become centred around one leader who exercises absolute control over the party.'[106] Such leaders and their associates are normally found to be:

> ..excessively interested in perpetuating themselves in power endlessly and in amassing wealth by making use of their position, [and hence] it became difficult for the parties to manage public affairs...Ruling parties are repeatedly voted out in elections due to the anti-incumbency factor. As popular pressures have increased on the parties, the party leaders have found out ways to win elections by resorting to huge expenditure to secure votes, the use of coercion, and the playing up of caste and community identities[107]

A flow-chart given in Appendix E portrays how once parties become some kind of a wanton victim of populism, their transformation into just an election-contesting machine is its simple logical corollary.

With winning elections being the sole purpose of democratic politics, and for that, amassing financial resources becoming a near-

---

[106] KC Suri, *op.cit.*
[107] *Ibid.*

must, parties no longer talk of bringing about any changes seriously. Corruption, for the purpose of mobilising financial resources, has become acceptable. In spite of the fact that corrupt practices have become rampant, there are hardly any instances of elected representatives being questioned by the party for such allegations. In fact, party bosses have lost the moral authority to examine party members about this. According to a senior member of a municipal corporation:

> Party leaders at times actively encourage law breaking among their subordinates as a kind of initiation into serious politics and as a means of guaranteeing their own untouchability if the political climate changed. On the rare occasion where an individual is actually punished for corruption, this is more of a sanction for lack of conformity to the system than for corruption itself.[108]

This has also led to some kind of a wanton criminalisation of politics. It is common knowledge that several elected representatives at the municipal level in Maharashtra do have some connections with criminal gangs. The situation is almost the same in other states and also other houses of representatives. Political commentator Amulya Ganguly has observed that seventy-two MPs amongst the total 542 (only in the Lok Sabha) have dubious antecedents and so do as many as 700 members of the legislative assemblies out of the 4,000 in the states.[109] Jayprakash Narayan (JN) echoes the same point:

> ...in last few decades political parties played into the hands of those who fought the elections with money, liquor and violence. In the process, even the crucial police system had

[108]As stated by a senior member of the Kalyan-Dombivali Municipal Corporation belonging to a national level party, in a focus group discussion, on condition of anonymity on 2 July 2005.

[109]Amulya Ganguly, '*The degeneration of Indian political class*' at http://news.monstersandcritics.com/india.

> become a tool in the hands of unscrupulous people...half of the people will withdraw from politics, the moment functional autonomy is given to the police system[110]

Another reason for conversion of parties into election-winning machines is that the parliamentary or legislature wings have almost overpowered the organisational ones. When in power, the entire decision-making power is vested with the leaders of the parliamentary wings and the organisational wings are reduced to just rubber-stamp authorities. In the Indian context, the Congress unabashedly accepted this supremacy of the legislative wing while the BJP attempted at giving due importance to the organisational wing, but only with limited success. Notably, the CPI (M) has fairly successfully ensured that sub-committees are constituted to 'monitor and guide'[111] the elected representatives of the party from parliament to local bodies, and thereby establish that the writ of the organisation runs on the elected representatives.

Tapering party identification lies at the centre of the existing vicious circle of party decline. Although systems and structures play no insignificant role, the reasons for this slump in party identification lie beyond them. These reasons could be found in factors like decreased confidence in social and political institutions, increased use of television, enabling the candidates to establish a direct rapport with the voters without going via the party organisation and also in the progressive ineffectiveness of family and other agencies of vertical socialisation. The emergence of scores of new groups and blogs on the Internet, as also encroachment of media in practically all aspects of human life has greatly affected our lives. In certain cases, well-meaning reforms have also contributed to the process of party decline. In the US, the federal funding of presidential campaigns, voted into law with a view to 'cleaning up' national politics, has greatly reduced the dependency of candidates on the party.

---

[110] http://www.thehindu.com/2006/09/17/stories/2006092707590500.htm.

[111] *Report on Implementation of Organisational Tasks,* CPI (M) Publication. November 2006, p.27.

A more practical explanation for party decline in India comes from a jurist, Justice Chandrashekhar Dharmadhikari.[112] According to him, with the beginning of the differentiation between public and personal character, the downfall of parties has started almost unstoppably. He adds that this disregard for personal character is the reason why women do not join politics in good numbers. Striking a perfect balance between being a people's representative and party representative is also a key to reducing the negative impact of petty partisan politics, he adds.

To summarise, parties have largely become wanton prisoners of a situation of their own making. Had there been a genuine commitment to the cause of the institutional character of parties on the part of politicians, parties could have easily freed themselves from these traps.

Impact of Party Decline

The decline of parties has paved the way for multiple crises in several countries. It's a fact that for a majority of the people in well established democracies, traditional forms of politics have lost credibility. Reforms remain the only way out but unfortunately, both the traditional parties in such democracies and their voters continue to take a status quo approach and puncture such efforts, overtly or covertly.

Party decline is also influencing inter-party relationships. For a sound and strong democratic polity, what is also essential is healthy inter-party relationships. When parties shun political extremism and take a centrist position, prepare themselves for negotiations and mutual cooperation and as a result, when political exclusivity and resultant 'untouchability' is fairly low, the chances of achieving a significant degree of consensus within the political elite become bright. There are instances in the history of democratic polities, that in the absence of all these factors, social and political polarisation of the very rigid type, plunges nations into crises

[112] As told in an interview to the author in Mumbai on 27 June 2007.

and tragedies. In India, this was witnessed in 1989 (Mandal Commission and Ayodhya dispute) and in 1999 (Mulayam Singh Yadav's refusal to support Sonia Gandhi mainly to claim the anti-BJP space amongst the minorities, exclusively).

The relationship between the party system and political system is that of interdependence. While it is true that political systems decide, to a considerable extent, the nature of political culture, the reverse is also true. Not too long ago, in Venezuela, as politicians became more unpopular and respect for them declined, reforms in the system became very difficult. In spite of the fact that there were many able politicians around, the system was such that it could prevent the introduction of any reforms.

Party decline has its impact on party-government relationship too. There are instances of (ruling party) governments eating into the vitals of the party's organisation. In India, it started with the Congress but has never been confined to it alone. In 1947, when Acharya JB Kripalani resigned as Congress president, he gave vent to his anguish for having been sidetracked by those in the government and thereby on the vexed issue of party-government interface.[113] This tension between party and government continued for a long time. In 1960, the then Congress President, Sanjeeva Reddy, tried to put it mildly, saying that the party's president is today not as important as he was when the freedom struggle was on and the party was not in power. Reputed journalist and commentator Frank Moraes has quoted a Congress observer who had pointed out: 'Since 1955, the Congress president has functioned as no more than a glorified office boy of the Congress central government, headed by the prime minister'.[114] Except for the CPI (M), to a reasonable extent, all other mainstream parties in India have suffered these tensions. While the CPI (M) has fairly successfully tried to establish the supremacy of the party organisation over the elected representatives through party

[113] *Congress Bulletin*, No.6. December, 1947, p.11-12, as quoted by Stanley Kochanek, 'The Indian National Congress',*The Journal of Asian Studies*, August 1966, p. 681.
[114] Frank Moraes, *India Today*, (Book) p.98.

committees to 'guide'[115] them, most other parties have either been less successful in handling these pressures properly or tried to manage them by keeping both the responsibilities—leader in parliament and party president—with a single person.

In the context of the USA, the withering away of parties had affected government functioning at least initially. Due to party decline, the principles of collective responsibility started dwindling while special interest groups became more and more important. As a result, not only in the US but also in other democracies, we have a system that articulates interests superbly but aggregates them poorly. Naturally then, the making of public policy has become complicated with no central direction, much less any coherence. David Broader, in fact, has concluded, '[In the US] the governmental system is not working because the political parties are not working.'[116]

The collapse of political parties has also led to the emergence of parallel and illegitimate power structures. Let us take the example of the Philippines. There, it has resulted in the return of the political clans as the principal agents of political mobilisation at the local level. Machine politics—a term that was once largely used to refer to political party machine—today, in the context of the Philippines, means a temporary coalition of local notables assembled by a presidential candidate in every place. The growing trend, of using hired individuals to replace genuine political activists, adds to the gravity of the situation.

Some commentators have observed that party atrophy has also resulted in non-party campaigns and movements focussing mainly on one single issue. Through them, people think that they secure a better return on their participatory investment by acting through specialist organisations matching their specialised concerns. This proves to be better because parties are seen as 'reluctant to

---

[115] As mentioned in the *Report on Implementation of the Organisational Tasks,* CPI (M) party publication, November 2006, p.27.

[116] Through the notes of David Broader's talk at Salzburg Seminar in June 2001, at Salzburg attended by the author personally.

identify with narrow causes for fear of upsetting other sections of party constituency.'[117] This has already given some impetus to the concept of a party-less democracy, regardless of its practicability. A Chennai-based organisation with an acronym SWACHID[118] has incorporated the idea of a party-less democracy in its 'manifesto'. World Prout Assembly,[119] an independent international organisation, is also engaged in promoting the idea of party-less democracy.

The serious disconnect that has developed between the parties and the people whom they claim to represent, is at the core of the whole issue. This has given birth to severe challenges that representative democracy is facing today. It is only through a set of systemic changes and the right kind of leadership that the political parties will be able to reconnect with the people again. Parties at all levels must include voters in their activities and their deliberations if they are to transform into vital institutions, performing a useful function in democracy. Without any involvement of self-motivated people, parties are bound to get reduced to machines. To overcome the weaknesses emerging out of it, parties are often seen as resorting to populism.

---

[117] Grant Jorden, 'Politics without parties: A Growing Trend?' in *Parliamentary Affairs* Vol. 51, No.4, 1998, p. 234.

[118] SWACHID means Soldiers for War against Corruption, Hunger, Ignorance and Disease. Their manifesto talks of 'keeping political parties away from local-self government bodies, trade unions, cooperatives and professional bodies'. However, the website is silent about how this could be ensured. http://www.swachid.com/gandhian%20thoughts.htmir.

[119] http://www.worldproutassembly.org/archives/2007/05/the_political_d.html; Progressive Utilisation Theory.

APPENDIX B

TABLE: DECLINE OF INDEPENDENTS

Year	Independent Candidates Contested in Lok Sabha Elections	Seats Won	Percentage	Percentage of Forfeited Deposits	Percentage of Votes Secured
1952	533	37	6.94	67.54	15.90
1957	481	42	8.73	67.36	19.32
1962	480	20	4.18	78.91	11.05
1967	864	35	4.04	86.26	13.78
1971	1134	14	1.23	94.00	8.38
1977	1224	9	0.74	97.22	5.50
1980	2826	9	0.32	98.87	6.43
1984	3878	5	0.13	98.79	7.92
1989	3409	12	0.32	98.90	5.25
1991	5546	1	0.02	99.69	4.16
1996	10639	9	0.08	99.70	6.28
1998	1906	6	0.31	99.11	2.37
1999	1945	6	0.31	99.13	2.74
2004	2377	2	0.21	99.37	4.25
2009	3831	9	1.66	99.35	5.19

Source: Data Unit, Lokniti-CSDS, Delhi and Election Commission of India website.

Appendix C

Table: Membership and Liking for Political Party

Class	Membership in Any Political Party	Liking for Any Political Party	Dislike for Any Political Party	Total
Very Poor	11	51	18	8101
Poor	13	53	22	9369
Middle	15	56	23	5186
Upper Class	18	56	26	4455
Caste/Community				
Upper Castes	12	58	26	4261
Peasant Proprietors	11	56	20	2221
Upper OBCs	19	53	23	5357
Lower OBCs	12	51	19	4315
SCs	14	56	21	4231
STs	13	44	13	2164
Muslims	12	53	25	2799
Others	13	50	19	1765
Education				
Non-literate	10	44	15	9477
Primary	13	55	21	6171
Matric	16	60	26	6483
College and above	19	60	30	4701
Occupation				
Higher Professionals	19	60	30	945
Lower Professionals	17	59	28	3336

Traditional Service	12	55	18	528
Workers	17	57	22	3093
Farmers	14	56	22	5535
Agricultural	12	53	21	5688
Workers				
Other Occupations	12	47	18	7984
Location				
Rural	14	53	21	21377
Urban	15	54	24	5735
Total	3710	14428	5823	27112
	13.7%	53.2%	21.5%	

All figures are in percentage points.

Source: National Election Study, 2004, Data Unit, Lokniti-CSDS, Delhi.

Note: If we exclude the respondents who have no opinion on these questions, the percentages would go up by 3 to 4 per cent.

Question wording:

Are you a member of any political party?

No Yes DK

Is there any political party, which you particularly like?

No Yes DK

Is there any political party, which you particularly dislike?

No Yes DK

Appendix D

Present Nature of Party Organisations

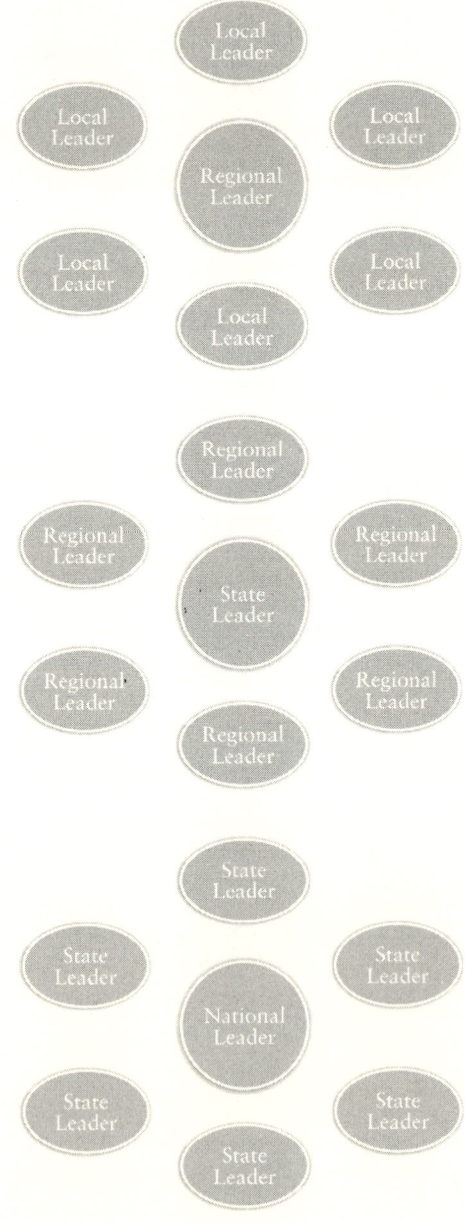

Appendix E

How Parties Become Victims of Populism and Electoral Compulsions

Parties fight elections.

↓

Parties win elections, many a time due to anti-incumbency.

↓

Parties attain power.

↓

Parties neglect organisations.

↓

Parties take shelter in shortcuts and compromises via populism.

↓

Parties, unsure of electoral gains, succumb to electoral compulsions.

↓

Parties master the technique of electoral success, thanks to a particular electoral system.

↓

Parties become machines.

↓

Parties become wanton prisoners of populism and electoral compulsions.

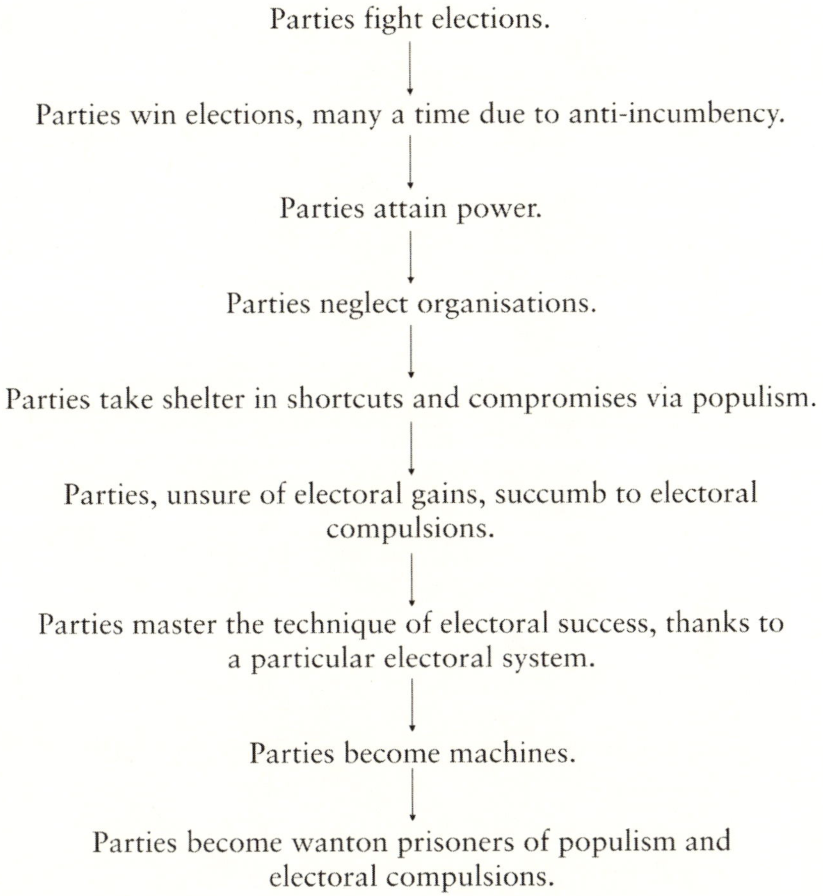

CHAPTER 5

The Lethal Cocktail: Populism and Electoral Compulsions

What is populism? What are electoral compulsions? How and why do politicians succumb to these pressures? How have these twin traits really afflicted democratic politics in India? How have they damaged the classical notions of representative democracy? Questions galore. Granted that populism is inherent to the concept of representative democracy, nonetheless, the magnitude of the damage it has caused is mind-boggling. More importantly, given the all-pervading cynicism about democracy almost all over the world, the indifferent approach of the democratic fraternity to the perilous impact of populism on democracy is simply inexplicable.

The Meaning of Populism

In the ultimate analysis, political democracy boils down to the rule of majority. Naturally then, people are sovereign at least in theory and popular opinion is of supreme importance. But this does not mean that in a democracy 'a majority would or should do anything it felt an impulse to do'.[1] The idea of restraints, checks and balances are

[1]Robert A Dahl, *A Preface to Democratic Theory*, p.36.

present everywhere, making the 'tyranny of majority' unacceptable in any democratic set-up. It is, therefore, imperative to review factors that may promote, overtly or covertly, a predominance of brutal majority, either natural or artificially cultivated through electoral techniques and strategies. Populism or populist politics is one such important factor and hence it is pertinent to know what it means.

According to *The Encyclopedia of Democracy*, populism is 'a political movement that emphasises the interests, cultural traits, and spontaneous feelings of the common people, as opposed to those of the privileged classes.'[2] It further explains that for legitimacy, populist movements 'often appeal to the "majority will" directly—through mass gatherings, referendums, or other forms of popular democracy—without much concern for checks and balances or the rights of minorities.'[3] *The Concise Dictionary of Politics* defines populism as '(More generally) support for the preference of ordinary people.'[4]

Arousing Raw Passions?

Beyond the obvious fact that the term *populism* has its roots in the word 'people', its connotations are largely contextual. In this characteristic vagueness lies the strength as well as the weakness of the term. In the context of politics, populism means a fine rallying cry, a unique combination of indistinctness and emotional reverberation. More importantly, it helps the politician to interpret facts differently and try to unite followers across formal party lines and to spread their appeal as widely as possible.

Populism could also be interpreted as a policy or a position, which people perceive as being in their favour for a short span of time, notwithstanding their larger interest in the longer run. The term connotes some compromises wantonly indulged in by the parties, solely for the purpose of seeking popular support for electoral success. It also means creating an atmosphere where voters get carried

[2]Seymour Martin Lipset, (Ed.), *The Encyclopaedia of Democracy*, p.985.
[3]*Ibid.* p.985.
[4]Iain McLean (Ed.), *The Concise Oxford Dictionary of Politics*, p.392.

away easily. This becomes easy mainly because the average voters are not necessarily and always capable of thinking about their larger interests or taking a long-term view while selecting a party or a candidate. In yet another shade of meaning, populism also means policies, slogans or declarations, which are made without any due seriousness attached to it and simply for the sake of garnering electoral support.

Before discussing the present-day meaning of populism, it would be useful to look into some relevant aspects of the classic definitions of the term. As mentioned by universally acclaimed political scientist Margaret Canovan,[5] one of the definitions states that populism is 'basically a rural movement seeking to realise traditional values in a changing society.'

It was political scientist Peter Wiles who emphatically advocated the idea of looking at populism as 'a syndrome, not a doctrine'. According to Wiles, 'Populism is any creed or movement based on the following major premises: virtue resides in the simple people, who are the overwhelming majority, and in their collective traditions.'[6]

Considering the present context in which the term populism is being used, it can reasonably be argued that what was considered to be a fairly genuine attempt to ensure the supremacy of popular opinion, has been converted into a mechanism for arousing raw and uncultivated or even ill-cultivated passions of the people, without making any efforts to enlighten them. In other words, modern day populism is an attempt to exploit the popular perceptions about the good of the people by way of endorsing them without critically examining the issues concerned. American political scientist Michael Kazin[7] had described populism as 'a flexible mode of persuasion' whereas Tom Brass,[8] in one of his essays, defines populism as 'essentially

---

[5]Margaret Canovan, *Populism*, p.261.
[6]*Ibid.* p.290.
[7]As quoted by Tom Brass, in 'The Agrarian Myth, the New "Populism" and the New "Right"', *Economic and Political Weekly*, Vol. xxxii. No. 4. January 25, 1997. PE-27
[8]*Ibid.*

a mobilising ideology, operating at the level of consciousness, where it serves to deflect discourse from class to non-class identity.'

History of Populism

A political movement built by Louis Napoleon, who staged a coup in France in 1851 and was able to attract an overwhelmingly popular support, is often described as a forerunner of populism.[9] His regime was seen as an early example of plebiscitary democracy, making a direct appeal to voter support with complete disregard to due legal processes. It has also been described as a combination of authoritarianism and mass consensus. Karl Marx called it Bonapartism. There is another view which traces the beginning of this phenomenon in the political world. According to *The Encyclopedia of Democracy*,[10] the term *populism* was first used in the 1870s in Russia. Populism referred to the thinking of a diverse group of theorists and politicians called *naordniki*. The members of this group were averse to any 'foreign' concept and were also vehemently against capitalism. They firmly believed in national popular traditions and institutions such as the village land-owning community, pioneered by Russian revolutionary leader and writer Aleksandr Herzen. Later, some elements of Anarchism, as interpreted by Mikhail Bakunin, another well-known Russian revolutionary, were also incorporated into this set of ideas. Mikhail Bakunin valued the spontaneity of the masses, including the large socially uprooted population in Russia, over the meticulous and deadening organisational skills of the Germanic Social Democrats.

In the US, populist tendencies asserted themselves through the formation of a formal political party, namely the Populist Party. Immediately after it came into being in the country in the 1890s, it based its major plank on agrarian issues. With demands such as free coinage of silver, an end to protective tariffs on manufactured goods, the abolition of national banks, introduction of a progressive federal income tax, direct election of the US senators and the regulation of railroads, it was clear that the party was trying to

---

[9] Seymour Martin Lipset (Ed.), *op.cit.*p. 987.
[10] *Ibid.*

play to the gallery. One of the most prominent demands was to abandon the laissez-faire policy by the government and take limited responsibility for the social well-being of American citizens. In 1893, the US witnessed a financial panic which quickly spread into one of the worst depressions. It aggravated the crisis of unemployment and fears about economic conditions and money supply grew. Jacob S Coxey, a Populist, organised a march to Washington DC by unemployed men. They demanded the hiring of unemployed youth for the construction of roads and bridges across the US. Not satisfied with just this, the Populists became the first political organisation to contest the elections nationally. They aggressively demanded that the size, activity level and, if need be, expense of the government should be increased to deal with the problems of a perplexing, complicated and modern nation. The very nature of these demands as also their aggressive tenor reveal how confident the Populists were of popular support.

While it is true that the Populists failed to win national office or displace either or both the major parties, they had a significant impact on the political and governmental systems in the country. Many of their demands, which were viewed as radical and extreme in the 1890s, were enacted shortly thereafter. By 1920, the scenario had changed considerably: US senators were elected directly, a progressive federal income tax was in operation, railroad regulatory efforts were strengthened significantly, protective tariffs were lowered and short term credits made available in rural areas.

The first wave of populism in the US also marked the emergence of the Jacksonian Movement.[11] This was an out and out populist movement, drawing its support from the firm popular belief that rustic wisdom (alone) was important as compared to the judgment of the highly-educated elites. Not surprisingly then, during Andrew Jackson's electoral campaign, a point was stressed emphatically by his campaigners that he had 'escaped the training and dialectics

---

[11] A movement in the US in 1830 for greater democratisation of government in the country. This movement grew out of the discontent over the growth of federal power and the protection given to Native Americans.

of the schools.'[12] Andrew Jackson, in a way, exploited the fact that people generally feel alienated from the elected representatives and politicians. He believed in direct connectivity with the electorate. His appeal to the American people was like that of a chieftain's to his tribe. In that sense, he was truly a people's president.

Just as in the US, in India too we have witnessed attempts at developing a contemptuous attitude towards all that is serious and academic in the name of the commoners and the downtrodden. The vocabulary used by politicians and those in public life, who are always keen to be politically correct, reflects a common disdain for the rich, elite and highly educated and this too is populist at the core. In the present day and age, several political leaders relish presenting themselves in public meetings as rustic, uneducated and poor and hence, more capable of understanding the agonies of the masses.

In the first half of the previous century, populism became more audacious in America. For all the shortcomings of representative democracy, populist democracy was presented as a remedy. It was during these turbulent times that the mechanisms of direct democracy, such as referendum and recall were introduced in some states in western USA. Even today, those who are demanding the introduction of direct democracy measures are banking upon a kind of restlessness born out of the deep distrust of traditional party politics and its limitations in offering genuine good governance. In the early twentieth century, the California Progressives, a political group on the fringes, openly asked the people to choose among the three alternatives: 'a government controlled by corporate interests, socialism or, if we have the courage, unselfishness and determination, [through] a government of individuals.'[13]

Since there are significant differences in the shades of meanings and connotations, it would be wrong to paint all branches of populism with the same brush. As rightly pointed out by Margaret Canovan, at times, populism of a particular kind serves as an

[12] Margaret Canovan, *op.cit,* p. 233.
[13] *Ibid.* p. 178.

appeal to the conscience of the people and eventually opens up the 'embarrassing gap between "the people" and their supposedly democratic and representative elite by stressing on popular values that conflict with those of the elite.' Canovan describes this kind of populism as 'Reactionary Populism' and asks, 'What are the enlightened democrats to do if "the people" in whose rule they are supposed to believe, utterly fail to share their views?'[14]

While discussing the various implications of populism, one must remember that it has become a seriously opinionated term, which also reflects the contemporary thinking among the intelligentsia. Most of the times, populism is perceived as negative and does not augur well, yet there are instances when it directly appeals to popular common sense. Of the several populist waves witnessed in the electoral history of India during the last sixty years, the one which favoured the restoration of democracy in 1977, could be mentioned as a case of positive populism.

It is popular perception that shapes populism. It has very little to do with genuine public interest. Social reformers in every society have had to struggle hard to convince people to accept reforms which are in their larger interest. From disciplining people participating in the festivities of Ganesh Chaturthi to convincing Muslims in accepting a common civil code, reformers have always faced stiff opposition to their efforts. At several instances, it has been observed that public spirited individuals and organisations find it easier to approach the judiciary to establish a few things, as against convincing the public itself about the larger public interest.

This gap between genuine public interest and the perception of the people about their interest is evident in every walk of human life. In that sense, populism is everywhere. From religion, culture and education to social issues and even technology, populism covers everything. The most glaring example of this fact can be seen in the infamous confrontation between science and popular religion, which began in 1925 and is continued in one way or the other to

---

[14] *Ibid.*

this day. The fundamentals of the Theory of Evolution propounded by Charles Darwin are clearly in conflict with the Biblical belief of Divine Creation. However, temptations of playing to the gallery and, more importantly, the fear of touching the religious sensibilities of the voters, have reflected in two compelling developments of that period. In 1923, the state of Oklahoma banned the teaching of the evolution theory in public schools. In Tennessee, John Washington Butler, a Baptist, contested the elections for the legislature on the plank of banning unbiblical teachings in the schools. Subsequently, thanks to the popular support he could mobilise, he got himself elected to the Senate, which ensured the passage of the bill. Even today, state administrations in the US are not able to rise above these populist considerations on the vexed issue of the Biblical theory of Divine Creation versus the Darwinian Theory of Evolution. This classic confrontation is important for another reason. It has rendered a devastating blow to yet another principle of democracy, that is, 'secularism'.

Populist Theories

Amongst the serious theorists, the most prominent was Jean-Jacques Rousseau, who came forward in staunch support of populist values. Through his *The Social Contract and Other Writings,* as also speeches, he not only advocated the rejection of progress, civilisation and inequality in political terms, but also looked at the entire elite section of society with utter contempt. He said, 'I hate books, they only teach us to talk about things we know nothing about.'[15] In his *Discourse on the Origin of Inequality,* he eulogised the 'Natural Man' as 'ignorant, solitary, completely uncivilised' but nevertheless 'equal, free and happy' and blamed civilisation for enslaving Natural Man. To sum up, it can be rightly said that Rousseau tried to present a theory of degeneration in opposition to the doctrine of progress through enlightenment. At the core of his theory was the view that 'Man is best when he is closest to nature, in societies that

[15] *Ibid.* p. 242

are simple, unrefined, and egalitarian, while he is worst where he has progressed furthest along the road to civilisation and inequality.'[16]

To the critics, Rousseau understandably appears to be confused and unclear. In his *The Social Contract,* on the one hand he eloquently defends the capacity of common men to manage their own affairs, while on the other he firmly asserts that 'a blind multitude' is not capable of working out its own laws. Therefore, he introduces a mysterious figure of the Lawgiver who is presented as a superhuman leader, presiding over the birth of the state, as Lycurgus did over that of Sparta.

The confusion on the part of Rousseau, betrayed by his writings, is in a way representative of the overall situation of the intelligentsia prevailing in those days. To defend populism or to denounce it was one of the serious dilemmas in the intellectual discourse. Many sought to adopt a policy of accommodation. Russian thinkers, who later came to be known as Russian Populists, struggled with this predicament very earnestly. Most noteworthy of them was Peter Lavrov, an academic who taught at the St Petersburg University in Russia in the 1850s. Through his *Historical Letters* Peter Lavrov created a feeling of being indebted to the masses whose toil had brought the intelligentsia closer to culture. On the other hand, it was the same Lavrov who stated that 'Progress consists in the development of consciousness and in the incorporation of truth and justice in social institutions; it is a process which is being accomplished by means of the critical thought of individuals who aim at the transformation of their culture.'[17]

Edward Shils, who is often described as the world's most influential sociologist, had pointed out one of the sinister aspects of populism—the distrust of the educated. This emanated from the firm belief of the populists that whatever the people want must be right, and which would dare the populists to sweep aside bureaucratic professionalism, constitutional restrictions and due process of law.

[16]*Ibid.*
[17]*Ibid.* p.242.

According to Shils, this very type of populism '...is the people's justice of a lynch mob, whereas the careful restrained sifting of evidence at a formal trial demands an unpopulist respect for the authority of law and lawyers. While distrustful of experts, however, and inclined to regard politicians as mere errand boys whose job is to carry out the people's will, populists are notoriously given to following demagogues, from Huey Long to Senator McCarthy.'[18]

Why Populism Thrives

The roots of populism can be found in the fact that emotional aspects continue to influence laypersons greatly, even today. Broadly speaking, populism thrives because the sentimentality of people still rules the roost. It was not for no reason that Abraham Lincoln once observed, 'With public sentiments, nothing can fail; without it, nothing can succeed.'[19] Before one looks into the history of populism, it would be interesting to understand as to why, after all, populism thrives. Peter Lyon, then Director of the Institute of Commonwealth Studies at London, had a very thoughtful comment to offer on this issue. When I interviewed him in London in 1998 on a quiet August afternoon, he said, 'When passive political classes are helped by an active media creating an illusion of popular public opinion, populism starts playing the role. But often, these opinions are very fickle and short lived since people themselves are fast changing their loyalties.'

In a democratic polity, populism thrives because the majority or numerical superiority is the cardinal rule there. Elections are the operative mechanism of democracy. Although elections were 'supposed to be a quantitative instruments designed to make qualitative choice, the quantitative emphasis [has] quickly usurped the place of the qualitative. The mechanism has taken control of the mechanic...That is to say, that instead of qualitating, quantity devaluates quality—an unhappy confusion of arithmetic with values.'[20]

[18] *Ibid.* p. 184.

[19] As quoted by Duane Elgin. 'Revitalising democracy through electronic town meetings', in Robert Diclerico and Allan Hammock, (Ed.) *Points of View: Readings in American Government and Politics*, p.48.

[20] Giovanni Sartori, *Democratic Theory*, p.104.

In a democracy, populism thrives mainly because voters have a tendency to get swayed by popular opinion. Under most of the democratic systems, the voting trend and the voters' tendencies have fuelled populist politics all along. Sir Ivor Jennings, in his book *Primer to Electioneering*, has laid down thirteen prepositions. He has made a noteworthy conclusion, 'most electors vote not for party policy but for a party image.'[21] In the Indian context, this influence of image could be explained through the illustration of the Congress. As revealed by the report presented by the Sachar Committee[22], Muslims continued to remain underprivileged during the last sixty-five years, in spite of the fact that the Congress was in power for most of that period. But thanks to the fact that it always took advantage of the sentimentality of the issues concerning the Muslim community—a separate Civil Code, promotion of Urdu language and refraining from the ban on cow slaughter—the Congress cleverly cultivated an image as that of the only party safeguarding the interests of the Muslims, without any result-oriented efforts for the spread of education and bringing social reforms amongst them.

There are some other sociological explanations as well. According to Gino Germany, a pioneer of research in populist politics in Latin America, populism is mainly a result of social mobilisation. Due to internal migration and improved mass communication, masses sever their traditional loyalties and associate with a new upsurge. A highly visible and charismatic person, who identifies him/herself with the dominant classes but sets himself against the elite, emerges as a leader. In India, the BJP's catapulting to power in 1998 can be traced to this process. Senior BJP leader and party president for several years, LK Advani, coined the word pseudo-secularism and successfully employed cultural symbols to foster nationalist spirit. He also trained his guns against the politics of offering concessions to the minority Muslim community, describing it as

[21] As quoted by YN Sukathankar in *Human Nature and Politics*, p. 6.

[22] A high-level committee, headed by Justice Rajinder Sachar was appointed by the Prime Minister in 2005, for the preparation of a report on the social, economic and educational status of the Muslim community.

'minority appeasement'. With LK Advani at the helm of affairs, the BJP could challenge the political elite while influencing the mindset of the huge emergent middle class, and eventually captured power.

As discussed earlier, one important reason for parties going populist is their willingness to compromise with their very *raison d'être*, resulting in a clear loss of focus. Generally speaking, parties have lost the essential urge to achieve their ends and have become complacent merely with the achievement of means. Partly, this tendency to compromise with accepted doctrines has its roots in the all-pervading confusion about major ideological blocks, the Left, the Right and even the Third Wayers. Also, there are instances when parties engage in a wanton compromise with the basics of their philosophy, mainly for the sake of power. Having tasted power once, most of the mass or catch-all parties give up their core doctrinal approach and try to appear like everything to everybody. This also influences their organisational character. As mentioned by Richard S Katz and Peter Mair, in a traditionally catch-all kind of party, relations between the ordinary members and party elite are top-down. 'Members are organised (merely) as cheer leaders for the elite.'[23] Understandably, this tendency converts party workers into mercenaries. This is abundantly evident in India as well.

In India, with lost focus, parties have been trying to encompass everybody and in that process either avoid taking a position on apparently divisive issues or take only those decisions which may bring votes. British political scientist and professor of government, Wicky Randal[24], points out that the leaders of the Congress in India, themselves span a wide Left-Right spectrum and aim to maximise the party's electoral appeal to make it catch-all. From Mahatma Gandhi, Jawaharlal Nehru, Indira Gandhi, Rajiv Gandhi to Manmohan Singh, there is a wide spectrum of policy perspectives, especially on economic issues and the Congress seems to have digested all of them

---

[23]Richard S Katz and Peter Mair, 'Changing Models of Party Organisation and Party Democracy', *Party Politics*, Vol.1 No.1, Jan. 1995 p.18.

[24]Wicky Randal (Ed.), *Political Parties in the third world*, p.182

to make it acceptable to all. Even parties like the BJP and the CPI (M) could not escape this lure, especially while in power.

One comes across a similar example in Zambia. The party led by Kenneth Kaunda—the president of Zambia during 1964-1991—whose humanism, 'combining capitalist, socialist, and populist strands...'[25], reflected the various elements within Zambian society. His party (the United National Independence Party, UNIP) sought to accommodate all the diverse interests and eventually combined them into a coalition government which was presided over by him.

Nature of Populism

The politics of populism and the way it is practised has come a long way since the times of Margaret Canovan. Refusing to take a long-term view or considering the larger interest of the people, and doing it 'right' in the name of the people is the principal characteristic of populist politics. Although sentimentality is at the core of populism, several contemporary issues and popular perceptions give shape and lend content to it.

Broadly, populism can be categorised into five different practices. These can also be described as the categories of applied populism. Since parties' indulgence in populism is the focus of this study, populist practices of littérateurs, artists and thinkers are not taken into consideration here. While populist practices certainly can be categorised, it has to be noted that a certain amount of overlap is bound to be there. Besides, one may describe a particular act of a party as part of economic populism while some others may interpret it as that of political populism.

Nationalist Populism

This kind of populism involves appealing to the national spirit with an extremist zeal and raising the tempo of jingoist emotions of the masses in such a way that rational analysis of an issue becomes impossible. While practising this, political parties create an impression

[25]William Trardoff, 'Political Parties in Zambia' in Wicky Randal (Ed.) *op.cit.*p.17.

that their unique and supremely important nation is being threatened by the onslaught of internationalism—endangering its identity as a nation and more importantly, its sovereignty. Traditionally, right-wing parties and groups practise nationalist populism. The lure of exploiting nationalist spirit and, more importantly, the fear of being dubbed as less patriotic drives even the non-Right parties into the trap of this category of populism.

Nationalist populism is also manifested in the overemphasis on the concept of 'one people'. According to Canovan, 'the people' serves as an effective battle cry 'and a particularly useful one for politicians who seek to blur established differences, to unite followers across former party lines and to spread their appeal as widely as possible.'[26] One of the principal arguments advanced by the British Liberal Party was that the Labour and the Conservatives perpetuate an unnecessary and damaging class conflict in Britain, whereas the Liberal Party stands for the people and not for any particular class.

Peter Worsley, in his book *The Third World,* has maintained that 'populism' was the characteristic ideology of the ex-colonial one-party states of Africa and Asia, and the unifying 'politician's populism' was the prominent common element. Elaborating upon the lurking dangers of this otherwise prudent approach of those who propound the 'one people' theory, Worsley observes, 'The populist asserts that there are no divisions in the community...since the society is undifferentiated, organic, undivided, it needs only one single political organisation to express its common interests, only one party...the party does not represent a particular, narrow, sectional interest; it represents everyone.'[27]

In India, Mayawati's slogan of *Sarvajan Samaj,* coined and propagated a little before and during the 2007 elections to the Uttar Pradesh assembly, the *Mee Mumbaikar* campaign attempted by Shiv Sena leader Uddhav Thackeray before the 2007 Mumbai Municipal Corporation elections and Narendra Modi's repeated reference to

[26] Margaret Canovan, *op.cit.*p.261.
[27] *Ibid.*p. 266.

'5.5 crore Gujaratis' are some of the notable examples of unifying populism practised by politicians. Obviously, here the focus remains on peppering over the cleavages—social in the case of Mayawati, linguistic in the context of Uddhav Thackeray and religious or communal for Narendra Modi, while creating an impression of the unity of the people. Sharad Pawar, in 1999, used the 'Nationalist' tag for populist purposes. In the same year, he chose the 'Nationalist Congress Party' as the name for his new party. He wanted to signify that while the Congress (INC) was being led by a foreign national, his party stood for real nationalist aspirations. The fact that he readily accepted Sonia Gandhi as the leader of the coalition government later, underscores the sheer populist character of his move of breaking away from the Congress.

There are positive aspects of this unifying populism too. Canadian activist-academic John Saul has observed that a populist emphasis on unity and solidarity might be politically useful without being true. He has further pointed out that such populism may 'represent an aspiration to make a particular view of the characteristics that unite people, prevail over any continuing awareness of the elements that divide.'[28] Researchers have also advanced certain examples of political strategies adopted by leaders like Abraham Lincoln, Mahatma Gandhi, Charles de Gaulle and Jimmy Carter of positive, unifying populism. Although there may be differences about the genuineness of the honest efforts for forging unity amongst the people, one cannot overlook the fact that populism can also be used with an 'above partisan' consideration, to promote harmony in society. Both in the Ekatmata Yatra (Integration Yatra) (1991) of Murali Manohar Joshi and Swarnajayanti Rath Yatra (Golden Jubilee of Independence Rath Yatra) (1997) of LK Advani, it was the 'Nationalist appeal' that was at the core, when BJP leaders embarked upon nationwide tours.

The examples of using nationalist populism in other countries are also worth noting. Popular movements like the one in Egypt

[28]As quoted by Margaret Canovan, *op.cit.*p. 267.

which installed the regime of Gamal Abdul Nasser could be classified as populist in nature. In the early Forties, Colonel Juan Domingo Peron of Argentina overthrew the conservative government of the country and acquired power through democratic means. It was a mix of nationalism and solidarity with the working classes that marked the core of his appeal.

In the recent past, many European parties have been seen as taking shelter in nationalist populism. Sieglinde Rosenburger has observed that 'many Europeans have been experiencing "Europeanisation" or "Globalisation" more as a loss of a sense of identity and belonging than as an opportunity to create a cross-national "European soul". In such a scenario, Nationalism's electoral success seems inevitable.'[29]

Identity Populism

While nationalist populism focuses on national identity, identity populism goes even further and appeals to the sub-national, ethnic or community identity. Obviously, this has a limited sphere of appeal but it is more focussed and sharp. As it is, back to the roots is a popular social trend today and powerful uprisings and congregations on caste or community lines have become the order of the day. The Gujjar agitation for a quota in Rajasthan and the first-of-its type convention of Chitpavan Brahmins held in Pune in December 2007 are the cases in point. When society is in turmoil and the electorate is restless, an appeal to the root insecurities of the people works and several politicians convert this into an electoral advantage.

In India, identity politics has often taken an ugly turn with passionate appeals addressed mainly to a particular section of the society, connoting a message of coming together against another group. This has resulted in a brazen caste conflict. In the Lok Sabha Elections of 2004, Sharad Pawar had touched a subtle communal

---

[29]Sieglinde Rosenburger, 'The other side of the coin: Populism, nationalism and the European Union', Harvard International, Interventionsim, Vol.26 (1) –Spring 2004, at http://hir.harvard.edu/articles/1210/2/.

chord while asking whether one comes across people with last names like Vajpayee, Advani or (Pramod) Mahajan speaking about farmers. Very obviously, Pawar wanted to underscore the upper caste background of Vajpayee, Advani and Mahajan through the mention of their last names. Several instances are available when political leaders or workers in India have uttered slogans which connote a subtle appeal to caste or community identities.[30]

It is a common experience that political leaders and even governments play upon the resonance of popular unity with a contempt for any divisive factional identity and use it as a ladder to climb up and acquire power. There are scores of examples of how leaders like Indira Gandhi, Narasimha Rao, Mulayam Singh Yadav, Mayawati or Mamata Banerjee have tried to use symbolisms and rhetoric to ride to power.[31]

Political scientist Prakash Sarangi has commented that, in India:

> Political parties have tried to relate themselves to people through various primordial linkages, through the cast, linguistic or regional groups...there is another qualitative change in the way the parties relate to people. Earlier, the party leaders used to argue that they 'represented' the interests of 'the people'. Now, since the parties tend to represent the primordial interests, they seem to claim that they themselves are 'the people'.[32]

---

[30]In several press reports, party workers of the BSP have been reported as airing slogans like '*Dalit, Muslim, Sikh, Isai...Hindu Kaum Kahanse Ayee*' and '*Tilak Taraju aur Talwar, Inko Maro Jute Chaar*'. In the case of the Samajwadi Party, their leaders have openly demanded a separate Muslim Pradesh within Uttar Pradesh.

[31]Indira Gandhi presented herself as *Gujarat ki Bahu* to the voters in Gujarat in 1975. Similarly, the slogans of *Telugu Bidda* (Narasimha Rao, Andhra Pradesh elections in 1994), Marathi *Manoos* (Maharashtra Nav Nirman Sena in Maharashtra) and *UP mein hai Dum* (an advertisement campaign in Uttar Pradesh elections in 2007) or *Poribartan* and *Ma Mati Manush* used by Mamata Banerjee in 2011.

[32]Prakash Sarangi.*op.cit.*

Identity-based politics has always remained central to the political scenarios of several states, including Tamil Nadu. According to many political observers, Jayalalitha's populism has always remained very audaciously calculative. All the time, her strong argument has remained that she alone can change people's lives for better and hence, she has been unabashedly adopting a paternalistic and patronising posture. On the other side, at least for the sake of using politically correct language, M Karunanidhi has been referring to social justice and similar terms. Both these trends were also evident, more or less, in the assembly elections which were concluded in 2011.

Issues like the border row between Karnataka and Maharashtra, with Belgaum at its centre, creation of a greater Nagaland in the North East, the Left parties' demand for a greater adivasi state combining parts of north Maharashtra and south Gujarat, are only a few of the innumerable instances of identity populism indulged in by political parties in India. The Congress and the BJP too have played with this card at one time or the other.

Economic Populism

While today it is rhetoric against globalisation and market forces, in the past it was shrill slogan-mongering against the rich and the powerful, the social and the economic elite that formed the plank of economic populism. In India, the issue of offering subsidies to farmers has been one of the popular measures under economic populism. In the 1997 elections to the Punjab assembly, the Akali Dal's promises of doling out freebies had run into several hundred crores, on top of an inherited deficit of ₹6,000 crore. Similarly, in the neighbouring state of Haryana, Bansi Lal's Haryana Vikas Party (HVP) had promised the lowering of electricity tariff in the run up to the elections in 1997, but later had to increase it substantially, inviting widespread agitation by the farmers. The Communists and also the Left-of-the-Centre parties have always tried to theorise what was, in most cases, a brazen indulgence in a kind of economic populism. Opinion makers and reformist-activists in the country, like Jayprakash Narayan (JN) have, without mincing words, assailed the economic populism which emanates from a socialist hangover. According to Narayan, 'During the past fifty years, in the name of socialism, we undermined true entrepreneurship.'[33] He further comments that it has strengthened and legitimised 'many imprudent economic policies'.[34] The continuing demands of the Left parties for lowering the prices of Liquid Petroleum Gas (LPG) and other petroleum products, regardless of the economic inadvisability inherent to the move, or slowing down the process of disinvestment as demonstrated in the case of the Neyveli Lignite Corporation[35] under the UPA-1, as well as the repeated switching from regulation to de-regulation and vice versa in the case of the prices of petroleum products by UPA-1 and 2, are some of the many examples of economic populism.

Indulgence in bashing the moneyed sections of society has been fashionable for decades. This also is a kind of economic populism. Even seasoned politicians like the then American President Jimmy Carter[36] could not resist the lure of rich bashing, mainly for the purpose of establishing a so-called solidarity with the poor and the deprived. The decades old debate about a free market economy versus state controlled economy offers several examples of economic populism. Individuals and organisations advocating either of these have often shown utter disregard for the fact that there are several grey areas in this debate and stereotypical thinking needs to be abandoned. Lack of courage on the part of political parties when it comes to taking any position where there is a calculated risk of misinterpretation involved, is most common. Parties are often seen as sticking to a position for they are not certain about their own

---

[33]Jayprakash Narayan (JN), '*Democracy, Populism and Free Lunches*' (The text of Sreeramulu First Endowment Lecture) at www.loksatta.org.

[34]*Ibid.*

[35]The UPA government halted the sale of 10 per cent equity in Neyveli Lignite Corporation, a public sector power-generating company on 6 July 2006 after DMK threatened a pull out from the government.

[36]Jimmy Carter's speech accepting democratic nomination in 1976 at www.jimmycarterlibrary.org/documents/speeches/acceptance_speech.pdf.

supporters accepting any apparent deviation. Apparently, it can also be said that party leaders doubt the ability of their own party cadres to approach their support base and convince their voters about the change in the party position. Consequently, beneath the make-believe atmosphere of mutuality, there also lies unease. Partha Chatterjee has rightly cautioned, 'In the context of the latest phase of the globalisation of capital, we may well be witnessing an emerging opposition between modernity and democracy, i.e. between civil society and political society.'[37]

Socio-cultural Populism

Social reforms are one of the important ingredients of any transformation in society. The key to these reforms lies in making consistent and indefatigable efforts for changing the collective mindset of society. To bring about such changes, organisations and their leadership fundamentally require a firm conviction, political will and a non-compromising approach. A well-thought-out strategy is also imperative to pursue the cause. This, undoubtedly, is difficult and hence, politicians routinely take recourse to compromises.

In Andhra Pradesh in 1995, the Telugu Desam party came to power on the promise of implementing a policy of total prohibition—restricting consumption of liquor—in the state. This attracted a huge number of women voters who firmly supported the TDP. Having exploited the popular view politically, within just three years thereafter, the TDP abandoned the policy on fiscal grounds. The same story was repeated in Haryana. Here, Haryana Vikas Party's Bansi Lal sought mandate in 1996 promising total prohibition and later withdrew the same in just two years, in 1998.

How the governments develop cold feet when it comes to popular feelings can be seen from an example in Maharashtra. In August 2005, the Supreme Court had ordered the state government to enforce strict controls over blaring loudspeakers, often used

[37]Partha Chatterjee, 'Beyond the Nation? Or Within?', *Economic and Political Weekly*, 4–11 January, 1997 p.33. Volume xxxii. No.1 and 2.

for religious and cultural celebrations. In its application, the state government submitted that a total ban on the use of loudspeakers, drums and amplifiers would disturb the sentiments of the people, which could lead to police-public confrontation, as there was no societal consensus on the issue.

In the recent past, India has witnessed the use of religion or religious symbolism for electoral gains. There is a history of politicians taking advantage of the presence of various religious or communal identities in India. The steadfastness with which subsequent Congress governments at the Centre have hesitated in bringing a common civil code, as illustrated very strongly by its approach to the Shah Bano case in the late Eighties, is a case in point. Several decisions of the governments headed by the Congress have made Hindus sceptical of their secular credentials. For instance, the government's stand vis-a-vis the large-scale illegal migration from Bangladesh (mostly by Muslims) was clearly visible when it introduced the Illegal Migrants Determination by Tribunals (IMDT) Act[38] in 1983. Later, in July 2005, when the apex court declared the IMDT act null and void, the government tried to circumvent the verdict through an administrative order. The Constituent Assembly of India[39] had deliberated the issue of religion-based quotas and very clearly decided against implementing these. This once-settled subject is being repeatedly revived by successive Congress governments in Andhra Pradesh through several attempts at introducing quotas for Muslims, with utter disregard for the court judgments. (The Supreme Court, on 13 June 2012 expressed doubts about the constitutional

---

[38]Illegal Migrants Determination by Tribunals Act of 1983 was promulgated under the regime of Indira Gandhi. Recently declared null and void by the Supreme Court, this Act is applicable in Assam alone and its provisions put the onus of establishing the illegality of a migrant on the complainant.

[39]Pandit Nehru, welcoming the decision of the Constituent Assembly, of accepting the proposal of the Advisory Committee on Fundamental Rights, thereby rejecting the communal basis of political reservations, had said that with this 'our destiny has taken a historic turn'. For details, see KM Munshi, *Indian Constitutional Documents–Volume 1: Pilgrimage to Freedom*, p.197.

validity of the UPA government's bid to create a 4.5 per cent minority sub-quota within the 27 per cent OBC quota).

This underscores the fact that mainly the Congress is exploiting religious populism to the hilt. It was against this background that LK Advani's talk of 'pseudo-secularism', 'Muslim appeasement' and 'minoritism' easily captured the imagination of a large section of Hindus, who have, of late, become more conscious of their religious identity.

There also have been some instances of meekly giving in to compromises with the cardinal principles of one's ideology. In 2003, when the government in Tamil Nadu decided to ban animal sacrifices in temples, it enraged Dalits and Backward Classes, for whom the ritual has special significance. It may be noted here that the DMK, the Pattali Makkal Katchi (PMK) and the CPI (M) supported this demand. These are the very parties that are otherwise keen on presenting themselves as rational parties. Similarly, in 2005, when cine star Amitabh Bachchan was hospitalised after an ailment, two buffaloes were sacrificed at the Kamakhya Temple in Guwahati to seek the goddess' blessings, by the leaders of the Samajwadi Party, whose public posturing is that of a secular, rationalist and socialist party.[40]

In India, examples of political populism thriving during the elections are aplenty. The latest example is that of the 2012 UP election campaign in which the Batla house 'controversy' was resurrected and the reported story of Sonia Gandhi bursting into tears over the alleged terrorists was circulated in the media. The history of electoral politics in India is replete with numerous examples of political parties competing in promising individual benefits such as social welfare pensions, loan waivers, housing, rice at ₹2 a kg etc. This list is now expanding rapidly to include modern consumer durables such as television sets, cell-phones and refrigerators, as witnessed during the

[40] Anuradha Dutta, 'Sacrificing Ideology', *The Pioneer*, New Delhi, 15 December, 2005.

2011 elections to the Tamil Nadu assembly and the 2012 Mumbai Municipal Corporation elections.

The result is an increasing trend towards competitive populism. This is a cancerous trend that threatens to engulf our democratic polity.

Another classic example of giving in to public pressures comes from the UK, where the supporters and opponents of blood sports were fighting for quite some time. Commenting upon the controversial issue of banning blood sports and how Prime Minister Tony Blair buckled under the pressure of populist demands, political scientist FF Ridley has made some noteworthy remarks. He says:

> There is probably a lesson about the society we live in here. Pursuit of self-interest appears to dominate. Indeed, an international survey just published claims that the British, from the childhood onwards, now rate material interests more highly than anything (including family life) and outstrip other Europeans in this respect. The result may be that latent emotions, if touched on a national scale, can bring disarray to our socio-political order (the Princess Diana case a portent?). Mr Blair, backing away from support of anti-blood sports legislation in the face of a mass rally of hostile future voters, may one day regret disregarding the quieter but much larger number of people that opinion polls show opposed to such sports.[41]

Political Populism

Over and above all the categories mentioned earlier, there exists what can be named as sheer political populism. This populism is brazenly power-oriented and parties or leaders who pursue this, do it unmistakably in the name of people's power. Plausible spontaneous upsurges of popular feelings, in wanton disregard for constitutional processes or established norms, could be described as the principal

---

[41]FF Ridley, 'Crusaders and Politicians', in *Parliamentary Affairs*, Oxford University Press, Vol.51, No. 3, July 1998, p. 309-313.

characteristic of this kind of populism. Those who practice this, ensure that everything they do is propagated in the name of being done for the benefit of the masses.

In India, political populism began with anti-Congressism in the late Sixties. In 1989, anti-BJPism started when the BJP became a force to reckon with. Anti-BJPism was practised by many regional parties in the name of consolidating 'secular' forces, forgetting the fact that they had fought elections against each other. The case was the same with the first Democratic Front government in Maharashtra, in 1999, when the Congress and the NCP joined hands after fighting a bitter election battle. In 2001, before the assembly elections in West Bengal, Mamata Banerjee tried to experiment with political populism by building a *Mahajot* (grand alliance) against the ruling Left Front.

Coalition politics can be described as one of the most important products of political populism. There is an oft-repeated allegation that parties push ideology to the back burner for the sake of power, attained through coalition politics. Citing the example of the Congress in India, veteran Indian journalist Cho Ramswami has commented:

> ...a political party to be successful in electoral politics in India, has to be like Hinduism. You can be a *Vaishnavite* (worshipper of Vishnu), you can be a *Saivite* (worshipper of Shiva), you can be a *Shakta,* (worshipper of Shakti) you can be a *Kaumara* (worshippers of Karthikeya) and you can even be an atheist and still be a Hindu.[42]

For a political party, to be everything to everybody may prove to be a good strategy, but the impact of the resultant dilution in their distinctness is not far to seek.

This tag of doing 'in the name of the people' has always helped dictators like Benito Mussolini and Adolf Hitler, who capitalised on their own commoner background and presented themselves as

[42]Cho Ramswami, 'Coalition Politics and the Death of Ideology', *VIGIL, 20th Anniversary Souvenir,* August 2003, Chennai, p.77.

representatives of the ordinary, common man. Hitler is on record having said that:

No one has set me above this people. I have grown from the people, I have remained in the people and to the people I shall return. It is my ambition not to know a single statesman in the world who has a better right than I to say that he is a representative of his people.[43]

Yet another twentieth century practitioner of political populism was Huey Long (1893-1935), who got himself democratically elected as the governor of the state of Louisiana in the US, but later became better known as a virtual dictator of the state. He had complete popular support and at no time did he lose touch with the commoners. But, as rightly commented on by Margaret Canovan, the fact remains that 'he was a cynical manipulator who used his popular appeal to gain wealth and power for himself, who had no respect for law or constitution, who would not brook opposition and who made himself virtual dictator in Louisiana'.[44]

Even in the recent decades, we have come across several instances of mobilising masses and acquiring power, often without bothering about scruples, in the name of the people. These upsurges are also labelled as revolutions or fights for freedom and/or self-determination. The ousters of the President of the Philippines, Ferdinand Marcos, in 1986, or that of the then president of Serbia and Yugoslavia, Slobodan Milosevic, in 2000 and in 2003 of the then Georgian President Eduard Shevardnadze, are all examples of such popular risings. Reviewing the events in Georgia, *The New York Times* had commented, 'It may not have been a constitutional process that brought him to power. But there was tough-minded strategy, organisation and hard work behind the chanting crowds in the streets.'[45] Again, a victory of populism over constitutionalism. It is understandable that rule-breaking can be tempting when the

[43] Margaret Canovan, *op.cit*, p.149.
[44] *ibid.* p.158.
[45] A despatch by Seth Mydnas, in *The New York Times*, New York, 7 January 2004.

democratic process bogs one down. However, popular revolts like this can also pave the way for a different set of problems.

PARTY-POPULISM NEXUS

Although not exactly based on the nature of populism, parties that have emerged out of populist-sounding processes have been broadly classified into four categories.[46] These categories, their class composition, characteristic nature of appeal and their broad examples, are elaborately explained in *The Encyclopedia of Democracy*. Its summary is given here:

Multi-class Integrative Parties	Middle-class Populist Parties	Working-class Populist Parties	Social Revolutionary Parties
Emergence through a nationwide confrontation against dictatorship or colonial rule.	Largely confined to middle-class and offer more scope for conservative sections of the society.	Emergence through movements of working classes.	Usually, based on Marxist-Leninist ideology and led by a strong, charismatic leader.
Mexican Institutional Revolutionary Party, Indian National Congress.	Aprista Party of Peru. Janata Party in India in 1977 and to some extent, the BJP.	Various Communist parties in India, and Social Democratics in Brazil.	Maoist parties in Nepal and CPI (M-L) in India, besides social revolutionary parties in Cuba and the Caribbeans.

It is amply clear from the chart that populism has played

[46] Seymour Martin Lipset, (Ed.), *op.cit*, p. 987.

some role in the emergence of most of the ideological-sounding parties; what causes concern is their continuous dependence on it. While populist politics do catapult parties to power, democratic process becomes hollow and as a result, popular faith in the concept of democracy itself is shaken.

Impact of Populism

The impact of populism on democratic polities has always remained long-lasting, far-reaching and wide enough to impact major walks of public life. Edward Shils, who was the first to proclaim that populist politics ultimately may lead to the death of liberty, has minced no words while outlining the perils of populist politics. He had gauged the depth and severity of the impact of populism. According to him, it:

> ...proclaims that the will of the people as such is supreme over every other standard, over the standards of traditional institutions, over the autonomy of institutions, and over the will of other strata. Populism identifies the will of the people with justice and morality.[47]

Nonetheless, he had no doubts that the lurking dangers of populism outweigh the benefits, as Nazism and Bolshevism and, of course, McCarthyism were all different forms of populism.

Populism's impact is twofold; it affects society in general as well as the democratic polity. It also eats into the vitals of political parties as institutions.

Impact on Democratic Polity and Society

Populism impacts democratic polity and society in certain ways which are now being discussed.

Shying away from responsibility: Thanks to populism, the political leadership first develops a habit of avoiding taking any

[47]As quoted by Margaret Canovan, *op.cit*, p. 183.

harsh decisions. As a consequence, the leadership also dithers in accepting responsibility and focuses more on shying away from it. Always under the pressure of winning elections, it consistently takes a politically correct position and in the process avoids the onus of decision-making. For example, in India, provincial leaders often find an escape in putting the blame for all their problems on the Union Government, regardless of the fact that, at times, their own party is ruling at the Centre. In countries like India, it is easier to hoodwink the electorate due to ignorance and lack of political education. From eradication of slums and shanty colonies in cities to disputes over sharing of river water, there are several issues about which voters have no knowledge as to which government is really responsible.

Similarly, in Europe it has been observed that when it comes to nationalist considerations and the apparent clash of interests between member states and the European Union, 'political parties and their leaders are eager to avoid responsibility for unpopular decisions made in Brussels. Both pro- and anti-European parties blame the European Union alike for decisions, even when they themselves play a large role in the decision-making processes.'[48]

Politicisation of inter-community relations: Margaret Canovan has pointed out that populism impacts more effectively on the polity when societies are sharply divided by communal differences, whether ethnic or religious. She has also expressed the apprehension that this may 'strengthen the stranglehold of the larger community'.[49] But this process is not always so very simple. There are instances of minority groups joining hands with a section of the majority and outnumbering those who are otherwise numerically dominant. In the Indian scenario, communities that have strong community bonds and hence are traditionally voting en bloc, Marathas, Dalits or Muslims,[50]

[48]Sieglinde Rosenburger, '*The other side of the coin: Populism, Nationalism and the European Union*', Harvard International Interventionsim. Vol.26 (1) –Spring 2004 at http://hir.harvard.edu/articles/1210/2/.

[49]Margaret Canovan, *op.cit.*p.203.

[50]Many political commentators and analysts perceive that Muslims, Dalits and some other marginal sections of society in India traditionally vote en bloc. Shafi Rafai,

prove to be gaining more than the numerically larger community, in this case, all other Hindu communities put together. This explains, partly at least, why the Congress government at the Centre could go resolutely ahead in introducing a Hindu Code Bill in the Sixties, but surrendered to the Muslim community and repeatedly dithered on the issue of introducing a Uniform Civil Code even in the face of a clear constitutional mandate and several judgments of the Supreme Court.[51] It can be reasonably argued that the best example of certain sections of the electorate voting as one unified group in favour of one party is the Muslim vote bank in India. All parties are aware of the strength of this section of the electorate and the impact that their votes can have on the electoral verdict. Although Muslims are in a minority here, the undiluted sway that the religious leaders have on the thinking of this community, has converted it into a vote bank. What Canovan refers to as 'Tyranny of the Majority' in actual terms proves to be the 'tyranny' of the 'more organised on communal lines', especially in a situation like India, where the majority community is divided on caste and community basis. This obviously influences inter-community relations.

Ineffective governance: With populist politics becoming the order of the day, parties develop a habit of playing to the gallery, always and on every issue. This afflicts some cardinal principles of the process of governance itself. Myopia continues to rule the roost, as parties and governments controlled by them tend to take a

---

President of the United Muslims of America has appealed to Muslims in the USA to learn good lessons from Muslims in India who 'voted en bloc for the Congress party for fear of the fundamentalist Hindu party without getting anything in return'. For reference, visit http://www.umanet.org/cms.cfm?fuseaction=articles.viewThisArticle&articleID=45&pageID=159. Also see *Indian Express*, Mumbai, 10 May, 1999, for a news piece, quoting leaders of the Muslim Coordination and Action Committee (MCAC) with the title 'Say Yes (to quotas for Muslims and releasing TADA prisoners) and Take the Muslim Vote En bloc'.

[51]Between the Shah Bano judgment in 1995, Sarla Mudgal judgment in 1995 and John Vellamtom verdict in 2003, the court had stressed the need for enacting a Uniform Civil Code, saying it would help forge national integration and remove dissimilarities. the Provision for a UCC is incorporated in Article 44 under the Directive Principles.

short-term view. Citing the example of the power sector, Jayprakash Narayan (JN) of Lok Satta laments:

> While concerted efforts are being made to address the crisis in the power sector, the recent political events have now led to a *domino effect*, deepening the crisis. Three of the better states have now announced free, unmetered power to agriculture and others will be compelled to follow suit. Maharashtra joined two other major states in reversing a rational management policy in power sector. The Congress swept to power in Andhra Pradesh with the promise of free power in May 2004. In Tamil Nadu, Ms Jayalalitha's government too reversed its earlier policy and opted for free power in the face of massive rejection of the ruling combine in the Lok Sabha election. The Central Electricity Act, forbidding unmetered power, or realisation of less than a minimum tariff, has been relegated to the dustbin.[52]

In such a case, it is not surprising that 'competitive populism and powerful commercial farm lobbies have converted almost all the State Electricity Boards (SEBs) to sick units'.[53] Thus, democratically elected governments with a mandate to rule, abdicate their responsibilities when populist considerations dominate. This leads to some kind of a governance vacuum, inviting other pillars of democracy to fill it. As pointed out by Pratap Bhanu Mehta, the weaknesses of a political process emerging out of populist considerations have provided ground for judicial activism. 'In many cases, governments routinely seek judicial dispensation to give them political cover for unpopular decisions they might have to make.'[54]

---

[52] Jayprakash Narayan (JN), *op.cit.*

[53] NJ Kurian in *Seminar* (Issue 509) January, 2002 p.65

[54] Pratap Bhanu Mehta, 'Parliament and Judiciary: Where should the line be drawn?' *The Economic Times*, Mumbai, 31 January 2006, p.13. According to him, court decisions on issues 'from waste management to clean air, admissions policy to fees structure, from property rights to religious liberty and many administrative matters', have shown extraordinary activism. This activism, although generally unacceptable

On the economic front, the impact of populism is too serious to be ignored. Populist politics has all along pushed the economy deeper into the debt trap. With poor standards of governance, successive non-performing governments are rendering democracy and its institutions outmoded. Slowly, but certainly, the Indian state is becoming a 'soft state' as described by renowned economist and Nobel laureate, Gunnar Myrdal. Even American political sociologist Barrington Moor Jr's words of 1960—Indian democracy is 'a case of peaceful stagnation'—have proved to be prophetic.[55]

IMPACT OF POPULISM ON PARTIES AS INSTITUTIONS

Populism affects the functioning of political parties in various ways which ultimately leave a mark on the entire democratic process.

Ruled-ruler relationship undergoes a change: The impact of populism, understandably, emerges from its roots. Paul Taggart pointed out, '... populism has its roots in a reaction of the ruled against the rulers'.[56] He further concludes that, 'increase in scope and complexity of representative politics provides more scope for representation and it also provides more possibilities and sources of populism'.[57] According to Edward Shils, populism inserts an 'inverted egalitarianism' since it 'is tinged by the belief that the people are not just the equal of their rulers; they are actually better than the rulers'.[58] As a consequence, with populist policies coming to centre stage, a constant interplay of a giver-taker relationship has dominated the mutual expectations of people from their representatives.

Populism influences the relationship between the representative and those whom he represents. In fact, Taggart considers populism as being 'hostile to representative politics'. If political parties are

---

and unexpected, is used by the politicians to their advantage as the buck can be passed on to the courts.

[55]DN Dhanagare, 'Civil Society, State and Democracy: Contextualising a Discourse' *Sociological Bulletin,* 50(2) September 2001, p.184.

[56]Paul Taggart, *Populism*, p.111.

[57]*Ibid*.p.112.

[58]*Ibid.*

organisationally weak and ineffective, in a constituency, populist politics can hijack the representative and effectively de-link him from the party. This is mainly because many practising politicians believe that voters are the masters and representatives their servants and at least at the time of elections, politicians have to impress the electorate. However, politicians like John F Kennedy were conscious of the hazards of this perspective. In one of his brilliant arguments, he stated:

> I cannot believe that the people of Massachusetts sent me to Washington to serve merely as a seismograph to record the ups and downs of popular opinion. I believe instead that those of us in public office were elected—not because the people believed we would be bound by their every impulse, regardless of the conclusions directed by our own deliberations—but because they have confidence in our own judgment, and in our ability to exercise that judgment from position where we could determine what were the best interests of voters as a part of the best interests of the nation. If we are to exercise fully that judgment, some times we may be required to lead, inform, correct, and at occasions even ignore public opinion in our states.[59]

Trivialisation of policy formulation process: With ideology pushed to the periphery and ideologically motivated cadre becoming a rarity, winning elections naturally becomes the one and only objective of parties. As a result, parties tend to assure what they cannot implement, and in the process the policy formulation mechanism within the party is trivialised. Consequently, manifestos lose their sanctity and importance. It is of no surprise then, that this trend of looking at the process of policy formulation with utter contempt for ground realities, trickles from top to bottom.

---

[59] From the text of 'Remarks by Senator John F Kennedy at Sigma Delta Chi Journalism fraternity dinner, Boston, Massachusetts, 27 October, 1955. http://www.jfklibrary.org

This casual approach has affected everything. From deliberations in party meetings, contents of the resolutions passed there and even the quality of the house proceedings in parliament and state legislatures, everything is done sans seriousness. Party manifestos are the first victim. It may be pointed out here that in India, in the April-May 2007 elections to the Uttar Pradesh assembly, '...the BSP (Bahujan Samaj Party) was the only player to have jumped into the election fray without a manifesto, so none will be able to blame (Mayawati) for not honouring pre-poll promises'.[60] What is more worrisome is the fact that none of the important national dailies felt the need of discussing this utter disregard of an important and established aspect of democratic electoral competition through their editorial columns.

In March 2011, the speaker of the Maharashtra Legislative Assembly, Dilip Walse Patil, blamed both the ruling and the opposition party for not taking legislative business seriously. He felt they were betraying the people who had elected the legislators.

This is happening in other democracies too. Not very long ago, parties across the globe used to give due importance to the process of preparing a manifesto and implementing it. Kay Lawson, a senior researcher on political parties, has in fact described the style of politics in New Zealand as 'manifesto driven'. Quoting political scientist Richard Mulgan, he recalls, 'How seriously Labour and National prime ministers before 1984 took the manifesto on which they had come to office. Copies would be brought to cabinet meetings to check off outstanding promises with the appropriate ministers'.[61] Lawson laments how the situation had changed thereafter, saying, 'Since 1984, however, a different view has been aired'. In 1987, the Labour Prime Minister David Lange had said, 'If anyone judged

[60] Sumanta Sen in 'Caste for Higher Things', in *The Telegraph,* Kolkata, 19 May, 2007.

[61] Geoffrey Debnam, 'Overcoming the Iron Law? The Role of the Policy Committees of the New Zealand Labour Party', in Kay Lawson (Ed.), *How Political Parties Work? Perspectives from Within* p. 59.

the incoming government on the basis of a manifesto after three years in office, they have to be very silly indeed...'[62]

Thanks to populism, political parties try and avoid taking firm and aggressive positions purely out of conviction and commitment, on any given issue, leaving sufficient room for policy shift. In India, the UPA government, in 2005, introduced the National Rural Employment Guarantee Bill (NREGB), which was passed with near total unanimity. As pointed out by Pratap Bhanu Mehta,[63] this unanimity was a part of 'consensus politics' with policies 'that no one can object to'. But, 'policies that no one can object to are often policies that no one can quite believe in. Hence, the paradox that the areas we have most consensus on are the areas where we achieve the least.'

Michael Gallagher, another political scientist, has observed that in some European parties, 'members, perhaps realising the pointlessness of spending their leisure hours discussing programs that mean little or nothing, do not show much interest in the formulation of the details of policy proposals'.[64] The case was the same with the British Labour Party, when it 'sought to engage its members and supporters in a major policy consultation exercise in the late 1980s, the result was an "embarrassing flop" as hardly anyone was interested in participating.'[65]

Since there is hardly any conviction, obviously there is no strong commitment to any cause on the part of the political party leadership. Such leadership also fails in taking courageous decisions and this has a cascading effect, which, more often than not, leads to a gradual erosion of the credibility of political parties. The disturbing evidence is revealed in the outcome of a National Election Study conducted by CSDS, New Delhi, in 2004. According to

---

[62]As quoted by *Dominion*, Wellington, 7 July, 1987.

[63]Pratap Bhanu Mehta, 'Sense and Consensus', *Indian Express*, Mumbai, 28 August, 2005.

[64]Michael Gallagher, Michael Laver and Peter Mair, *Representative Government in Modern Europe*, p.252

[65]*ibid* p. 252

this study report, 'Only 9 per cent of Indians have faith in politicians. All democracies view their politicians with some derision. But if over 90 per cent of people have no real faith in politicians, it is a danger signal.'[66]

Spoiling of intra-party relations: Populism is like telling a lie. One tells a lie and to hide the truth, keeps on fabricating the story. Populism catapults a party to power and to continue to remain at the helm of the affairs, politicians adopt more and more of populist practices. More often than not, those in the party organisation who are nowhere closer to power indulge in openly assailing those with authority. Several parties in India—from the Congress and the BJP to innumerable smaller ones—have experienced this divide.

Several instances of this dissent between the party's elected representatives and office bearers of the party organisation are seen in modern times. The repeated surfacing of tensions between the BJP, while it was in power at the Centre and its mother organisation, the RSS, can be seen in this perspective. When the BJP consciously decided to compromise and keep the three contentious issues of Ram Janmabhoomi, Article 370 and Common Civil Code[67] out of the National Agenda for Governance in 1999, understandably, it added to the chasm between the party leadership and supporters from the ideological movement. Earlier, during the years immediately after Independence, a similar kind of hiatus existed between Gandhians or those running the Sarvodaya movement and Congressmen in power. Acharya JB Kripalani was disillusioned with the abandonment of the Gandhian ideals by the Congress. This rift within party workers

---

[66] A CSDS National Election Study Report at http://www.lokniti.org/projects.htm#nes.

[67] Ram Janmabhoomi is the vexed issue of building Lord Ram's temple in the area widely recognised as his actual birth place, where a disputed structure known as Babri mosque stood till December 2002. Article 370 is a provision in the Indian Constitution which grants greater autonomy to the Government of Jammu and Kashmir and was considered as temporary. The Common Civil Code is also a part of the guiding principles of the Indian Constitution. It is meant for all the Indian citizens, regardless of their religion.

widened with the exit of Acharya JB Kripalani from the Congress. After leaving the party, he founded the Kisan Mazdoor Praja Party which subsequently merged with the Socialist Party of India to form the Praja Socialist Party. Justice Chandrashekhar Dharmadhikari, while discussing this split in the Congress, blamed the trend of self-seeking amongst some of the ideologically-motivated activists. He told me in an interview as to how the lure of position amongst the Congressmen used to be ridiculed by many in different ways. One of the popular sayings of those days used to be '*Chune to Minister, Gire to Governor, varna Vice-Chancellor nahi to Sarvoday hai hi…*' (If one gets elected he seeks ministership, if one is defeated, he seeks governorship or Vice-Chancellor's position. If nothing of these comes to him, he seeks solace in the Sarvodaya movement.)

Perhaps pre-empting such tensions, Shiv Sena Chief Bal Thackeray had, in 1995, openly proclaimed that his party's Chief Minister Manohar Joshi will abide by his dictates completely. In declaring so, Thackeray wanted to signal that the party leadership ultimately would call the shots.

Disconnect between principles, policies and manifesto: Like in several other democracies, in India too, the preparation of a manifesto is not taken seriously for multiple reasons. It is firmly believed that voters don't care for the contents of the manifesto. Since the voters are anyway unconcerned about the contents of a manifesto, it can contain any impracticable promise. Compromises and bargaining are a necessary part of politics, therefore voters do not mind even if certain commitments are not kept. Consequently, many election manifestos initially serve the purpose of documentation but later, simply gather dust from the moment they are published. In this process the distance between the principles of the party, its policies and the assurances given in the manifesto obviously grows.

Neglect of organisational health: When populism produces a bumper crop of votes and parties happily return to power, their leadership gets more convinced that organisation-building is redundant. In the absence of any well-knit organisational structure, parties tend to heavily depend upon some kind of a technique for winning elections. The very technique creates an atmosphere where real problems get relegated to the back-burner and thereafter into oblivion. Unsurprisingly, concerns like unstoppable corruption and criminalisation of politics often take centre stage, until the elections. People realise later that solutions continue to elude them for want of a strong political will.

This takes us to a situation where democracy fails to deliver. Elections take place, governments get elected, but issues continue to remain the same. All this put together, results in what Dr Mahesh Chandra Sharma has termed, 'parties losing their character and identity as parties. Today, parties are in newspapers, not in localities, they conduct public meetings, although they are otherwise absent in the mohallas'.[68]

Political parties come into existence mainly for the purpose of attaining power. This fundamental fact is stretched too far when they tend to disregard their own organisational norms to gain authority. In the mid-Sixties, a leader of the then Praja Socialist Party, Ashok Mehta, decided to join the Congress and accept the membership of the Planning Commission of India at the Centre. He and his colleagues were accommodated in the Congress by relaxing some provisions of the party's constitution. They were allowed to join the party without having been primary members for two consecutive years.[69] In 1964, this compromise with the party's constitutional provision made news for the *Congress Bulletin*, today, thanks to many such arrangements and relaxations, it certainly has lost any news value.

Lastly, the most serious impact of populism is with regards to popular faith in democracy. HM Patel, India's illustrious finance minister in the late Seventies, had cautioned, saying:

> If the leadership think only of the immediate advantages and pander to the popular weaknesses and prejudices, they

---

[68] As told by Dr Mahesh Chandra Sharma in an interview to the author on 1 February 2004.

[69] Indian National Congress, *Congress Bulletin* Nos. 10, 11, 12. October-December 1964.p.396.

> would not only be doing disservice to the country, but also—and this is more serious—destroy the faith of people in democracy...more serious still, the people (in India) have genuinely begun to doubt the value of the democratic form of government, almost as if it was that form of government which has been responsible for their disillusionment.[70]

ELECTORAL COMPULSIONS

Electoral compulsions can be described as a kind of compulsive behaviour of political parties, when elections are just round the corner. While populism is an omnipresent trait in the process of political decision-making, electoral compulsions are strategic public postures of parties, which are more immediate in a given situation, topical, short-lived and at times not with a very long-lasting impact. By definition, these are the demands of the situation and it is presumed that had there been a sufficient time gap between the elections, the decision-making would have been qualitatively different.

There are two distinct sets of electoral compulsions. Those compulsions that work at the time of selecting a party candidate are described as organisational-electoral compulsions. The second set is prominent during campaigns and actual voting and they could be described as real-time electoral compulsions.

Organisational-electoral Compulsions

Although political parties are considered to be mass organisations, with gaining power becoming supremely important, cadre-building also now acquires some kind of electoral orientation. Compulsions of electoral politics have long started affecting the character and composition of the organisation. Leaders often perceive the party only as a device to make electoral success easier. Instead of looking at the party organisation as a living organism, they desire to develop it as a group of persons with unflinching personal loyalty and total surrender before an individual and not an ideology. Naturally then,

---

[70] HM Patel, *Democracy at Work in India*, p.16.

they try and cultivate storm troopers in place of cadres who have the ability to think independently. All this has given birth to a culture of personal loyalists and sycophants, consequently leading to a deep-rooted factionalism, so much so that 'an individual refusing to align with a faction is generally not acceptable since every faction leader suspects him'.[71] It must be noted here that at least some mature leaders are trying hard to prevent this culture from getting any further fillip. Former BJP President Nitin Gadkari, in his very first press conference in December 2009, had openly denounced the practice of touching the feet of party higher-ups and leaders regardless of the age factor.

To contest an election is becoming more and more expensive and both individuals as also the party organisations, require huge funds for the ultimate success. In the process, individuals who have the capacity to collect funds, by hook or by crook, grow in stature. As observed by Shivraj Patil, persons who collect capital 'become more powerful and decide the directions the party should take. Those who contribute also expect some returns. In the process, things happen which should not happen and are not appreciated by the common man'.[72] Many in the BJP also admit that this did happen to their party too. The rise of politicians like Suresh Kalmadi and Kanhaiyaalal Gidwani in Maharashtra of the Congress, Sureshdada Jain of the Shiv Sena are some of the cases in point. With fundraisers gaining prominence, parties tend to become more elite oriented. In the process, hard core organisers in political parties are sidetracked and feel dejected. More importantly, when fund collector-turned-party leaders with whom commoners cannot connect get disproportionate limelight, the party's base amongst the masses begins to dwindle.

When elections are fought just for the sake of winning and acquiring power, and not for any lofty ideal or an ideological goal, the choice of candidate zeroes in on the one who stands a maximum chance to get elected.

---

[71]An observation endorsed by leaders of different parties including Vasant Sathe (Congress), Mahesh Chandra Sharma (BJP) and AB Bardhan (CPI).

[72]Shivraj V Patil, *Emerging Vision of India* p.11.

Aloo J Dastoor, renowned political scientist from the University of Mumbai, has observed that during the last sixty years after Independence, when it comes to selecting the candidates for the political parties, 'The ruling criterion has been the possibility of success. This tendency has become more conspicuous with every succeeding election.'[73] Several politicians, functionaries and thinkers in India too have deplored this fact while interacting with the author.[74] Dr Mahesh Chandra Sharma observes:

> Election has become the foundation of politics today. An easy combination of vote banks and hero worship is the surest formula for electoral success today. In a situation of this kind, when a party decides to offer candidature only to those who are capable of winning, individuals will succeed, but parties as democratic institutions are bound to lose.[75]

AB Bardhan, the General Secretary of the CPI, agrees with this, saying:

> Undue importance to electoral merit has accelerated the process of degeneration of political parties. Money and muscle power dominates [political power] today. There was a time when elements like these used to help others get elected. Now, they themselves fight elections and get elected.[76]

Vasant Sathe argues that generally speaking, what is called the electability of a candidate does not always influence the common man.[77]

---

[73]Aloo J Dastoor, 'Indian Democracy revisited: Looking back to look ahead', in Nawaz Mody, Kannamma S Raman, Louis D'Silva, (Ed.), *Revisiting Indian Democracy*, p.25.

[74]Interviews with Shivraj Patil, Vasant Sathe, Dr Mahesh Chandra Sharma and AB Bardhan, besides Govindacharya, in New Delhi.

[75]*Ibid.*

[76]As told by AB Bardhan to the author in an interview on 8 February 2004.

[77]As told by Vasant Sathe to the author in an interview on 9 February 2004.

Preferring electability to ability has become a universal phenomenon. This happens practically everywhere. According to Andrew Imlach of the Commonwealth Parliamentary Association, in many political parties all over the world 'the struggle between ability and electability has reached its crescendo, and democracies today have failed to attract good candidates'.[78] Helmut Scholz, German politician and a senior functionary of the Party of Democratic Socialism (PDS), has admitted candidly that 'while selecting, candidate's electability overrides several other considerations'.[79]

Electability, in the ultimate analysis, boils down to possessing resources and a certain level of skilfulness and abilities. It is interesting to know what Jayprakash Narayan (JN) has observed in this context. During the last twenty years, 'family connections, abnormal money power, criminal activities and exploitation of sectional interests of caste and religious groups became the chief qualifications for candidate selection.'[80]

In today's electoral politics, only those who have a particular kind of dexterity stand a good chance of winning an election. This requisite set of skills includes: Image building, resource mobilisation, good relationship with the high command and the ability to manoeuvre the withdrawal or entry of candidates in the party.

A candidate's image plays an extremely vital role in determining the outcome of an election. The image of an individual is perhaps the key factor in today's electoral politics. This is partly because of the media boom, including the growing importance of social media like Facebook and Twitter. The hold of media on the public opinion-making processes is increasing by the day. Besides, the importance of an individual candidate as compared to the party's organisation is also growing. Noted American political scientist, Gerald M Pomper, has

[78] As told by Andrew Imlach in an interview to the author in London, August 1998.

[79] As told by Helmut Scholz, in an interview to the author in Berlin, on 14 August 1998.

[80] As told by Jayprakash Narayan (JN) in an interview to the author in Hyderabad on 27 July 2006.

pointed out that the standing of candidates is now certified not by their support among party leaders or their particular office, but by a small group of reporters and commentators for newspapers, magazines and television.[81] Since image has acquired disproportionate importance, it has also become an extremely fragile factor. Any trivial thing can either make or break it and therefore, individual politicians, especially those contesting elections, have to be extra cautious and hyper sensitive about their image. Wolfgang Weeg, senior functionary of the SPD party of Germany says, 'They [voters] see something on a TV talk show in the night, immediately send an angry e-mail next day in the morning and expect that they should get a reply within a day. If not, they are free to say all blah-blah things about our alleged sensitivity.'[82] This is evident from the responses and reactions on Twitter and Facebook too.

Over the years, the concept of resourcefulness has undergone a change and is not confined to just money and material resources. Today it also includes the ability to have a professionally functioning set-up which can pre-empt the likely impact of certain developments on the voters. According to Vasant Sathe, 'A politician today, more than ever before, is extra-sensitive about people who have a nuisance value. To that extent, although he/she is more resourceful than in the past, he/she is also more vulnerable and hence insecure too.'[83] Since voters are exposed to several factors on which no politician can possibly have any control, he has to be extremely cautious and keep track of the things that shape public discourse. He should be able to turn it to one's advantage or else at least ensure that no damage is done. Hence, the concept of overall resourcefulness comprises good connections with media persons, voluntary organisations, opinion makers, religious leaders, musclemen and even leaders of the opposition parties. While there is nothing wrong in being resourceful, the tricks and tactics that some politicians employ

---

[81] Gerald M Pomper, 'The Decline of Partisan Politics' in Louis Maisel and Joseph Cooper (Ed.), *The Impact of the Electoral Process*, p. 14.

[82] As told by Wolfgang Weeg in an interview to the author in Bonn on 8 August 1998

[83] As told by Vasant Sathe in an interview to the author in 9 February 2004.

is a matter of concern. The most worrisome aspect is the ability of politicians to cause inconvenience even to law abiding people when they refuse to fall in line. As revealed by some conscientious municipal councillors, some of them take up environmental issues not out of any genuine concern for ecology but simply to create deterrence in the minds of those who break the law and exploit them monetarily. Unfortunately, this has also been true in several instances of whistle blowers and those who have been using the Right to Information (RTI).

Since electability becomes the be all and end all, organisational considerations take a back seat. As a consequence, for the party high command, only those leaders matter who, in their own judgment, have the ability to get elected. Obviously, when it comes to the application of a very subjective yardstick such as 'judgment', personal equations are bound to influence the process. Pratap Bhanu Mehta observes that this dominance of those who can get elected 'ensures that newly mobilising groups and leaders at the local level are not attracted to the party, since the path to the top depends so much on the caprice and loyalty tests of one leader rather than clear and settled procedures. The party, even at the level of local units, remains in the hands of individuals who have more access to the top echelons of the party than knowledge about voters. There is no solution to these challenges other than systematic intraparty solutions.[84]

This, understandably, provides a fertile ground for politics of coterie, rampant sycophancy, nepotism and decisions on the basis of personal likes and dislikes, to grow.

In a no-holds-barred competition today, a politician also needs to possess the ability to manage the contestants of an election. This means an ability to manoeuvre the entry or withdrawal of a candidate from the electoral fray. This is more in the context of the FPTP system, under the Westminster model of democracy. To ensure electoral success, a kind of strategic division of votes

---

[84]Pratap Bhanu Mehta, in 'Where's the party?' in *Indian Express*, Mumbai, 29 June, 2005.

becomes essential. Let us take a hypothetical case. In a constituency where a particular caste, for instance Maratha, is dominant to the extent of 60 per cent in the composition of registered voters, a party may strategically select a candidate belonging to other less dominant groups, say the Brahmins, with 30 per cent presence. The ability of the Brahmin candidate on two counts adds to his electability. First, he should be able to manoeuvre the entry of many more Maratha candidates to ensure greater division of votes in the rival camp. Second, he should ensure withdrawal of other Brahmin candidates, if any, to bring about a consolidation of votes. This cannot happen without a well-cultivated relationship with community leaders and an influential network of inter-party connections. No wonder then, candidates who possess these abilities easily score over others.

Parties have started believing that unless they rake up an emotional issue, it is hard to win an election. In India, when a sitting Member of Parliament (MP) or Legislature dies, giving a party nomination to the deceased member's widow or his progeny simply to exploit sympathies, has become an established practice. The emergence of Veena Sharma, widow of slain Maharashtra BJP MLA Premkumar Sharma and Sunita Nayak, wife of another slain Maharashtra BJP MLA Ramdas Nayak or that of Priya Dutt, daughter of Sunil Dutt and Sachin Pilot, son of Rajesh Pilot, as MPs, are some of the instances.

Also, there are occasions when parties give up their positions and bow down before a strong wave of popular feelings. In Maharashtra, the Bharatiya Jan Sangh, which had earlier opposed the reorganisation of states within India on the basis of language, changed its stand later and joined the Samyukta Maharashtra bandwagon while upholding the 'necessity and profitability' of the electoral alliance amongst the opposition parties aligned against the Congress.[85] A similar realisation of groundswell of emotive support to the cause of Samyukta Maharashtra in the late Fifties

[85]Bharatiya Jan Sangh, *Report of the General Secretary for the year 1958.*

forced the Scheduled Caste Federation (SCF) of Ambedkar[86] to change its stand and join the chorus for a separate all-Marathi state. At the national level, Indira Gandhi rode the wave of popular support while exploiting emotional support generated by the victory in the Bangladesh War. History repeated itself when, in 1984, her son Rajiv Gandhi succeeded in the elections, out of sympathy towards him immediately after her assassination. Similarly, in 1991, PV Narasimha Rao could snatch victory from the jaws of defeat, mainly because of the sympathy wave generated after Rajiv Gandhi's untimely demise. Atal Bihari Vajpayee could get re-elected in 1999 mainly thanks to the emotional upsurge after the Kargil victory.

In modern times, this has been a common feature in several election campaigns of major democracies. Ronald Reagan in 1988 and Bill Clinton in 1996 in the USA, as also Tony Blair in 2005 in the UK focussed relentlessly on feelings rather than facts.[87] Such is the power of emotional appeal that, in 1998, Gerhard Schroeder's Social Democratic Party in Germany had hired Detmar Kharpinski, creative director of a renowned Hamburg-based advertising agency, with the clear objective of ensuring greater impassioned appeal all through the campaign.

When one election follows the other, important and apparently unpopular policy decisions become extremely difficult. LK Advani, the deputy prime minister of India in 2003, observed while intervening in a debate in Lok Sabha that his experience of the past five years had made him 'conscious of the fact that the continuing election mode, in which the ruling party is, has made a serious handicap to good governance of the country'.[88] His candid observation explains as to what forced the NDA government to

---

[86]Dr BR Ambedkar, *Thoughts on Linguistic States* as quoted by AG Kulkarni in his unpublished doctoral thesis 'A Study of Political Parties in Maharashtra with special reference to the period 1947-67', March 1968, p.201.

[87]Edmund L Andrews, in *International Herald Tribune*, London, 16 September 1998.

[88]As quoted by C Chandra Mohan in 'Drawbacks of a Perpetual Election Mode', *The Financial Express,* 7 August 2003.

go slow on the implementation of Value-Added Tax (VAT) or the continued dithering on the part of the UPA-1 on sending the Indian troops to Iraq in 2004-06.

Much against the well-articulated policy perspective given by Jawaharlal Nehru,[89] clearly against quotas on the basis of religion, the Congress government in Andhra Pradesh repeatedly pushed the proposal for five per cent reservation for Muslims, mainly for electoral purposes. A similar example is that of the proclamation of the Congress to bring 'Christian Socialism'[90] in the state of Mizoram at the time of the state assembly elections in 1989. The BJP also has its own share of succumbing to the pressures of electoral politics. During the 2004 elections to the Andhra Pradesh assembly, it had desisted from supporting the demand for carving out a separate state of Telangana, simply to keep the Telugu Desam in good humour, regardless of its policy supporting smaller states. The number of instances where several other parties have given up their policy

---

[89] In his speech 'Why are we opposed to communal reservations' (delivered at Mumbai at the Convention against Faith Based Reservations, on 14 August 2004, LK Advani said: 'In his five-volume monumental study *Framing of the Indian Constitution*, B Shiva Rao records, "A lengthy discussion took place on these proposals of the Advisory Committee. The majority of the speakers—and these included members from all communities—Muslims, Christians, Anglo-Indians, Scheduled Castes, as well as Hindus—offered full support to the proposal to abolish reservations on communal grounds. Jawaharlal Nehru described the proposal as a 'historic turn in our destiny'. Nehru added: 'A safeguard of this kind would have some point where there was autocratic or foreign rule; it would enable the monarch to play one community off against the other. But where you are up against a full-blooded democracy, if you seek to give safeguards to a minority, and a relatively small minority, you isolate it. Maybe you protect it to a slight extent, but at what cost? At the cost of isolating it and keeping it away from the main current in which the majority is going—I am talking on the political plane of course—at the cost of forfeiting that inner sympathy and fellow-feeling with the majority' ".' http://www.bjp.org/.

[90] Subir Bhowmik quoted from the Congress Manifesto issued for State Assembly elections in 1989 at Aizwal, in his essay on 'Ethnicity, Ideology and Religion: Separatist Movements in India's North-east'. This paper could be accessed at http://www.apcss.org/Publications/Edited%20Volumes/ReligiousRadicalism/PagesfromReligiousRadicalismandSecurityinSout.

positions under the compulsions of electoral politics is also not small. The lack of enthusiasm betrayed by the AGP on the issue of immediate scrapping of the Illegal Migrants Determination by Tribunals (IMDT) Act, after it returned to power twice in Assam or the withdrawal of the anti-conversion bill by the AIADMK government led by Jayalalitha in 2004, immediately after her defeat in the Lok Sabha elections are only some of the few examples of this trend.

Governments of the day in India in the past two decades have demonstrated as to how electoral compulsions play havoc with policy issues. When new governments come to power, they are keen about economic reforms and try to make some changes in the initial two years of their tenure. Later, when anti-incumbency trends start appearing, they develop cold feet and eventually try to put a lid on reforms. As pointed out by Sanjay Sinha,[91] this half-hearted attempt at reforms was witnessed in the regimes of successive governments starting from Rajiv Gandhi up to the current UPA regime. A very insightful observation about how succumbing to electoral pressures has a cascading effect on the quality of governance, comes from HM Patel. He says:

> Under pressure of so-called public opinion, as interpreted by ministers, often acting under the influence of elected representatives or interested lobbies, our top civil servants tend to act without paying attention to the large number of reports of commissions of investigation, evaluation reports and surveys. Inevitably, their policy decisions tend to be defective.[92]

Realtime Electoral Compulsions

Most of the realtime electoral compulsions are basically those that parties indulge in covertly and defend them in the name of competitive violation of ground rules. It is true that all these violations are officially condemned by one and all and yet most of the parties

---

[91] Sanjay Sinha, 'Electoral Compulsions versus Growth' *The Economic Times*, Mumbai, 17 May 2007.

[92] HM Patel, '*The First Flush of Freedom—Recollections and Reflections*' p.120-21.

continue to use them and only in that sense one can label them as 'compulsions'. Generally speaking, these may not be considered as electoral compulsions, but for the fact that practically all grass-roots level political party workers have accepted that these are also compulsive acts on the part of most of the political parties. These compulsions include electoral malpractices of two kinds. Alluring voters through incentives in cash or in kind is the first category. This involves distribution of goodies to the voters, en bloc purchase of community or locality votes, or organising vehicles for the voters. In the 2011 elections to the Tamil Nadu Assembly, both the DMK and AIADMK brazenly indulged in promising freebies. The DMK promised 35 kg of free rice every month for below-poverty-line families, on the other hand the AIADMK assured 20 kg of free rice for all ration card holders. While the DMK wanted to give women free mixies and grinders, its rival added fans to the list. The ruling party had promised laptops to students in their first year of college. Jayalalitha had assured them one even as early as their eleventh standard. The one-upmanship continued throughout the campaigning exercise.

The other set of electoral compulsions include the use of muscle power for the purpose of terrorising the voters or for similar acts that are brazenly illegal and anti-democratic.

A senior functionary of a national political party in Mumbai, who was otherwise known for his high moral standards, ethical behaviour, and non-corrupt and clean operations while in the Maharashtra cabinet in the late Nineties, once frankly commented about the electoral compulsions that he faced over the years. He told me that much against his desire to be a stickler for values and ethical code, he was compelled to allow party workers to distribute money in the slum areas in his constituency, simply to out-manoeuvre his rival candidate.

Practices like these have led to a culture of competitive compromises by various actors in the political process. What should be causing more concern is the fact that the decision-makers are fast losing the sense of judgment while accepting a compromise. In this process, compromises have become the rule. The difference between a one-time compromise and a total surrender before the compulsions of the situation is quite blurred.

Quite understandably, an atmosphere of helplessness surrounds all parties involved in politics. All are playing politics, which is bereft of issues and a competition for seeking power has acquired centrality. Generating a debate or even setting an agenda is hardly an important concern. In the recent past, hardly any national political party has passed a resolution on the vexed issue of electoral reforms or judicial reforms, let alone pursuing the matter. What commentator Pratap Bhanu Mehta[93] has said in the context of the Congress is true in the case of most of the political parties. He says, 'It suggests that for all its talent, the party (Congress) cannot set the terms of debate or an agenda. And a party that cannot set this agenda is unlikely to be able to break the current mould of politics.'[94] That the parties have almost lost the desire to 'break the current mould of politics' is perhaps a stark reality.

WHY DO PARTIES NEED TO RISE ABOVE POPULISM AND OVERCOME ELECTORAL COMPULSIONS?

Certain schools of theorists have unhesitatingly accepted that parties are bound to be populist and hence, it is natural for them to succumb to electoral compulsions, because winning elections is the most important goal before them. These theorists, prominent amongst them being Leon Epstein, Anthony Downs and Joseph Schumpeter, have, in fact, stressed their point by using economic analogy. Schumpeter sees no reason why political parties need to be ideologically distinctive. According to him:

> ...for all parties will, of course, at any given time, provide themselves with a stock of principles or planks and these principles and planks may be as characteristic of the party that adopts them and as important for its success as the

[93]Pratap Bhanu Mehta, 'Where's the party?'*op.cit.*
[94]*Ibid.*

> brands of goods a departmental store sells are characteristic to it and important for its success. But the department store cannot be defined in terms of its principles.[95]

What is noteworthy here is the unhesitant acceptance of power-seeking, or a self-interest axiom as the cornerstone of their arguments. Obviously then, their 'emphasis is on the competitive struggle in the political market place, political leaders viewed as entrepreneurs, candidates for public office are the commodity, voters are the political consumers, and votes and influence are the medium of exchange.'[96] Anthony Downs is very clear in his mind when he states: 'our model could be described as a study of political rationality from an economic point of view' in which there is a recognition of the fact that parties, 'so as to attain their private ends, formulate whatever policies they believe will gain the most votes.'[97] Here, it may also be noted that this brazenly 'self-seeking party' model is referred to as a rational-efficient model while the traditional view about political parties is referred to as party democracy model. That a section of political scientists should be accepting that power seeking is the only rationale behind the existence of parties and hence name such parties as rational-efficient, also speaks volumes about the prevailing biases in the scholarship. Notably, Maurice Duverger is considered to be staunchly in favour of the party democracy model, while Epstein is known for his bias in favour of American parties and hence, a proponent of the rational-efficient model.

It must also be pointed out here that all this discussion about these two models is more than half-a-century old. One will have to look at this analysis of political parties when universal suffrage was not commonplace, people were still a little sceptical about democracy and hence, the idea also might be that recognising the self-seeking attitude of politicians and parties may help the process of consolidation of democracy. Now that democracy has been tried,

[95] Joseph A Schumpeter, *Capitalism, Socialism and Democracy*, p.283.
[96] William E Right, *A Comparative Study of Party Organization*, p.19-20.
[97] Anthony Downs, *An Economic Theory of Democracy*, p.295.

tested and a new bout of scepticism about its ability to deliver has gripped the discourse in the political science fraternity, recognising the crass self-interest of parties may not help in the consolidation of democracy at all.

Populism and electoral compulsions underscore the centrality of elections, electoral politics and electoral success in any party's organisational set-up. This contributes to the process of converting the entire organisational activity into a more pronouncedly election-oriented one. This adversely affects the process of institution-building within the party framework. After the introduction of democratic decentralisation in Maharashtra in the early Sixties, through the establishment of Zilla Parishads and other Panchayati Raj institutions, the formal organisational structure of the Congress below the districts became almost defunct. 'The Maharashtra party leadership was obviously worried and had expressed concern about this fallout of electoral competition at the grass-roots level'.[98]

Any discussion about populism would be incomplete without covering the question of leadership. After all, a leader is expected to lead the masses and refuse to be led by them. On the contrary, populism promotes leaders who are willing to be led by the masses. Focussing upon the concept of a people's representative, a couple of centuries earlier, Edmund Burke[99] too had stressed the need for a leader who refuses to be guided by the wishes of his electorate. Expressing his gratefulness towards the electors from his birthplace, Burke told them candidly that, 'but the sphere of my duties is my true country'. Responding to his opponents, who criticised him for refusing to subordinate his will to the opinion and instructions of those he sought to represent, Burke was blunt. He told them that electors may have opinions and inclinations, 'government and legislation are matters of reason and judgment and not of inclination'. Mahatma Gandhi had expressed similar views. He wrote in *Harijan*:

> In theory, a leader of democracy holds himself at the beck

[98] Maharashtra Pradesh Yuvak Congress: *Rahuri Shibir Visheshank*, July 1965.
[99] As quoted extensively by Arun Shourie, in *The Parliamentary System*, p. 239-242

> and call of the public. It is but right that he should do so. But he dare not do so at the sacrifice of the duty imposed upon him by the public...their gesture of simplicity, necessary as it was as a preliminary, will avail them nothing if they will not show requisite industry, ability, integrity, impartiality and an infinite capacity for mastering details.[100]

As much as on other factors, the success of democracy heavily hinges upon the leaders too. Integrity and ability are the principal pillars on which democratic leadership can effectively lean. Populism and electoral compulsions are the two most influential factors facilitating the election of those whose integrity is dubious and ability questionable. When such leaders are elected to govern, their failure erodes the trustworthiness of democracy itself. This is a price too heavy to compel the voters to pay, for their share of fault is marginal.

Elected representatives in a democracy are no doubt accountable to the people but this loyalty should not exist only in the formal sense. Populism and electoral compulsions are powerful levellers and thanks to them, true choice is eroded for voters. This negates the element of accountability in actual terms. But there is also a silver lining to these black clouds. Most voters understand that there is no such thing as free lunch. Now there is greater realism that it is difficult to sustain populism. One can only hope that this realisation becomes stronger and a way towards politics through a reformed system is found sooner than later.

The effect of populism and electoral compulsions need not be accepted as a fait accompli. In certain electoral systems, the overall role of populism and electoral compulsions is limited and hence their impact is less damaging.

---

[100]MK Gandhi, 'Gandhiji Expects' p.126 (Quoted from *Harijan*, 9 October, 1937).

CHAPTER 6

Re-examining the Form of Government and Electoral System in India

Do forms of government and types of electoral systems have an impact on the democratic polity in general and parties in particular? To answer this question, one has to explore the nexus between the form of government, electoral systems and the quality of democracy, especially in the context of the overall efficacy of political parties.

While the form of government is like an outer functional set-up, at its core lies factors like the number of houses of elected representatives (unicameral or bicameral) as also the vesting of executive authority (president or prime minister) and the control over it by the elected houses (of representatives). In any representative democracy, the way candidates are elected determines the electoral system. An electoral system means, 'Any set of rules whereby the votes of citizens determine the selection of executives and/or legislatures.'[1] As explained by Michael Saward:

> If all citizens in a given political community must have

[1] Ian McLean (Ed.). *The Concise Oxford Dictionary of Politics*, p.154.

> an equal, effective input into decision-making, then we are immediately faced with the task of devising a rule by which the felt wishes of the citizens can be aggregated into a decision of the community.[2]

And an electoral system is an instrument to do just that. Every form of representative democracy has to perform with the help of any given electoral system. One can come across a particular form operating with two distinct electoral systems in two different countries. For example, parliamentary democracy in Germany functions with proportional representation, whereas in the United Kingdom and in India, it operates with FPTP electoral system. Representative democracy has several variations. Hence, forms of government have no direct and fixed relationship with factors such as the number of chambers (houses of representatives) or the division of power between the executive head of government and the supreme constitutional authority.

Influence of Forms and Systems

However, it is generally accepted as an established fact that both the form as well as electoral system greatly influence the democratic polity and, more importantly, parties and party system. While only one particular aspect like form or electoral system can never be held singularly responsible for either the success or failure of a democracy, its ability to influence the fate of democracy is indeed beyond doubt. This relationship is significant since in any representative democracy, parties have to shoulder the crucial responsibility of forming the executive government. Understandably then, parties always try to seek maximum popular support. Certain forms of government and/or electoral systems facilitate this for political parties, while others make it difficult for them.

Both the form as well as system significantly contribute in shaping the nature of the relationship between people and their representatives. Features such as methods of casting votes, frequency

[2] Michael Saward, *The Terms of Democracy*, p.68.

of elections, funding for electoral campaigns, stability of governments vary from one form or electoral system to the other and they make a great impact upon the characteristics of polity in a given democracy. A wide range of factors manifests this effect of form and/or electoral system. Some of them could be the state of party organisations, overall influence of party politics on the masses, promotion and control of social cleavages, quality of party and leadership and condition of governance in general.

Forms of Governments under Representative Democracy

To start with, let us understand the presidential form. Later, we will analyse the parliamentary form as the discussion here is mainly about India. Under both the presidential and parliamentary form of government, the concept of the role of a party remains the same, yet there are factors that distinguish their functional character.

In the presidential form, the president is more likely to control party organisation whereas in the parliamentary form, if the party president is assertive then the prime minister is less likely to dominate, although a confrontation always remains on the cards. In the presidential system, the organisational wing has a comparatively marginal role as against the parliamentary form, where there is always a greater possibility of the independent existence of party organisation. Similarly, between the two forms, elected representatives have a comparatively limited role under a presidential system. As a consequence, under the presidential system, elected representative-people linkage is more likely to be weak.

It is noteworthy that every form has its own limitations and customised reforms may ultimately provide some solutions. In this context, the experience of the Philippines is worth analysing. President Joseph Estrada was ousted in 2001 and immediately the country witnessed a fresh constitutional debate. The roots of the growing demand, for a shift from the presidential to a parliamentary system of government, were in the provision for fixed term of the president's office. The prevailing system allowed for the removal of a mal-performing president only by way of an impeachment.

In an article, Jurgen Ruland[3] has argued that such a shift does not necessarily solve the problems blamed on the 1987 Constitution of the Philippines. The problems could be listed as the rigidities of the presidential term, executive-legislative gridlock, presidential concentration of power, political instability, a weak party system, populism and patronage. Ruland has advocated 'incremental reforms by amending the 1987 Constitution...without scrapping the presidential system of government'.

Between the presidential and parliamentary system, which one is more susceptible to the pressures of populism? Before trying to find an answer to this, it must be noted that parliamentary democracy has long remained the overwhelming choice of the older democracies. Countries with parliamentary systems have always outnumbered countries with presidential systems. In India, it was the Nehru Report of 1927 that settled the question of opting for the parliamentary system. Apart from familiarity, 'avoiding the risk of perpetual cleavage, feud or conflict between the legislature and the executive'[4] were the compelling reasons cited for this conscious decision.

PARTIES UNDER PRESIDENTIAL FORM

In a presidential democracy, the president is the executive head of government while in a parliamentary democracy, he is more of a decorative or titular head. Presidents may be directly elected, indirectly elected or appointed. Under the presidential form, legislatures and executives are elected separately and often for different terms, hence it is not uncommon for them to be controlled by different parties. Thus, the presidential political system is characterised by a separation of powers, where the executive and legislative branches are independent of one another. This influences the role of the ruling political party to a great extent. In the presidential form, parties tend

[3] Jurgen Ruland in 'Constitutional Debates in Philippines: From Presidentialism to Parliamentarism?' in *Asian Survey*-May/June 2003, Vol. 43 No. 03, Pages 461-483.

[4] This statement is attributed to Sir Alladi Krishnaswami Aiyar and has been quoted by AG Noorani in *India's Constitution and Politics* p.56.

to be less structured than in the parliamentary system. One of the key areas of difference between presidential and parliamentary systems is about the power to remove a chief executive or to dissolve the legislature. In a parliamentary democracy, unlike the presidential form, the chief executive's term is directly linked to that of the legislature.

Lesser Scope for Sectarian Appeal

For the president's election in the presidential form, the entire nation is the constituency and the population, having attained the age of majority, are the voters. Both these characteristics demand that parties with a pan-national appeal alone can successfully contest these elections. As a result, this form leaves comparatively lesser scope for mobilisation on caste, communal and ethnic basis. The presidential system also serves as an antidote to voter mobilisation on consideration of primordial loyalties of caste and region since a party aspiring for support for its presidential nominee is forced to coalesce and go with a broad, pluralist plank. Advocates of presidential systems like PM Kamath, a senior political commentator, have argued that a presidential system in India 'will de-emphasise caste and community considerations within the political system,'[5] and hence, may effectively prevent further fragmentation of society.

Balancing between Constituency Demands and Party Pressures

One of the important built-in features of presidential democracy is the scope it offers to achieve some kind of equilibrium between party organisation and constituency. An elected representative is simultaneously accountable to both, his party and the electorate in his constituency. Under this form, failure to vote with one's party does not threaten to bring down the government, and therefore, it leaves a space for actually representing the electorate, regardless of the party's view. Besides, as said earlier, the legislature and

---

[5]PM Kamath, 'A quest for a Democratic Alternative: A Case for Presidential Government' in Nawaz B Mody, Kannamma S Raman and Louis D'Silva, (Ed) *Revitalising Indian Democracy*, p.171.

executive are elected separately in the presidential form and often for different terms. Consequently, to be controlled by different political parties is considered as a normal practice for them at particular times. Generally speaking, this element goes in favour of the overall health of the democracy, as inter-party cooperation becomes a mutual need. The presidential form promotes a kind of loose party structure. Enforcing discipline is comparatively more difficult in such an informal organisational structure. However, this has some clear advantages too. Here, both the president and individual members are directly accountable to the voters.

Of course, there is also a lurking danger. Elected members in the presidential form can easily take the liberty of identifying with regional, ethnic, economic or other divisions when considering policy issues. Since the presidential form can afford less structured and more resilient parties, this feature is less likely to harm the institution of parties.

In effect, the presidential form can also arrest the trend of growing fragmentation of the polity as constitutionally, presidency remains at the centre of executive power.

Less Prone to Populist and Electoral Compulsions

In the context of governance too, there are several merits of a presidential form. It provides greater scope for making it free from populist considerations and electoral compulsions. Enabling the appointment of talented persons to public positions regardless of their low electability, is one of the main advantages of this form. This also affects the party-government interface in a positive way. Besides, with such prevailing provisions as term limit under many presidential democracies, elected members are less likely to develop a vested interest in continuing in the legislature and turning service into profession.

Another significant feature of presidential democracy is the fixed term of the government's tenure, which brings greater political stability. During 1966-69, India witnessed the installation and collapse of four governments at the Centre. This led to a discussion about switching over to a presidential form, mainly because of the perception that it brings in a more stable government. It may be noted here that France, after experiencing twenty-five governments in twelve years, when the country was under the parliamentary system as a part of the Fourth Republic, changed over to the presidential system in the Fifth Republic, mainly to secure political stability.

As is very obvious, democracies with directly elected presidents tend to favour larger parties. With the entire nation as a constituency and the presidency as the biggest political prize to be won, only large parties have a realistic chance of winning it. The popularity and charisma of a leader play key roles in this pattern too. Here, since the entire nation is the Electoral College, the image of a candidate becomes extremely important. Naturally then, the chances of considerations for ability dominating over electability are comparatively greater.

There is a widespread impression that after the electoral verdict is out, parties under presidential democracy are left with only little or almost no role to play. But the US experience in this regard is far from this. As pointed out by VO Key Jr, in the US, 'party appears to be the strongest and most persistent factor associated with the actions of Senators and Representatives'.[6] One may also observe that presidential democracy provides the necessary resilience and a much-needed ability to rise above partisan considerations. There is an inherent mechanism to avoid a clash of interest between party policy and constituency interest. As Key further mentions, '... in the presidential form of democracy, the institutional apparatus accommodates itself to the interplay of centripetal and centrifugal forces within each major party, yet permitting neither to triumph completely...in the working of Congress, the forces of particularism, of section, of class of all types of subgroups within the party enjoy comparatively free play—a luxury made tolerable by the stability introduced into the government by an executive whose tenure is beyond reach of mercurial parliamentary majorities'.[7]

---

[6]VO Key Jr., *Politics, Parties and Pressure Groups*, p.727.
[7]*Ibid.* p.741.

In the context of the ability to influence party functioning, on the part of the different forms of democracy and electoral systems operating under it, the presidential system in the US deserves special mention. Under the prevailing electoral system in the USA, the practice of nomination through direct primary seems to be adding to the pace of the further decline of political parties for obvious reasons. Now, for campaigning, candidates depend upon not their own party canvassers, but those who organise it systematically through the mass media or locally, by unions and public employees' organisations. Since party cadre is fast disappearing from the scene, quite understandably, the voters now respond less to their weakening appeals.

It is in this setting that 'vote for the man, not for the party' has become one of the significant electoral appeals today. As against this, those who favour parliamentary system argue that highly organised parties under this system can act as a link between party leaders and the constituents at the local levels. This can also serve the cause of both, the party as also the constituency.

PARLIAMENTARY FORM: GREATER ROLE FOR PARTIES

The functional aspects of parliamentary democracy have an inherently influential role for parties. Disraeli had made this point as early as in 1848 when he said, 'You cannot choose between party government and parliamentary government. I say you can have no parliamentary government if you have no party government.'[8] Philosopher and former president of India, S Radhakrishnan,[9] felt that disciplined parties and devoted and patriotic leadership are the sine qua non of a successful parliamentary democracy in any country. It is widely recognised that the parliamentary system is highly conducive to the emergence of disciplined 'programme parties'. This is mainly because parties in a parliamentary democracy are bestowed with

---

[8] As quoted by Elaine Thompson, in the research paper, *Australian Parliamentary Democracy After a Century: What Gains, What Losses?* (Parliament of Australia Website) from HC Debates, Vol. 101.cols 205-6,30 August, 1848, at http://www.aph.gov.au/Library/Pubs/rp/1999-2000/2000rp23.htm.

[9] As quoted by Deendayal Upadhyay in *Political Diary* p.114.

the onerous task of installing a government and provide it a lasting support. It is under this system that the chances of parties adopting coherent programmes, and thereby shaping cohesive organisational structures, are much higher. As against this, the mutual independence of government and parliament renders a kind of secondary role to parties under the presidential system.

With the element of collective responsibility of the cabinet, which is answerable to the parliament, parties in a parliamentary democracy have a greater and more proactive role. Since the government in a parliamentary system survives on the support of the elected representatives, there is an inbuilt mechanism in this system to influence its functioning. Consequently, political parties can wield greater influence on the government under this form.

In a parliamentary democracy, the executive head of government is either directly elected by or has to have a demonstrable majority support in the house of representatives or in certain cases, at least in the lower house of parliament. Theoretically, parliamentary democracy provides a considerably large scope for parties to play a significant role. Since continued cooperation between the executive and legislature is required for the government to survive and to be effective in carrying out its programmes, party organisations could play a niche role.

A parliamentary form of government is extremely demanding in the context of parties. Highly structured parties that tend towards unified action, have distinct party platforms and a disciplined party organisation, are the pre-requisites for the parliamentary form to be successful. Contrary to the presidential form, for the survival of a government under the parliamentary form, a perfect cohesion and synergy between the party-organisation and party-government is a must. Ideally, important policy decisions have to be made within the party structures, such as party caucuses, rather than within the legislature itself. It should be kept in mind that at the conceptual level, parliamentary democracy presupposes that the decision by a majority is the underlying principle. The individual members are considered to be free to apply their own judgment before casting their vote on any given issue, and hence, no party or group can take its support base in the house for granted. This aspect of the parliamentary system is crucial because 'the guarantee of responsible government in a parliamentary system is the individual member who exercises his own judgment.'[10]

Here, it must also be noted that an uneasy relationship between the organisational and parliamentary wing of a political party has become one of the universal characteristics of parliamentary democracy. Strong pro-organisation puritans, whom Maurice Duverger has described as 'militants', are 'always suspicious of the elected representatives but they envy them'.[11] Duverger has further observed that elected representatives are generally more capable and they can easily outsmart the party organisational leaders. All over the world, socialist parties have succeeded in establishing the supremacy of party-organisation over the elected 'deputies' and the communist parties in India are not an exception. Duverger feels, 'To a Communist it is quite obvious that a member of the central committee is much more important than a member of a parliamentary group...being himself trained in a attitude and himself convinced that the Party (with capital P) is far superior to the bourgeois Parliament...'[12]

Under a parliamentary democracy, if the party organisations are not strong enough, elected representatives become the party unto themselves and overrule their organisational heads. In India, the first case in point is the rebellion of Indira Gandhi, who as leader of the parliamentary party, almost hijacked the party organisation in 1969 and relegated senior party veterans to the periphery. Sharad Pawar also did the same thing in Maharashtra and staged a coup to become the state's chief minister in 1978. In more recent times, HD Kumaraswamy seized control of the legislative party and joined hands with the BJP to become the chief minister of Karnataka in early 2006. Ironically, his own father and the chief of

[10]FA Mechery and Maneesha Tikekar, *Constitution, Polity and Society – A study of Indian political system*, p.266

[11]Maurice Duverger, *Political Parties*, p.195.

[12]*Ibid.* p.201.

the Janata Dal (S), HD Devegowda, had expelled him from the party initially, only to pardon him later. Similar instances are in abundance in India's political history in almost all states. One can safely conclude that a strong, confident and charismatic leader can easily sway the legislature party, leaving the official organisational wing and its leaders in the lurch. Therefore, in a parliamentary democracy, only those parties that have a strong organisational base which no leader can usurp, can sustain themselves for a longer term.

Legitimate Space for Opposition

The parliamentary form of democracy also provides a legitimate political space for opposing the ruling party. Occupying this opposition space aggressively has become extremely crucial in the context of anti-incumbency voting. With the growing trend of alternating between the two principal political parties almost firmly set in the Indian polity, it is expected that parties in the opposition behave like an opposition. When a party fails in utilising this space, an impression gains ground that it has a tacit understanding with the incumbent party; consequently it loses credibility and popular support. The results of the assembly elections in Uttar Pradesh in 2007 and 2012 are a testimony to this. Analysts believed that both the Congress and the BJP failed to influence the electorate as a genuine 'opposition party' and hence, an alternative to Mulayam Singh/Mayawati. Eventually, both the parties lost.

Parliamentary Democracy with FPTP: Shortcomings

Over the years, in countries like India, where parliamentary democracy combined with a First-Past-The-Post (FPTP) electoral system is in practice for more than fifty years, serious shortcomings of this combination have come to the fore. Some of the major shortcomings that merit discussion are given here.

Inherent Conflict between Representatives' Own Judgment and Party Discipline

Under the parliamentary system, with the introduction of devices like the party whip and several anti-defection laws, the freedom of an individual member to exercise his own judgment has been curtailed to a considerable extent. These measures are also seen as a clear case of crass violation of the fundamentals of 'representative democracy'. There are several instances of individual members being forced to take a stance much against the desires of the people whom they are expected to represent. All this is done with a view to abide by the party whip.

Under the parliamentary system, it's a three-legged race. An elected representative has to listen to the demands of his constituency, go by the policy perspectives of the party and also apply his/her own judgment. This often turns out to be a test of his dexterity. In the absence of any well-laid mechanism to resolve the inherent clash of interest on a given issue, representatives easily tend to have their own way. The emerging confusion also leaves enough scope for them to take shelter in pressures either from their party or constituency. These factors often camouflage the representative's selfish interests too.

It is true that the anti-defection laws have at least partly arrested the growing trend of switching sides as and when convenient, due to the mandatory character of party whips. Nevertheless, there are some negative aspects of this system too. Party whip as an instrument of parliamentary control prevents the protection of the constituency's real interest. David Kilgour, a Canadian MP, has said that the notion of party discipline precludes an elected person's ability to represent his constituents. According to him, 'In our current electoral system, the ability of an elected official in government to represent constituents is seriously impaired by the high degree of party discipline prevalent in the Canadian system…the reality of our present system is that the will of the constituents is often trumped by party discipline.'[13]

Albeit, there are practical difficulties in letting the interest of an individual constituency dominate at the cost of a democratically evolved policy perspective of a party. Today, parties and even non-party informal groups or a combination of both can survive in the

---

[13]David Kilgaour, *Whither Democracy in Canada*. At http://www.david-kilgour.com/mp/Whither%20Democracy%20in%20Canada.htm.

government only because there is a reasonably justifiable mechanism to take its own members for granted. Parties are recognised as an organised unit in a house of representatives and this unit governs the parliamentary behaviour of individual members. In India, and anti-defection law is in place and under it every individual member has to be in conformity with the party whip. In effect, this deprives a member of the freedom to vote as per his conscience. Initially it was thought that such tough measures would considerably reduce the instances of defection. Unfortunately, the experience during the last few decades suggests that it has had only a marginal impact.

Fragmentation

Several researchers have pointed out that parliamentary democracies often lead to the fragmentation of political parties. The ever-increasing number of political parties in India is a testimony of this observation. As per the Election Commission of India's notification in March 2011, there are a total number of 1196 registered as well as unrecognised parties in the country. Besides, many new parties take birth just before the elections. For example, *The Indian Express* reported the mushrooming of 150 additional parties in the run-up to the assembly elections in Uttar Pradesh in 2007.

CHART 1: STEADY INCREASE IN THE NUMBER OF PARTIES[14]

Year	1980	1996	2006	2011
Number of National Parties	6	8	6	6
Number of Regional/State Parties	19	30	43	51
Registered Unrecognised Parties	11	171	827	1139
Total Number of Parties	36	209	876	1196

[14]CSDS-Lokniti Database at www.lokniti.org/WPS-1.pdf and Political Parties in India–2006, an official publication of the Election Commission of India and data available at the Election Commission of India website.

This steady increase in the number of political parties is mainly due to the fact that almost every minor caste, religious or social group in the country has now started asserting itself politically. In the process, these groups claim a separate identity and subsequently an independent and exclusive representation.

In the recent past, the leaders of various caste and social groups have developed a calculated strategy. The underlying thinking has been that if they support a major political party like the Congress, or the BJP, they may not get adequate representation in the Cabinet. But if they form their own political party, it is likely to ensure not only some seats in the Lok Sabha or the state legislatures, but also some berths in the Cabinet. 'This process of fragmentation has led to the registration of thirty-six parties with the term Congress in it, like Kerala Congress, Nationalist Congress, etc.'[15]

Coalition politics has added to the complications of representative democracy. Consequently, a trend of coalition politics with competitive political bargaining—largely on sectarian lines—at its core, is gripping the political scenario. Thanks to the phenomenon of identity politics, several smaller parties are out in the electoral malls to shop for votes.

As a consequence, small parties have become more prominent with their concentrated pockets of influence. While parties and candidates are theoretically compelled to appeal to the widest possible base to get elected, in reality the plea is narrowed down further. Arun Shourie underscores this point. According to him, several recent electoral verdicts bring forward three main features of the present situation, namely, 'the electorate splintered, the splinters frozen, small swings in votes having such pronounced consequences for the share in seats—lead the politician to the same operational lessons: somehow exacerbate divisions, somehow swing a small fraction of the electorate; somehow stitch up the small sections.'[16]

---

[15]PM Kamath, 'A quest for A Democratic Alternative: A Case for Presidential Government', in Nawaz B Mody, Kannamma S Raman and Louis D'Silva (Ed.), *Revitalising Indian Democracy*, p.168.

[16]Arun Shourie, *The Parliamentary System*, p.58.

Several political parties in India could be described as dominated mainly by a single community. The Samajvadi Party in Uttar Pradesh has a clear Yadav domination whereas the Rashtriya Lok Dal is considered as a party dominated by the Jats. The Shiromani Akali Dal is primarily a Sikh party while the Vannia community dominates the Pattali Makkal Katchi (PMK) of Tamil Nadu.

It is also true that while these community satraps do represent community interests, they rarely are sincere and honest to pursue resolutely the cause of their community's development. As a result, dishonest and secret deals at the cost of genuine community interests remain the basis of coalition partnerships. Eventually, the entire process of on-ground and off-ground electoral adjustments often leads to multiple fragmentations of public opinion, communities and society at large.

Instability

After more than three decades of parliamentary democracy, an anti-defection law was enacted in India in 1985. It banned individual defections but permitted and condoned party splits. Paragraph three of this law said that if one-third of the members broke away from a party and formed a separate faction or block, they would not attract the provisions of the Anti-Defection Law. But it failed to curb defections. Subsequently, the ninety-first amendment in 2003 made defections more difficult and almost did away with the provisions approving mass defections. Ever since, any MP or MLA who 'splits' a party loses the membership of the House he belongs to. And yet, these systemic efforts to halt the process of political fragmentation have not yielded any significant success. This is evident from the fact that in 2004, Gegong Apang, the chief minister of Arunachal Pradesh, defected to the Congress, en-bloc with the entire cabinet and legislature party.

This has also led to political instability, ultimately endangering the very credibility of democracy in India. As Ivor Jennings, British lawyer and academic, has rightly commented, 'Frequent resignations (of governments) involve frequent party splits and party splits lead to short and weak governments, which in turn lead to distrust of the democratic system.'[17]

Former Chief Minister of Goa, Pratap Singh Rane, had once rightly remarked, 'The danger of instability is more pronounced in small states like Goa. Here, from 1963 to 1990, six assemblies had only three chief ministers and three to four ministers. But, since 1990, this system has provided us with thirteen chief ministers and not a Cabinet of less than twelve to fourteen in a forty-member House.'[18] This explains as to why he himself had argued for suitably amending the Constitution.

Parliamentary democracy is considered to be prone to political instability. Every time a motion of 'no confidence' is passed, elections are normally called for. During the Fourth Republic in France, the elections were conducted after every five months, while in Italy it was at even shorter durations. Understandably, the Constitution was amended in France mainly to overcome political instability.

Dilution of Party Distinctions Due to Coalitions

Splintered votes are throwing up splintered verdicts, making coalition almost mandatory. In India, apart from at the Centre, coalition governments are in power in as many as at ten states today. While the coalition era has brought at least a semblance of political stability, the perils are too many to ignore.

Coalition too brings instability to the political set-up. Out of the eight coalition governments at the Centre witnessed in India since 1989, only four could last full terms. Fractured verdicts invariably lead to post-poll coalitions, more often than not, violating the popular mandate. With post-election coalitions, parties get a license to keep their manifestos in cold storage, blaming it on 'insufficient

---

[17] As quoted by PM Kamath from Ivor Jennings, *Cabinet Government*, Cambridge University Press, Cambridge, 1951. p.261 in his essay 'A quest for A Democratic Alternative: A Case for Presidential Government' in Nawaz B Mody, Kannamma S Raman and Louis D'Silva (Ed.) *Revitalising Indian Democracy.*

[18] Then Goa Chief Minister Pratap Singh Rane in an interview with rediff.com at http://www.rediff.com/news/2003/may/27inter.htm.

popular mandate'. While accommodation is the foundation of coalition politics, it also paves the way for compromises at the ideological and policy level. And once compromise is accepted as a virtue, what commences is 'competitive compromising' under the garb of the spirit of accommodation.

Besides, coalition politics also negates the absoluteness of the freedom of choice bestowed upon the voters, especially in the case of post-poll coalitions. Let us look at an example. When a voter opts for party B out of the available choices such as A, B and C, the decision simultaneously rejects both A and C. But, one fine morning, after the election and at the time of the government's formation when the voter sees B joining hands with A, he/she is bound to feel betrayed. Coalition politics not only accepts political compulsions but also indirectly legitimises the inherent element of betrayal, making the whole system appear helpless in so far as truly respecting the voters' freedom of choice is concerned.

Arrogance of Winning Parties

One of the weaknesses of parliamentary democracy is that large majorities often lead the winning parties to arrogance. The leaders often tend to forget that however big the majority, one single party cannot claim to be the sole representative of the people. We come across several such instances of arrogance in India, generally manifested through the statements of party leaders. Former president of the Congress, Dev Kant Baruah's infamous phrase: 'Indira is India' and Rajiv Gandhi's statement that he will make his adversaries remember their grandmother (*Nani yaad ayegi*), are some of the widely discussed examples of brazen arrogance on the part of winning parties. Political commentator Madhu Kishwar, in one of her blogs, has noted how Mayawati's interaction with her own party people betrayed arrogance and disdain.[19]

Fillip to Adversarialism

Many believe that opposition for the sake of opposition has made

[19] www.indiatogether.org/manushi/xddx Cissue111/women-pol.htm.

an adverse impact on democratic polity. Commenting on the party scenario in the Sixties, an Australian political analyst had remarked that 'major parties were seen as rigid and the adversalism between the parties was seen as excessive and actually subverting the process of good government—it was argued that what was in the public interest was too often secondary to the adversarial battle of the parties.'[20] Naturally then, in certain situations, the parliamentary form acts as a disincentive to coalesce, as the power depends on the parties' strength in the chamber of representatives. Many a time, it is the contemporary ground situation that influences the level of adversarialism. In the Indian context, the UPA and the NDA have changed their positions contrary to their earlier positions when in power.

This apparent dishonesty also perplexes the voters. Understandably, in many democracies, people feel that all politicians are covertly hand-in-glove with each other, regardless of their party differences. The notion that the differences amongst the political parties are contrived and far from genuine is fast gaining ground in the popular mind. Many believe that should this popular feeling persist, it will not only add to the growing cynicism but also bode ill for the future of democracy in general.

Protection of Incompetence

The parliamentary form not only facilitates but also protects incompetence. For the sake of ensuring the inclusive and representative character of a cabinet or a legislative body, every section of society needs to be accommodated. True, that quality and competence need not always be the sole decisive factor in a representative democracy, but the system should also not promote contempt for competence. Under the parliamentary system, it is unrealistic to expect that the ministers possess either professional knowledge or

---

[20]Quoted from Elaine Thompson, in the research paper, *Australian Parliamentary Democracy after a Century: What gains, What losses?'* from HC Debates, Vol. 101.cols 205-6,30 August 1848 at http://www.aph.gov.au/Library/Pubs/rp/1999-2000/2000rp23.htm.

practical experience of a particular portfolio. The distribution of portfolios among them is often solely on the basis of their political standing in the party and the confidence they happen to enjoy with the prime minister. Shail Chaturvedi, noted Hindi poet, has brilliantly commented upon the state of democracy in India, where faith in god is considered enough for running governments.[21] *The Sunday Standard* had once sarcastically mentioned:

> What makes you say politicians are not qualified? They have first class degrees in clichés and pious platitudes, they have done courses in fabrication, they are PhDs in the arts of sycophancy and expediency, they have diplomas in feathering their nests and they serve themselves with dedication, sincerity and sedulous hard work...perfect qualifications for politics.[22]

More Prone to Intra-party Friction

Ample scope for friction between the ministerial wing and the party bosses—the parliamentary and the organisational wing—is yet another problem area in the parliamentary system. The history of parliamentary democracy in India is replete with examples of a continued tug of war between the prime minister or chief minister and the party's president. Starting from the 1969 split in the ruling Congress on the issue of presidential candidature[23], at the national level to HD Kumaraswamy's coup in 2006 in Karnataka, there are

---

[21]In one of his brilliant poems, often quoted by many politicians, Shail Chaturvedi has commented that only a trained driver can drive a car while governments could be run (only) with a firm faith in god. (*Yeh car hai, sarkar nahin, jo bhagwan bharose chal sakti hai.!)*

[22]'Situation vacant, Politicians Wanted; Qualifications: Nil' (*The Sunday Standard*, 15 April 1979, Bombay)

[23]Then Prime Minister Indira Gandhi rebelled against the official candidature of Sanjeeva Reddy and extended support to VV Giri in the Presidential election of 1969. This led to a vertical divide in the party leading to the emergence of Congress-I and Congress-O (Organisation).

several instances of the heads of the parliamentary or legislature wing usurping the organisational leadership. A continued struggle to establish one-upmanship has always afflicted both the performance of the government as also the organisational health of the party.

Decline of the Parliament

Questions like 'Is Parliament becoming obsolete?' are being asked for a long time now, not only in India but also in the UK. Shortening the duration of sessions of the Parliament and legislatures has become an established trend in India. The quality of business is deteriorating very fast, resulting in greater scepticism about not only parliamentary debates but also the entire functioning of the Parliament. According to CV Madhukar of the Centre for Policy Research, New Delhi:

> Technically, Parliament passed fifty-nine bills in 2006, which is a shade better than the average fifty-eight bills per year over the past five years. However, if one were to take the percentage of time spent on legislation as an important indicator of Parliament's focus on legislation, the numbers are not very encouraging. Over the past seven sessions of Parliament, the time spent on debating legislative issues was approximately 20 per cent in the Lok Sabha and 23 per cent in the Rajya Sabha. In fact, in the winter session of 2004, less than 15 per cent time was spent on legislation in the Lok Sabha.[24]

A second indicator that is of concern is that Parliament passes a number of bills with little debate. In the year 2006-07, over 40 per cent of bills were passed in the Lok Sabha with less than one hour of debate. Rejecting the argument that discussions in parliamentary standing committees takes due care of the scrutiny of bills, Madhukar counter argues that 'In any case, closed room deliberations of

---

[24]CV Madhukar, 'House this for debate?', *The Indian Express*, 3 January 2007.

committees cannot substitute for healthy and well-researched debates on the floor of Parliament on important legislation.'

Having realised that debates in parliament or legislature cannot throw the government out, the powers that be often seem to become careless and insensitive to the content of parliamentary deliberations. Similarly, often the opposition tends to go overboard, realising full well that their views are going to make the least impact on government decisions. These very approaches pave the way for further devaluation of the institutional characteristics of parliament and legislature.

Hamid Ansari,[25] Vice-President of India, has very passionately spoken about the decline of parliament and state legislatures in his speech at the Conference of Party Whips in Mumbai in February 2008. According to him, 'The yardstick of public expectations is the only way to measure the effectiveness of the functioning of our legislatures. How successful have our parliamentary institutions been in making the system work?' He also expressed anguish over the facts that the number of sittings in the Rajya Sabha has come down from an annual average of 90.5 in the first decade, 1952-61, to 71.3 in the last decade of the last century, 1992-2001, a decline of 20 per cent. The comparative figures for the Lok Sabha are 124.2 and 81.0, a decline of 34 per cent. Pointing out that 'the picture in regard to the state assemblies is even more revealing, with the average now being in the range of 20 to 50 sittings every year', he pointed out, 'The annual average of the number of bills passed by Parliament has come down from 68 in the decade 1952-1961 to 49.9 in the decade 1992-2001. Assurances given on the floor of the House are being fulfilled with lesser regularity.'

A glance at how parliamentary means are being used in lesser and lesser numbers is an eye opener. The reasons for this could be found in the habitual attitude of both the ruling as well as the opposition parties. The unresponsive and callous approach towards legislative business of the respective governments on

[25] http://vicepresidentofindia.nic.in/content.asp?id=132 as.

the one hand and insistence on 'playing to the gallery' on the part of the opposition on the other are to blame for this situation.

The decline of the Parliament also has something to do with populism. In several interactions with MPs and MLAs, I was told that since the pandemonium brings headlines the next day, members indulge in it. Once the media decides to ignore the commotion and publish only reports about neatly conducted debates, the Parliament and legislatures would start functioning without disruptions.

According to British political scientist Peter Lyon, parliamentary democracy today is under severe threat. He observes, 'The challenges before the parliamentary system are too many. Firstly, it is the loyal opposition; secondly, the growing lure of extra-parliamentary means and thirdly, the fact that nobody wants to play the game as per the agreed principles. Opportunism is being defended as a part of compulsions.' The situation described by him causes more concern when most of the things mentioned by him are defended as 'competitive compromises'. Just because one political party commits a wrong, the other also follows the same way without thinking of opposing the former. In the Indian context, there are instances which show how the opposition and the ruling parties are often hand-in-glove, especially at the level of local self-government institutions. In Maharashtra, way back in 1997, an enquiry committee was set up to look into the corruption charges against members of the municipal corporation belonging to all major political parties. Known as the Nandalal Committee,[26] it clearly established how members of all the parties join hands when it comes to indulging in corruption and other illegal activities. Ironically, this could be described as a new form of 'cartel politics' if not 'cartel parties'.

All this adds to the overall decline of parliament, legislatures and their members too. A survey conducted in Canada in 2003 brought to light the contemporary electoral mindset. As much as 74 per cent of the respondents felt that those elected to parliament soon lose touch with the people, while 67 per cent felt that commoners

[26] *The Indian Express*, Mumbai, 30 December 1998.

do not have any say about what the government does. As Canadian researchers and political scientists, Kenneth Carty, William Cross and Lisa Young have noted in *Rebuilding Canadian Party Politics*, 'Public opinion and survey data confirm that at the outset of the new century, large numbers of Canadians continue to believe their politicians and political institutions are out of touch and unresponsive, and are increasingly dissatisfied with the performance of parliament and political parties.'[27]

While it is true that the ground realities of politics influences parliamentary form, the form also affects the polity in general. Changes in ground realities have afflicted the effectiveness of parliaments. Many believe that on the one hand parliaments have lost their monopoly in representing the society, while on the other, governments have lost their exclusive right on decision-making. Hence, re-examining the fundamentals and exploring the possibility of introducing reforms remains the best way. In this context, some of the recommendations made by the eminent expert in parliamentary affairs, Dr Subhash Kashyap,[28] are worth noting. According to him:

> Parliamentary reforms would have to include: building a better image of Parliament as belonging to the people and not to MPs and establishing a new rapport between the people and Parliament; improving the quality and conduct of members; reducing expenditure on Parliament, improving information supply and efficacy of committee scrutiny; legislative planning and improving the quality of laws; setting up standing committees on the Constitution and codifying privileges; improving working of parties, floor management and parliamentary time table; and rationalising and modernising rules of procedure to meet today's needs.

---

[27] As quoted by David Kilgour, *Whither Democracy in Canada* at http://www.david-kilgour.com/mp/Whither%20Democracy%20in%20Canada.htm.

[28] Subhash Kashyap, 'Parliament, reform thyself' in *The Tribune*, Chandigarh, 24 September 2005.

ELECTORAL SYSTEMS

Elections are extremely important, but one has to understand that there are obvious and inherent limitations to the process of elections itself. According to Robert A Dahl, this is especially true in the case of the American presidential elections. He is convinced that 'on matters of specific policy, the majority rarely rules'. He has further noted that election can best be described as a technique 'for insuring that governmental leaders will be relatively responsive to non-leaders'.[29] Considering the limitations of what we describe as electoral verdict or mandate, one can reasonably argue that all an election brings forward are the first choices of only some sections of the citizens and that too within the options of the candidates available.

All in all, what it comes down to is 'not minority rule, but minorities rule'.[30] It is against this background that one cannot but agree with Dahl's observation—with such flawed electoral mechanisms, no matter the form of government, democracy itself is reduced to 'the steady appeasement of relatively small groups'.[31] Coming out in full support of Dahl's observations, Howard Zinn, historian and civil rights activist, World War II bombardier and author of *A People's History of the United States*, raises some very thought-provoking questions primarily in the context of the US, but with a universal relevance. Zinn enquires:

> What anti-smoking consumer group in the election year of 1996 could match the five million dollars donated to the Republican Party by the tobacco interests? What ordinary citizen could have the access to President Bill Clinton that a group of bankers had in May of that election year when they were invited to the White House?[32]

[29] Robert A Dahl, *A Preface to Democratic Theory*, p.81.
[30] *Ibid*.p.131-32.
[31] *Ibid*.p.146.
[32] Originally from *The New York Times*, 26-27 January 1997, and referred to by Howard Zinn in Robert E Diclarico and Alan S Hammock, (Ed.), *Points of View: Readings in American Government and Politics*. p.6.

He further says, 'If these relatively small groups turn out to be the aircraft industry far more than the aged, the space industry far more than the poor, the Pentagon far more than the college youth—what is left of democracy?'[33]

In an ideal situation, electoral systems are expected to minimise the impact of these inherent limitations of elections and hence, they are extremely crucial.

One of the most crucial aspects of representative democracy—where elected officials take decisions on behalf of the people—is how these officials are being elected. This translation of the citizen's votes into representative seats is performed through elections and by way of using an electoral system. When it comes to election, the strength of numbers comes into play. Ideally, it is expected that an electoral system should reflect the strength of numbers without leaving any scope for distortions. An electoral system is thus the most fundamental element of representative democracy. Commenting on the Jenkins Commission Report about changing electoral systems in the UK, political commentator David Beetham explained why a country must select its electoral system carefully. According to him:

> As growing numbers of people are becoming alienated from the political process, the debate needs to focus on which electoral system can best empower voters by extending the range of political voices, by treating all voters equal, by offering an effective choice between parties and candidates, and by providing an incentive to vote.[34]

Observing that under the parliamentary system, with just one act of voting, a voter elects a parliament and also chooses a government, Beetham rightly prescribes three important counts for judging the effectiveness of an electoral system, viz. ability to perform

---

[33] *ibid*

[34] David Beetham, *In for the count* at http://www.redpepper.org.uk/dem/x-nov98-beetham.htm.

functions democratically, ability to further empower the voter and ability to equalize the value of the vote.

Selection of the right kind of electoral system is crucial for several reasons. Elections and voting are perhaps the only avenues rightfully, commonly and easily available to each and every citizen for participating in the decision-making process. The very spirit of democracy will come to naught if people think that a particular electoral system is depriving them of their right to opinion and right to be heard. This will naturally make them feel that they are being given a raw deal. Needless to say, a widespread feeling of this kind may lead to the erosion of public confidence in the concept of democracy, afflicting its participative character. Arend Lijphart, who has several seminal studies on this subject to his credit, rightly underscored the importance of electoral systems for two distinct reasons. They are:

> First, they have important consequences for the degree of proportionality of election outcomes, the party system, the kind of cabinets that can be formed, government accountability and party cohesion. Secondly, they are more easily manipulable than any other elements of democratic systems, that is if one wants to change the nature of a particular democracy, the electoral system is likely to be the most suitable and effective instrument for doing so.[35]

The electoral system is the most important equipment for translation of popular will into votes. However, there are obvious difficulties in the task of determining the electorate's will. There are many who recommend that a referendum is the only effective way of comprehending the popular mindset. One can just not dispute British historian, statesman and diplomat James Bryce's observation that even in a country 'which clings to and founds itself upon the absolute supremacy of its representative chamber, the notion of a

[35] Seymour Martin Lipset (Ed.), *The Encyclopedia of Democracy*, p.412.

direct appeal to the people has (still) made progress'.[36] The popularity of referendum is growing, regardless of many constraints. Some of them are the limitations of understanding a particular issue on the part of the people and the durability of popular will. According to Sir Douglas Wass, who was permanent secretary to the treasury in Britain, 'Without a good deal of education and enlightenment, public opinion (polled in this way) could be a poor guide to policy—poor not in the sense that it would not correspond to elite opinion—but poor in that it would be ill-informed and in the long run unacceptable even to those expressing it.'[37]

A case in point is California. It has used Referendums on specific issues for many years and the mess of the state's finances is attributed to this method. Many in California say that they just do not have the time to read the lengthy explanations, which are given when they are asked to vote on many propositions. Undoubtedly, direct democracy or a system facilitating direct votes or Referendum just cannot be a substitute for dialogue. With weakening party organisations, parties are seen to engage less with the masses and when they attempt to do so, it is often very symbolic and superfluous.

The whole exercise, therefore, boils down to the best available electoral system in a given situation. In such a scenario, the choice of an electoral system has to hinge upon factors like practicability, participative character and the ability to reflect genuine public opinion. Recognising that the selection of an electoral system is one of the most crucial aspects of any functional democracy, New Zealand's Royal Commission on Changing the Electoral System, in its report in 1986, strongly recommended that a referendum be held on this issue, since 'a country's voting system affects the most basic aspects of its democracy'.[38]

---

[36] James Bryce, 'The Electoral Madness', 1988 'The American Commonwealth', as quoted in Jack Lively and Adam Lively (Ed.) *Democracy in Britain, A Reader*, p.63.

[37] Douglas Wass, 'Referenda—A Critical View (1983)', in 'Government and the Governed' (BBC Reith Lectures) as quoted in Jack Lively and Adam Lively (Ed.) *op.cit*,p.65.

[38] As quoted from the report by Poll Harris, at http://janda.org/c95/news%20articles/New%20Zealand/ZNswitch.htm.

Electoral and party systems influence each other greatly. Sharing his general conclusion, Lijphart has said: 'Electoral systems are strong—but far from fully determining—influence on party and political systems.'[39] In fact, it is widely recognised that the electoral systems are, if not the sole, one of the most crucial determinants of party systems. Douglas W Rae[40] has focussed on certain key aspects of links between electoral and party systems. Basing his arguments on the studies of Rae, Lijphart has pointed out three different trends that have refused to vanish, no matter which electoral system a country opts for. These trends are:

- Continued disproportionality in electoral outcomes.
- Reduction in the number of parliamentary parties as compared to electoral parties.
- Scope for manufacturing a parliamentary majority, regardless of the majority support of the voters.

What Lijphart concludes after a comparative analysis is more important. According to him, 'All three tendencies are much stronger in plurality and majority than in PR systems.'[41]

An electoral system determines who should vote, and how constituencies are to be demarcated and how winners are decided. As a consequence, it influences aspects like the structure, behaviour and likely success of the parties in contention. As pointed out by Jack and Adam Lively, in Britain, 'Successive electoral reforms in the nineteenth century...had profound effects on the party system and more recently, those who had wished to restructure the party system, have looked to electoral reforms as means.'[42] In fact, electoral systems influence everything in a party organisation, from the level of local activism, organisational network to policy decisions. In India too, when parties like the CPI(M), BJP and Shiv Sena—known for

---

[39] Seymour Martin Lipset (Ed.), *The Encyclopedia of Democracy*, p.421.

[40] As quoted by Arend Lijphart, *Patterns of Democracy: Government Forms and Performance in Thirty-Six countries*, p.92.

[41] *Ibid.*

[42] Jack Lively and Adam Lively (Ed.), *op.cit, p.153.*

their organisational networks—think of setting up a party at the grass-roots level, the primary unit has always been the booth-level committees.

There are several countries that have either switched from one electoral system to other or are seriously debating the matter. In 1997, Israel adopted a different form of government, combining the presidential and parliamentary and also a new electoral system, by switching over to the runoff. New Zealand also replaced the majoritarian with a proportional representational system in 1993. In the UK too, the nation witnessed earnest debates on selecting a more suitable electoral system. While every system has its own positive and negative aspects, the main electoral systems that merit elaborate discussion are: Plurality system, Majoritarian system and Proportional Representation (PR) system.

PLURALITY ELECTORAL SYSTEM

The plurality system is more popularly referred to as the FPTP system. Under this, in a multi-candidate election, the largest single total number of votes for any candidate determines the victor. In the US, such an arrangement is often referred to as a plurality system because the candidate with a plurality and not a majority of votes is the winner. Some political scientists refer to this as a system of single member districts with plurality elections.

Whatever the name, there appears to be greater unanimity about FPTP not being suitable for determining the electoral wishes. There are several instances from all over the world, suggesting as to how FPTP produces results that fail to reflect the genuine popular opinion. Many have criticised the single member district feature of FPTP where every constituency has to elect only one representative. Political scientist and an authority on voting systems, Douglas J Amy has called this a 'distortion in Representation'.[43] According to him, the FPTP offers one the right to vote but not necessarily the right to

[43]Douglas J Amy, 'What is PR and why do we need this reform?', at http://www.mtholyoke.edu/acad/polit/damy/BeginningReading/whatispr.htm.

be represented. He further elaborates that the single member district system, 'routinely denies representation to a large number of voters, produces legislatures that fail to accurately reflect the views of the public, discriminates against third parties and discourages voter turnout.'[44] There are several examples supporting Amy's observations. In the Indian context, the example would be the verdict of the parliamentary elections of 2004. While the BJP-led alliance with 34.83 per cent vote share got 185 seats, the Congress-led alliance with 34.59 per cent votes was able to achieve 219 seats in the Parliament. Though the aggregate vote share of the Congress alliance is less than that of the BJP's, the former ended up with thirty-four more seats. The electoral history of India is replete with such instances. In the 2011 assembly elections of Uttar Pradesh, the difference between vote share of the two principal contenders was not commensurate with the seats won or vice versa. The Samajwadi Party got 29.16 per cent votes and 56 per cent seats while the Bahujan Samaj Party's vote share was 25.92 per cent with 20 per cent seats. Way back in 1959, Gandhian thinker and leader Jayaprakash Narayan (JP) in one of his books had pointed out this fundamental flaw in our system.[45]

Analysing this, Arun Shourie has pointed out two clearly emerging trends. They are:

- Shares of parties in seats are often out of proportion to their vote share.
- Small swings in votes trigger a large swing in the number of seats.

The charts[46] given here clearly bring out how just a small shift in the preferences of voters makes a great turnaround. This analysis is just an example and there are many more such cases, which underscore the fact that the disproportionality is inherent to the FPTP system.

---

[44] *Ibid.*

[45] Jayaprakash Narayan (JP), *Bharatiya Rajya Vyavastha ki Punarrachana: Ek Sujhav* (Hindi), p.65.

[46] Source: Arun Shourie, *The Parliamentary System*, p.50, 52.

PERFORMANCE OF MAJOR PARTIES IN THE ELECTIONS TO THE ANDHRA PRADESH ASSEMBLY

Year	Telugu Desam Party		Congress	
	% Votes Polled	Seats Won	% Votes Polled	Seats Won
2009	28.12	92	36.56	156
2004	37.6	47	38.6	185
1999	43.9	180	40.6	91
1994	44.1	216	33.8	26
1989	36.5	74	47.1	181
1985	46.2	202	37.2	50

PERFORMANCE OF MAJOR PARTIES IN THE ELECTIONS TO THE RAJASTHAN ASSEMBLY

Year	Congress		BJP	
	% Votes Polled	Seats Won	% Votes Polled	Seats Won
2008	36.81	96	34.27	78
2003	35.6	56	39.2	120
1998	44.9	153	33.2	33
1993	38.3	76	38.6	95
1990	33.6	50	25.2	85
1985	46.5	113	21.2	39

While the beneficiary party may change, distorted representation continues to be a part of our political reality.

This disproportionality of the FPTP system is an universal phenomenon. In spite of the fact that Labour had won a majority of the votes polled, the Conservatives secured a majority of fifteen seats in the House of Commons in the UK in 1951. In 1974, the Conservatives had most votes but the Labour leaders were called to form government, simply because they had the largest number of seats. The Labour Party secured 27.6 per cent of the votes polled while winning 32.1 per cent of seats in 1983. In the same election, despite securing 25.4 per cent of the votes polled, the Liberal and Social Democrats could win only 3.5 per cent of seats.[47] This history has been repeating itself in the US. In the 1996 elections for the US House of Representatives, the Democrats won 66 per cent of the votes in Massachusetts, but received 100 per cent of the state seats, whereas even while securing 33 per cent of popular votes, the Republicans, in terms of seats, drew a blank. In the same year, in Washington state, the Republicans took second place with 47 per cent of the votes, but won six out of nine of the House seats.

The plurality system is considered as flawed mainly because it enables a candidate to win an election without winning a majority. The National Commission to review the 'Functioning of the Constitution', in its report published in 2002, has observed, 'In some cases those who would otherwise have forfeited their security deposit have been declared elected as they had obtained the highest number of votes amongst the candidates.'[48] A glance at a chart given in Appendix F, concerning the 2004 Lok Sabha election results in Uttar Pradesh, vividly brings about how members get elected by a minority of votes.

In spite of its several inadequacies, many still prefer FPTP, because it is one of the simplest electoral systems. Besides, it does handicap third parties, and eventually helps to produce a two-party system. The emerging bi-polar character of the polity in India, more particularly in some of the states in the country, is also a pointer. It is also observed that with an amplified majority of party members in the legislature, FPTP helps governments to meet the criterion of effectiveness. There are several political scientists and thinkers like Harold Laski, who never supported measures like PR, referendum or recall. Laski was also in favour of a territorial mode of representation

---

[47] http://www.bransdle.demon.co.uk/vote/listPR.html.

[48] As quoted by Arun Shourie, *op.cit*, p.32

in a legislature.[49] With all its inadequacies, FPTP continues to be in practice in several democracies for decades together. The Presidents of countries like Iceland, Nicaragua, the Philippines and Venezuela are elected through this system. Also, members of the lower houses of legislatures in India, UK, Canada and the US are elected through FPTP.

MAJORITARIAN ELECTORAL SYSTEM

In a Majoritarian system, in a multi-candidate election, voting is held twice so as to determine who enjoys the support of more than 50 per cent of the voters. This is also known as a majority-runoff or double-ballot system. A second ballot is held in this system to decide who scores more between the two most-voted-for candidates from the first ballot. A majoritarian electoral system is adopted in presidential elections in Austria, Brazil, Chile, Peru, Poland and Portugal.

As observed by Everett Carl Ladd, in a majoritarian system, politicians tend to 'practice an almost promiscuous majoritarianism that rejects ideological distinctiveness and stresses representation of the tastes of many.'[50] Consequently, the distinct ideological identity of parties is jeopardised. Since this system ultimately restricts the choice to only two top candidates, it is considered unjust and arbitrary, especially to those contestants and parties who have strong secondary support in the electorate. A solution to this is alternative or preferential voting, where voters are expected to vote for all the candidates on a ballot while indicating their preferences by way of putting preferential numbers before the names. It has been used for presidential elections in Ireland and Sri Lanka and also for the election of the Australian House of Representatives.

One of the important reasons for the worldwide review of the majoritarian system and the Westminster model is the clear and mandatory division it calls for between ruling or treasury and opposition. Nobel Prize-winning economist Sir Arthur Lewis has

[49] GL Mehta, *Harold Laski Revisited*, p.16

[50] Everett Carl Ladd, *Where have all the voters gone?* p.69.

forcefully pointed out that the majority rule and government-versus-opposition pattern of politics that it implies, may be interpreted as undemocratic because they are principles of exclusion. According to him, the primary meaning of democracy is that 'all who are affected by a decision should have the chance to participate in making that decision either directly or through chosen representatives.'[51] Although democracy means a decision by majority, he feels 'to exclude the losing group from participation in decision-making clearly violates the primary meaning of democracy'.[52] Perhaps, it is this particularly consensual character of democracy that made Lewis strongly recommend PR for the plural societies of West Africa.

PROPORTIONAL REPRESENTATION (PR) ELECTORAL SYSTEM

Considered to be an invention of the nineteenth century, the Proportional Representation (PR) system was adopted by most European democracies that were using plurality or majoritarian systems at the turn of the twentieth century. The fact that, of the twenty-three countries—which have been democracies since 1950 without any major interruptions—fifteen have used mainly PR speaks volumes about the system. Of the remaining eight, while Japan has used a semi-proportional system, only seven other countries have used plurality-majoritarian systems. In 1999, when Scotland and Wales had elections for their newly created parliaments, they both chose PR instead of the traditional single-member plurality system. Again, in 2004, the entire United Kingdom, along with other European countries, switched to a PR voting system when it came to electing representatives to the European Community. Even in the US, a considerable amount of support in PR's favour is emerging steadily. In the Nineties, two large cities of Cincinnati and San Francisco voted on a referendum to adopt PR and secured 45 per cent votes in favour of the same although the proposition as such was narrowly defeated.

---

[51] As quoted by Arend Lijphart, *Patterns of Democracy: Government Forms and Performance in Thirty-Six countries*, p.21.
[52] *Ibid.*p.21.

As far as the proportional system is concerned, there are several varieties of it. According to the *The Concise Oxford Dictionary of Politics*, a proportional system means 'any system, which seeks to ensure that each function, group or party in the electing population is represented in the elected body in proportion to its size.'[53] Important branches of proportional representation include additional member or mixed member proportional (MMP) system, party list (PL) system and single transferable (ST) vote system. Germany, Italy, New Zealand and Venezuela practise MMP whereas PL is prevalent in a large number of countries including Austria, Belgium, Denmark, Finland, Switzerland and the Netherlands. Countries like Ireland and Malta have gone in for ST vote system. Experts like Arend Lijphart have categorised the single non-transferable vote, once practised in Japan, as a semi-proportional system.

One of the notable observations about the PR system is that it often produces so many competing and conflicting parties and alliances in the parliament that majority coalitions are extremely difficult to form and they remain highly unstable. This hampers the effectiveness of government and Italy is cited as one such example. However, this may not be always true. With the introduction of several changes in the system, democracies such as the Netherlands and some Scandinavian countries have emerged as models of pragmatic reform combined with stability. Also, one of the arguments advanced in favour of the PR system is that it often promotes some kind of a 'consensus democracy'. In this type of a democracy, no one is able to monopolise the power and no one is left outside the elected government. Swedish democracy operates very much on these lines, in spite of the fact that every government there is a minority and yet it tries to implement policies that are liked by the plurality. Principles of mutuality and responsibility within the participating parties can be the basis for any such coalitional experiment. The government, which is elected through a PR system, has been referred to as 'deliberative democracy'.

---

[53] Ian McLean, (Ed.) *The Concise Oxford Dictionary of Politics*, p. 409.

On the one hand it is said, and it merits consideration, that PR 'allows the electorate to avoid making choices, and so the country is prevented from following a clear path. It provides the worst of both the worlds—consensus politics, the absence of clear direction and the sacrifice of all convictions in the interest of consensus'.[54] On the other hand, it is also true that the main strength of the PR system is that it provides for the sharing of power in the government. This also 'inculcates attitudes which spread outwards into society so that power in the economy and in industry also comes to be shared.'[55]

Those who prefer PR to any other system often claim that this is best suited for a democracy, since it is about the will of the people and PR does not allow any distortions to creep in. It is to do with a pure choice, about voters having the chance to vote for a party that genuinely reflects their views and not a lesser evil. More importantly, the system enables new movements and new parties to find a place in the political set-up. It is not for no reason that Australia, New Zealand and South Africa decided to opt for PR after a great deal of debate, taking into consideration all the merits and demerits of this system.

Australia decided to go the PR way in 1948. This move was mainly out of the realisation that discontent with the major parties could be reflected institutionally because PR gave new parties and independents the chance to be the elected groups of a reasonable size.

In 1986, when the report of New Zealand's Royal Commission on Electoral System recommended Mixed Member Proportional Representation (MMP) in place of the existing FPTP system, it took into consideration as many as ten criteria. The commission believed that MMP had 'comparable, though sometimes, different advantages over FPTP in relation to effective government, effective Parliament, representation of constituents,

---

[54]V Bogdanor, 'What is proportional representation?' as excerpted in Jack Lively and Adam Lively (Ed.) *op.cit* p.164.
[55]*Ibid.* p.165.

effective parties and political integration'.[56] In recommending MMP, the report recognised that this system facilitates 'the essential role [that] political parties play in modern representative democracies in, for example, formulating and articulating policies and providing representatives for the people.'[57]

The African National Congress (ANC) of South Africa opted for PR after a careful analysis of the positive and negative aspects of the available options. Its National Policy Conference, which was held in October 2002, had clearly favoured the PR system, stating:

> We adopted this (PR) system during negotiations before 1994 because we wanted an inclusive system and the representation of minority views, in the interest of nation-building and national unity.[58]

Rubbishing scores of arguments in favour of the FPTP and mixed PR system, ANC argued strongly in support of a pure PR system. It had strongly rejected the observation that under PR:

> 'Voters feel removed from their elected representatives and feel that they are not accountable to them'. This notion ignores the fact that 'alternative systems' do not in practice remedy the problems...there may well be ways to improve accountability and communication and we should also look at, our own selection and constituency deployment processes.[59]

ANC strongly endorsed the PR system also on the count of its inherent ability to promote party structures.

---

[56]Poll Harris, Chief Executive, Electoral Commission of New Zealand. 'New Zealand's Change to MMP' at http://janda.org/c95/news%20articles/New%20 Zealand/ZNswitch.htm.

[57]*Ibid.*

[58]African National Congress (ANC) Submission on Future Electoral System to the Electoral task Team (17 October, 2002) at http://www.anc.org.za/ancdocs/misc/ electsub.html.

[59]*Ibid.*

The co-chair of a commission set up in the UK to look at the experience of PR since 1997 in the devolved bodies in the country, Peter Ridell, in 2005, had indirectly advocated this system in the light of the fact that henceforth, 'neither Labour nor Tories will be able to win an overall majority in the Commons on their own. While the huge built-in advantage to Labour in the electoral system is partly unwinding, Tories still have a mountain to climb in both votes and seats.'[60] For some time now, there has been a clamour in the UK for switching over to PR. A campaign called 'Make My Vote Count' was aggressively conducted. According to Nina Temple, director and front-liner of this movement, 'First-Past-The-Post worked reasonably well when it was a two party culture in Britain, but now we are a multi-party democracy (and) it produces results that are skewed and unrepresentative of people's views'.[61] She has further observed that it is time the government 'embraced reform as a positive means of reconnecting politics to the people.'[62] Patrick Dunleavy of the London School of Economics had, in fact, predicted that the UK's moving to a PR system was now inevitable and that the transition to reform had already begun.[63] UK citizens voted in a nationwide referendum on 5 May 2011, on whether to adopt the Alternative Vote, in which the proposition was defeated. Many experts are of the opinion that this proposition failed mainly because of a complicated voting format, the conservatism of the Whigs and Tories and, above all, a deep-rooted mistrust of coalition governments.

Why is PR Preferred?

Advocates of PR also point out that all those countries where it is in practice have enjoyed high voter turnouts, vigorous multi-party competition, fair representation for political, ethnic and

[60] Peter Riddell, 'Lets do it, lets start flirting with PR', in *Times online*, 19 May, 2005 on http://www.timesonline.co.uk/article/0,1053-1617884,00.html.

[61] As quoted by *The Independent online*, published on 7 June,2005 at http://news.independent.co.uk/uk/politics/article224786.ece.

[62] *Ibid.*

[63] *Ibid.*

racial minorities and practically no gerrymandering. Studies have established that in Cincinnati and other places in the US, where PR is in practice, they have produced fairer representation for racial and ethnic minorities. In so far as gender justice is concerned, again, PR stands out. Results of elections in Germany and New Zealand under the mixed-member form of PR are a testimony.[64] In 1994, in Germany, 13 per cent women were elected in the single-member district while the number of those elected from the party list PR contests was 39 per cent. In New Zealand, in 1996, those numbers were 15 per cent for single-member district contests and 45 per cent for party list PR. According to the New Zealand Parliamentary Services, between 1999 and 2008, in four national elections held under the PR electoral system, the percentage of women elected to the Parliament has consistently remained around 30, which is remarkably higher than the previous elections. Besides, the fact that in New Zealand all parties that crossed the threshold in 1996 and 1999 (six and seven, respectively) and also received a share of seats in close proportion to their share of party votes, provided an evidence to the claim that a good PR enhances proportionality. The threshold has affected the composition of Parliament. The two traditional parties, Labour and National, have emerged as predominantly constituency parties while the newer parties have gained due to the list system. On the social front, parties were forced to go for 'balanced' party lists, making them more socially representative. Additionally, the MMP system has also resulted in aboriginal communities like the Maori getting representation, commensurate to their percentage in population. Representation of women has increased from 21.2 in 1993 to 30.8 in 1999. There is now greater inter-party dialogue and coordination in New Zealand. Although an adversarial approach continues unabated, prominent parties are more in a mood to listen to small partners.[65] While it is true that voters have expressed dislike

[64]Douglas J Amy, 'What is PR and why do we need this reform?', at http://www.mtholyoke.edu/acad/polit/damy/BeginningReading/whatispr.htm.

[65]www.citizensassembly.bc.ca/resources/Weekend%20Session%20Readings/Weekend5Session2McLeayPrint.ppt.

towards dual candidature and list the MP system, since candidates elected under this are likely to be less accountable to the electorate, but in any of the newly PR-converted countries no serious movement has gathered steam to abolish this system. This singularly proves beyond doubt that PR is considered to be more flawless and hence more acceptable too.

The percentage of voting has a clear impact and a tangible result, when it comes to the formation of government. There are studies that have proved that a PR system contributes to a higher voter turnout compared to non-PR systems.[66] A study conducted by IIDEA shows that average voting participation is about nine percentage points higher in a PR system than in non-PR systems. The lower turnout in a non-PR system is usually explained due to the fallout among voters who do not support a party with a real chance of winning the election and therefore do not participate at all. As far as the recruitment of women parliamentarians is concerned, according to several studies, the list-proportional representation system provides the most political opportunity to women.[67] In western democracies, the proportion of women parliamentarians is increasing, with the greatest surge being in proportional systems.[68]

QUALITY OF DEMOCRATIC GOVERNANCE UNDER DIFFERENT SYSTEMS

Parties, the quality of their electoral performance and the ability to offer good governance, are all intertwined factors. In that context, electoral systems do matter in so far as governance is concerned. As pointed out by the report of the Royal Commission on Electoral Systems (New Zealand), an 'electoral system should allow Governments…to meet their responsibilities. Governments should have the ability to act decisively when that is appropriate, and there should be reasonable continuity and stability both within and between governments.'[69]

[66] *Voting Turnout from 1945 to 1977: A Global Report on Political Participation* International IDEA, Stockholm, 1997.

[67] *Ibid.*

[68] *Ibid.*

[69] Report of the Royal Commission on Electoral System (New Zealand).http://www.aceproject.org/main/english/es/esy_nz.htm.

In New Zealand, after the country's switching over to the MMP system, Parliament has become more assertive over the executive, particularly through select committees.[70] Plurality or majoritarian systems are best operated in a two-party system and this argument is also extended when it comes to governance. It is often argued that two party systems are more likely to produce single party governments, which are internally united and hence strong and decisive. On the other hand, coalitions often produce weak and unstable governments. There are some studies that have attributed the failure of the Weimar Republic in Germany, in the first half of the twentieth century, to its PR system. However, there are equally strong counter arguments about the same, attributing the Weimar failure to an ineffective threshold, other institutional weaknesses and grave socio-economic conditions.

According to Lijphart, while majoritarian systems can produce governments with a majority support, the other pattern could be that of a government by 'as many people as possible'.[71] He refers to this model as a 'consensus model of democracy'. Further, he comes out with a theory, of which PR is an essential ingredient. According to him:

> ...while the majoritarian model concentrates political power in the hands of bare majority—and often merely a plurality instead of a majority—whereas the consensus model tries to share, disperse and limit power in a variety of ways. Exclusivity, competitiveness and adversarial nature are the characteristics of a majoritarian model, while in the case of consensus model it is inclusiveness, scope for bargaining and compromise. Kaiser has rightly termed this model as 'negotiation democracy'.[72]

---

[70] Paul Harris http://janda.org/c95/news%20articles/New%20Zealand/ZNswitch.htm.
[71] Arend Lijphart, *Patterns of Democracy: Government Forms and Performance in thirty-six countries*, p.123
[72] *Ibid.*p.131.

The test of the delivering aspect of democracy is in its ability to make a difference. On this count, Lijphart has said in conclusive terms that 'consensus democracy makes a big difference with regards to almost all indicators of democratic quality'.[73]

Researchers like Benjamin Reilly have reviewed electoral systems in the context of conflict management. In his recent work, *Democracy in Divided Societies,* Reilly has advocated the Australian system of preferential voting, basically as an incentive for 'office seeking politicians to campaign for these secondary preference votes and thus to bargain, cooperate and compromise in search of electoral victory.'[74] Reilly has also elaborated upon how the alternate vote system, when experimented with in Papua New Guinea between 1964-75, made a positive impact, leading to a clear centripetal incentive towards cross-ethnic bargaining and multi-ethnic coalitions and inter-ethnic moderation.

AN IDEAL PARTY THROUGH RIGHT FORM AND ELECTORAL SYSTEM

It is only under ideal democratic circumstances that ideal parties can emerge. On this count, there are many studies which deal with the quality of democracy in different models. Robert A Dahl has attempted to review democracy's condition across 114 countries. According to the ratings given by Dahl, consensus democracies (with PR as an essential element) have done better than the majoritarian or pluralist electoral systems.[75] As a part of the larger objective of this study, the attempt is to find out as to which form of democracy and electoral system is best suited to empower the political parties, subsequently to enable the prevailing democratic edifice, deliver the goods and transform the lives of the people, at least to a certain extent.

Empowering a political party basically means enabling and encouraging parties to offer a distinct political alternative.

[73] *Ibid.* p.161.

[74] Benjamin Reilly, '*Democracy in Divided Societies*', p.56.

[75] Robert A. Dahl, *Polyarchi*, 1971. p.231-45, as quoted by Arend Lijphart, *op.cit.*p.149.

Generally speaking, this can happen only in the case of parties having a distinct political ideology, a specific goal and a road map to improve the conditions all around with the help of a strong, enduring network of organisation. Although ideology per se is on the wane, revisiting doctrinal positions, restating philosophies and motivating cadres while re-emphasising distinct ideological issues can alone re-invigorate political parties as institutions. On the count of strong organisations, PR certainly yields more. As pointed out by Lijphart, 'Greater proportionality means better minority representation...also in terms of better representation of religious and ethnic minorities. Moreover, the representation of women—a political rather than a numerical minority—is much stronger in PR than in plurality systems.'[76] Again, on the basis of various ratings offered by political scientists, he has pointed out that the percentage of women's parliamentary representation is 6.7 per cent higher in consensus democracies than in majoritarian systems.[77] Lijphart has also concluded that 'citizens in consensus democracies are significantly more satisfied with democratic performance in their countries than citizens of majoritarian countries'.[78]

A wider scope for a greater representative character is the inherent strength of PR and it naturally adds to the organisational robustness of a party. Also, since the probability of a vote going waste is far too less in a proportional system and because it offers a greater choice to a voter, PR automatically encourages higher turnout. Besides, in a plurality system, a party can well afford to ignore particular regions with an inconsequential number of constituencies. However, this is not possible in PR and hence it naturally encourages nationwide party activity.

What are the indicators of the sound health of political parties? While works on political parties have rarely deliberated at length on this issue, one can certainly enlist them as factors such as

[76]Arend Lijphart in *The Encyclopedia of Democracy*, p.421.
[77]Arend Lijphart, *Patterns of Democracy: Government Forms and Performance in Thirty-Six countries*', p.150.
[78]*Ibid.* p.153.

internal democracy, absence of any personality cult, cohesion and collective leadership, value-based selection of candidates, and non-compromising approach towards policies and principals.

In so far as party cohesion is concerned, it is naturally at a high level when members of the same party are not forced to fight against each other. The plurality system absolutely negates this possibility. In the open-list category of the PR system also, this possibility is minimised. On the count of a generally cohesive and non-divisive polity, PR is likely to yield more than any other system since it promotes greater inter-party cooperation and dialogue.

While systems shape the parties, parties also decide the fate of a given system. In Australia, for example, an extraordinary degree of stability of governments could be achieved mainly because of some political conventions that parties adhered to. During the first six decades of the last century, elected members would always vote along party lines and this became a strong convention. The domination of Parliament by a disciplined bipolar party system meant that the House of Representatives came to be seen at worst as a theatre of meaningless ritual and at best as an institution often coming under the influence of the executive.

CHANGING PARTY SYSTEM VIA ELECTORAL SYSTEM

Electoral systems also play a role in determining the number of parties. It is largely believed that while PR generates a multi-party system, all other systems tend to establish a two-party system.

One of the most effective ways of influencing a party's system, profile and organisational character could be by adopting a closed party list form of political representation. It enables party leaders to vigorously dictate the composition of their party lists. In some countries, where parties would have exploited issues like ethnic and social diversities that result in the widening of cleavages, party lists appear to have worked well.

> In Singapore, for example, most MPs are elected from multi-member districts known as Group Representative Constituencies, which return between three and six

> members from a single list of party or individual candidates per constituency. Of the candidates on each party or group list, at least one must be a member of the Malay, Indian or some other minority community, thus ensuring a degree of multi-ethnicity on party slates.[79]

Similar changes in the designs of the electoral system in South Africa in 1994 and later in the Philippines in 1998 have also proved to be successful in encouraging greater representation of different ethnic groups. Other examples of similar exercises are from Fiji and Papua New Guinea where, with a view to developing a 'more aggregative party system', a new system of alternative vote was adopted. In order to promote cross-ethnic parties, definite provisions in the electoral system, requiring parties or individual candidates to garner specified support levels across different regions of a country for getting elected, have also been tried. Some of the successful experiments in this regard include Nigeria, Kenya and Indonesia for the direct election of president and vice-president. But these efforts continue to remain experiments for various reasons. This explains the disagreement amongst scholars and other observers about the impact of such measures, 'with some interpreting them as impotent and even harmful mechanisms which can subvert democratic consolidation, while others seeing them as potentially important mechanisms for muting ethnic conflict and ensuring the election of broad, pan-ethnic presidents'.[80] Requirements of cross-national membership and support have greatly helped reduce the number of contesting parties in Indonesia. Some forty-eight parties had contested the election in 1998, while in 2004 the number dropped to just six.

While analysing the strong points as well as the weaknesses of electoral systems, one needs to bear in mind that there are obvious

---

[79]Benjamin Reilly, '*Political Engineering of Parties and Party Systems*', the text of a speech prepared for delivery at the 2003 Annual Meeting of American Political Science Association. From APSA website at http://www.bt.undp.org/Democracy/Political Engineering.

[80]*Ibid.*

limitations to saying anything in absolute, conclusive terms in this regard. Several factors vary from country to country. While promoting a culture of party coalitions can be considered as a strong point of PR systems, in certain conditions it may prove to be a weakness. As has been discussed earlier, party discipline is important in several respects, but it is also true that it weakens the 'representative' function, causing voters to feel ignored. However, this also can be looked at from a different angle. In October 2002, the ANC, while reviewing the PR system prevailing in South Africa, came out in full support of the existing system and found no fault with party dominance, '[P]olitical parties are the main vehicles for the representation of various interests. The trend is for voters to find a home in the ideology and policies of a particular party and to vote for the party or its candidate at all levels.'[81]

Besides various principal electoral systems such as Pluralist, Majoritarian and PR, other methods for articulating public opinion such as Referendum and Initiative are also important. They too make an impact upon polity in general and political parties in particular. While it is true that Referendum and Initiative are confined largely only to the US, people who have a very frustrating experience of democratic regimes, may soon be tempted to try such devices and hence, one needs to look into their impact on parties. In the context of India, all those who had taken to the streets for the Jan Lokpal Bill in April 2011 were in a way clamouring for some kind of a referendum. Notwithstanding the merits of the methods used by some leaders of the India Against Corruption, Anna Hazare's movement has certainly served as an eye opener, making us realise that India's representative democracy is increasingly being seen as not so representative.

INITIATIVES AND REFERENDUM

Resorting to Initiatives and Referendum is one of the new trends in US politics. It is being considered a threat to meaningful

[81] Discussion document prepared for the National Policy Conference of African National Congress in October 2002 at http://www.anc.org.za/ancdocs/misc/electsub.html.

representative democracy by many. But one must not forget that the degeneration in the quality of representative democracy itself is responsible for the emergence of this trend. Political scientist Joseph F Zimmerman sounds correct when he observes, 'If all elected officers adhere to the highest ethical percepts and are guided only by *res publica* (the public good) and the views of citizenry at large, voters would have no need for corrective devices other than to vote to replace elected officers.'[82] It is believed that in the combination of Initiatives and term limits, what one sees is the clearest expression of revolt against representative government.

In the absence of any ability to mobilise organised opposition on the part of both the political formulations, how a provision for Initiative can be exploited to the hilt is seen from the examples of medical Marijuana Initiatives in the USA. An Initiative proclaiming, 'If you are not suffering from a debilitating illness such as cancer, AIDS or glaucoma, then you cannot use medical marijuana,' was passed in the state of Nevada in the late Nineties. Many political scientists and politicians in the US feel that this device of Initiative was made a part of the Constitution because it was supposed to offer people a way of overriding special-interest groups. But it has turned one-hundred-eighty degrees and now the special-interest groups use the Initiative process for their own purposes. David Broder has succinctly put forth the remedy to this crisis, when he says, 'Admittedly, representative government has acquired a dubious reputation today. But as citizens, the remedy to ineffective representation is in our hands, each Election Day. And whatever its flaws, this Republic has consistently provided a government of laws. To discard it for a system that promises laws without government would be a tragic mistake.'[83] The circulation of a large number of Initiative petitions is an indicator of discontent and protest. The electorate is clearly unhappy due to the sheer disregard of legislative bodies to their concerns.

---

[82] Joseph F Zimmerman, *The Referendum –The People Decide Public Policy*, p. 283.
[83] David S Broder, *Democracy Derailed-Initiative Campaign and the power of money*, p. 242

Quotas

Yet another device which is being employed in several countries with a view to ensuring proportionality in representation, especially for the weaker sections and women, is the quota system. India, like many other countries, has now 30 to 50 per cent seats reserved for women at city and village level bodies. According to a Harvard University research conducted in 2011:

> [A]verage female representation among legislators stands at 22 per cent among countries with any type of gender quota versus 13 per cent in countries without a quota. [84]

The same research has further concluded that quotas have guaranteed an increase in female leadership. While it has significantly improved the disbursal of gender and social justice, it also has its own set of side effects. As observed by a number of municipal councillors in Thane and Mumbai in group interviews and discussions with the author, to a certain extent, quotas also adversely affect the element of accountability. Under the existing quota system in India, which is implemented at the level of municipal corporation or council, constituencies are reserved on a rotation basis. When a constituency is suddenly declared a reserved constituency, the motivation of the incumbent representative to perform vanishes. Often these decisions happen through a lottery system.

Since the objective behind this work is to examine the impact of different models of democracy and electoral systems on political parties, it would be pertinent to enquire as to how direct democracy or methods under it affect political parties. This is crucial because, in the last few decades, direct democracy has become far more popular. The use of referenda has increased and many believe that direct democracy is a panacea for increasing disenchantment with politics, politicians and political parties. According to a study

---

[84] http://www.hks.harvard.edu/fs/rpande/papers/Gender%20Quotas%20-%20April%202011.pdf.

published by *Party Politics*,[85] the widespread impression that direct democracy weakens political parties cannot be generalised and hence is not correct. The study further states, 'In the Swiss case at least, direct democracy should not automatically be held responsible for comparatively weak parties; at least as far as organisational aspects are concerned'.[86] In India, Gram Sabhas at village level and Ward Committees in the municipal corporations are the only meaningful quasi-direct democracy devices that are in use. The Constitution provided for a Gram Sabha after the 73rd Amendment of 1993 was promulgated. Accordingly, the entire population of the village is expected to gather and resolve issues. Unfortunately, these Sabhas have not made any significant impact. According to a study,[87] 25 per cent of the Gram Panchayats in southern India did not hold any Gram Sabhas during the year 2003-04 while a majority of them held just one. The attendance at these meetings, on an average, remained a bare 20 per cent. The level of participation of women was also very low. In Andhra Pradesh, for example, these meetings lasted for barely fifteen-twenty minutes.

About ward committees, it is enlightening to understand the observations of a report prepared for the Ministry of Urban Development, Government of India. The report says, as per section 343-S of the 74th Amendment Act, it is mandatory for the legislature of the State to make provision by the law for constituting ward committees in all metropolitan areas having a population of 3 lakhs or more. However,

- Not all the states have enabling state legislation for constitution of ward committees.
- Not all the cities in states having the legislation, have ward committees.

---

[85] Andreas Ladner and Michael Brandle, 'Does direct democracy matter for political parties?' An Empirical Test in Swiss Cantons, *Party Politics*, Vol.5 No.3, July 1999, p. 302.

[86] *Ibid.*

[87] Based on a study by Vijayendra Rao on the state of Gram Sabhas in four South Indian states at http://ias.berkeley.edu/southasia/democracy07/docs/vrao.ppt.

- Wherever the ward committees are functioning, they are not delegated proper functions and finance.

While quotas help to enhance greater proportionality and the element of social justice, in constituencies that are rotationally being reserved, they do hamper the principle of the elected representative's accountability. The strongest argument in favour of the Westminster model is that it usually brings about a strong one-party government even when no one party has any absolute majority. But then, the Westminster model also invites some kind of a political duopoly, paving the way for 'executive dictatorship'. Several political scientists, including Vernan Bogdanor[88] and others, have supported PR on the count of its ability to encourage power-sharing and consensual politics. It is also considered perfect as far as a true reflection of proportionality of social groups is concerned but then it also brings in greater party control, affecting the representative-constituency relationship.

Plurality systems have some inherent threats. Plurality is likely to lead to a confrontationist approach. In a society where cleavages exist, this system may add to fragmentation. India provides the best example of this where, for electoral purposes regional, religious and sectarian feelings are routinely stoked and vote bank politics is heavily attempted. Organised minorities—under caste and community labels—are made to feel that they are separate from the vast majority and their identities are endangered, hence, they must vote for a particular party. This is true for Muslims, scheduled castes, various OBC groups and communities including Jats, Kurmis, Lingayats and Marathas. In this situation, extreme identity politics is bound to get a fillip, ultimately leading to further fragmentation of the polity.

WANTED: CONSENSUS ON CONSENSUAL DEMOCRACY

Pursuing the path of consensual democracy is the only way to

[88]Vernan Bogdanor is a professor of government at Oxford University, England and a fellow of Brasenose College. He is one of Britain's foremost constitutional experts and has written extensively on political and constitutional issues. He is an advocate of constitutional reform including PR.

overcome this challenge. To do so in fact will be going back to the basics. This is mainly because it has been widely accepted that in the non-Western societies, folk traditions and folk life have always stressed consensus, accommodation and a give-and-take approach. In most of the ancient cultures and societies, including India, consensual democracy was well entrenched in the villages. In fact, the basis of the traditional Indian system of Panchayati Raj also lies in this consensual democracy.[89] Sayings in different Indian languages suggest that when five wise individuals come together and decide (unanimously), it is like a divine decision.[90] This may not be always practicable but the point that 'superiority of headcount' was never an overriding principle of community life in India, is a fact that has been well accepted by the likes of Rupert Emerson. In his *From Empire to Nation*, Emerson has said that the majority's 'right to overrule a dissident minority after a period of debate does violence to conceptions basic to non-Western people.'[91] Accepting that there is a wide-ranging variety between the traditions of African and Asian peoples, 'their native inclination is generally toward extensive and unhurried deliberation aimed at ultimate consensus. The gradual discovery of areas of agreement is the significant feature and not the ability to come to a speedy resolution of issues by counting heads.'[92] Similar observations have also come from Filipino statesman and

[89] There are scores of examples of this consensual democracy in practice. One of them is village Charnaund in Hissar, Haryana, where none of the 1,200 inhabitants has ever approached the police or any court of law for the redressal of any grievance. A dispute is referred to the panchayat. According to the Sarpanch, all members work with a consensual approach. The contentious issues are also resolved with mutual agreement (*The Tribune*, Chandigarh. Nov. 21, 1998). Similarly, there is Samaras Gaon in Gujarat where villagers have unanimously elected a Sarpanch and other office bearers. In 2007, a scheme for promoting conflict-free villages was launched in Maharashtra.

[90] For instance, the famous saying in Marathi: *Panchamukhi Parameshwar* means when five persons collectively think or opine or decide on something, it is like a divine order or decision.

[91] As quoted by Arend Lijphart, *Patterns of Democracy: Government Forms and Performance in Thirty-Six Countries*, p.166.

[92] *Ibid.*

scholar Raul S Manglapus[93] and Nigerian scholar Adebayo Adedeji. Adedeji has said, 'Africans are past masters in consultation, consensus and consent. Our traditions abhor exclusion. Consequently, there is no sanctioned and institutionalised opposition in our traditional system of governance. Traditionally, politics for us has never been a zero-sum game.'[94]

Just as in Africa, traditional societal moorings in India too yearn for a consensus, a spirit of accommodation and a shared ethos. Based on this background, there could be a two-pronged approach: To introduce massive institutional reforms with a view to salvage the existing Westminster model of parliamentary democracy, and a change in the system too should be considered—switching over to the PR system prominently, based on the agenda of public discourse in India.

Unfortunately in India, discussions and debates about the electoral system are rare and peripheral. It is a fact that successive Congress governments at the Centre did not think of reviewing the functioning of the Constitution in a structured manner. The NDA government, led by the BJP thought of it, but the contents of the report submitted in March 2002 were neither seriously discussed nor debated. Several parties opposing the BJP had questioned the government's move of setting up a commission to review the functioning of the Constitution of India. The opposition parties protested against the exercise, calling it unnecessary and expressed doubts about the intentions of the ruling coalition. Some of the non-NDA parties opposed the doing away with the system of No-Confidence Motion, as it formed an effective means of ensuring the day-to-day accountability of the executive to Parliament. Some of them also rejected the idea of having a fixed term for the Lok Sabha (meaning that the lower house cannot be dissolved before

---

[93] In his book *Will of the people: Original Democracy in Non-Western societies,* Raul S Manglapus, (1987,69, 78,82,103,107,123,129) has said, 'the common characteristic (is) the element of consensus as opposed to adversarial decisions'. He also refers to 'concern for Harmony'. He has been quoted by Arend Lijphart, *op.cit.*

[94] *ibid*

the completion of its five year term in any case) on the ground that it would render the elected representatives unaccountable to citizens for the entire period of five years.

Opposition to review the functioning of the Constitution later became more partisan. The Congress and other opposition parties raised a hue and cry in public and on the floor of Parliament that the strategy was a ploy to take away the constitutionally guaranteed rights of the SCs and STs, the OBCs and minority groups in the country. The legislative assembly of the Union Territory of Delhi passed a resolution rejecting the government's programme. The Samajwadi Party and the Republican Party of India viewed it as an insult to Dr B R Ambedkar. The Congress organised huge rallies and meetings on 14 April 2000, which it designated as 'Save the Constitution Day'.

In spite of the inclusion of many non-partisan experts in the commission, the adversaries saw the move only through a biased angle. There has not been any wide-ranging discussion in the public on the question of switching over to any other electoral system. Most of the political parties have either not applied their mind or have refused to come clean on this subject.

Understandably, in an atmosphere like this, no serious debate on the electoral system has taken place. Thankfully, independent organisations like *Janadesh*, Vote India, Lok Satta and Association for Democratic Reforms (ADR) in India are engaged in evolving awareness about the ills of the present electoral system and shaping public opinion for changing it. One can expect that their efforts will ultimately compel intellectuals, academics and also political leaders in the country to think about the matter and at least join the cause, if not accept the demand for a particular systemic change. Unless a strong public discourse is developed on this issue, moving closer to actual change would certainly be difficult.

Appendix F

Uttar Pradesh, 2004: Lok Sabha: Some Key Constituencies

Votes Polled by Winners as Percentage of Electors[95]

Constituency	% Votes	Constituency	% Votes
Bareilly	17.3	Jhansi	15.6
Pilibhit	19.9	Hamirpur	18.6
Shahjahanpur	17.8	Banda	14.4
Kheri	15.6	Fatehpur	12.8
Shahabad	16.7	Chail (SC)	13.2
Sitapur	13.3	Allahabad	15.0
Misrikh (SC)	16.8	Phulpur	18.8
Hardoi (SC)	16.8	Mirzapur	12.4
Lucknow	19.8	Robertsganj (SC)	11.4
Mohanlal Ganj (SC)	11.6	Varanasi	13.9
Unnao	13.7	Chandauli	12.9
Pratapgarh	17.9	Saidpur (SC)	15.1
Sultanpur	17.9	Meerut	19.0
Faizabad	15.6	Bilhaur	16.3
Bara Banki (SC)	16.2	Kanpur	14.8
Kaiserganj	17.3	Farrukhabad	12.9
Bahraich	13.3	Firozabad (SC)	16.3
Gonda	18.1	Agra	17.0
Basti (SC)	11.0	Mathura	14.7
Domariaganj	15.0	Hathras (SC)	14.4
Khalilabad	16.8	Aligarh	12.5
Bansgaon (SC)	12.5	Khurja (SC)	14.7
Maharajganj	17.4	Hapur	13.0
Padrauna	13.8	Jaunpur	14.5
Deoria	15.1	Machhilishahar	16.1

[95] Arun Shourie, *The Parliamentary System* p. 34.

CHAPTER 7

Breaking the Vicious Circle through Reforms

More than sixty years after India became a republic, we have succeeded fairly in sustaining representative democracy. However, it is imperative that we revisit the premises, review the progress, analyse our strengths and weaknesses too, and plan for necessary reforms. Lest status-quo-ism grip our thinking, we must audit the performance of our democratic system.

The objective of the entire analysis so far has been to find out some systemic methods to overcome the challenges before our democratic polity, more particularly that before our parties. All through the discussion, the focus obviously has remained on the twin issues of populism and electoral compulsions. Hence, when one talks of breaking the vicious circle through systemic reforms, the solutions are also majorly concerned with liberating political parties from the lure of populism and electoral compulsions.

Normally, any discussion about political parties in India unfolds on expected lines, ending up with underscoring the bankruptcy of our political leadership. However, we are purposely looking at political parties in India as victims of circumstances, taking their genuine aspiration for providing good governance for granted.

It is easy to paint the politicians dark but what is more important is to examine the reasons behind the degeneration of political parties in India and suggest ways and means to prevent it. Undoubtedly, the problems being faced by India as a democratic polity could be resolved by adopting multiple measures. Focused reforms, with a clear objective and a strong political will to implement them, are central to all these efforts.

Revisiting the Questions

At the beginning of the book, we had posed a set of questions. Before the discussion moves to solutions through reforms, it would be pertinent to revisit those queries.

Are political parties in India really in the grip of populist politics? Have they become wanton victims of electoral compulsions? Are political parties as democratic institutions declining?

Most of the parties in India are, indeed, entangled in the web of populist politics. Party leaders are aware that populism is ruining party politics and thereby the democratic process and yet, no serious attempts have been made to come out of this trap. They are also conscious about the lack of serious efforts for party-building and functioning. Earnest measures for party building are, more often than not, pushed to the back burner as elections—to state assemblies in one state or the other—are held almost every year. Also, there appears to be an unarticulated conviction that elections can be won through 'technique', even if the basic organisational network is absent. Electoral success has replaced the ideological objective of sustained party activity. Besides, with winning elections overriding all other aspects of party life, there is hardly any 'felt need' for genuine measures to strengthen internal democracy.

Let us examine the sets of questions in the light of the discussions in the previous chapters. One has to start with: How is party decline likely to affect the ability to deliver on the part of democratic governance? Will it also affect popular faith in democracy?

Parties decline when they lose their distinct identity. Factors such as erosion of distinct ideological and policy positions have greatly contributed to the process of party decline, not only in India but also in several established democracies. As a consequence, the party cadre is unaware and unconvinced about the basic purpose of their party and its politics. This has led to growing similarities between parties, reducing, in effect, the choice available to the voters. As is obvious, when parties profess a distinct ideology, voters get to select between say yellow, green, blue and red. But when parties start behaving alike, voters are constrained to select between yellow, yellow and yellow again. This almost negates the very element of choice, which is so very central to the idea of democracy. When parties fail to offer any distinct option, democracy becomes a form without substance. This further adds to the all-pervading cynicism, which is harmful for the popular faith in democracy.

Why do Indians have a peculiar love-hate relationship with politicians? Is their mindset governing this relationship a cause of or a consequence of 'politics of patronage' leading to populism?

At the macro level, many people in the country hate politicians. But at the micro level, the same people try and seek a slice of the patronage cake that a politician can offer. Politics of patronage is thriving because politicians consider it easy to offer small, timely and at times illegal favours to individuals and groups of people rather than make any systemic changes. Shrewd politicians bank upon popular complacency and devise a strategy to sustain it. Besides, people are scared of the nuisance value of a politician. They know that a politician perhaps may not help them, but they also know that politicians are powerful enough to harm them. This leaves all the bigger issues of fundamental democratic rights almost unattended. From littérateurs to artistes, economists to technocrats, thinkers to educationists, all blame politicians and many a time relish ridiculing them. They rarely make any serious attempt to analyse the situation and find methodical ways to combat it.

Could political parties in India be saved from succumbing to populist pressures and electoral compulsions? Would the political class accept such solutions? Is the overall absence of any structured efforts to salvage party politics in India from its present mould, a result of inertia and helplessness?

Political parties could certainly be saved from populist pressures and electoral compulsions through a slew of systemic reforms. Except for a section of political leaders who have developed a vested interest in continuing with the status quo, a majority of the politicians feel that systemic changes are required. Not too long ago, political parties showed rare unanimity on the question of creating the three new states of Uttarakhand, Jharkhand and Chhattisgarh. They were also unanimous in passing the 91st Amendment[1], limiting the strength of the Cabinet. These are the two noteworthy examples of how political parties can bring in effective changes, provided there is a will to do so.

The tendency to succumb to populist pressures, with power-seeking becoming the principal purpose, party building continues to be neglected all along. We have also seen how the politics of compromises has heralded an erosion of the party leadership's moral authority. There are scores of examples suggesting how the inability of weak leaders to withstand populist pressures has led to a poor quality of governance. Needless to elaborate, all this has validated the basic premise talked about at the beginning of this work.

Populism thrives because of several reasons. However, it cannot be denied that people, their understanding, awareness or the lack of it plays an important role in the political process that gives a fillip to populism. Likewise, it is an established fact that electoral compulsions are mainly the creation of systems that have been adopted. Both these factors cannot entirely, and in every situation, be ascribed to political leaders. True, that politicians, and more particularly parties, can do a number of things to check populism, but it is certainly not the making of the political class alone. Today, parties are more forcefully driven by survival instincts than the actual will to work for people's welfare. Most of the factors that have contributed to this degeneration of political parties are embedded in

[1]On 7 July 2004 the 91st Amendment to the Constitution, limiting the size of the Council of Ministers at the Centre and the states to no more than 15 per cent of the numbers in the Lok Sabha or the State Legislature, came into effect.

the system itself, and it is this very system that creates a powerful inertia which ultimately prevents even simple reforms.

Innumerable examples suggest that parties wantonly walk into the trap of populism and electoral compulsions. Often, they refuse to look at the big picture and compromise on the fundamentals of representative democracy. Largely, it is myopia and lack of seriousness about the entire democratic process that are at the root of this situation. Parties find an escape route because of the flawed systems that contribute to the process of democracy's perversion. While looking into the systemic solutions, the objective is to generate a discussion about the ways and means of plugging this escape route. Once this is done, parties could be held squarely responsible and that may pave the way for reforming the party system and thereby prevent the degeneration of the political culture in India. This may reinstate the credibility of the political class and eventually restore the confidence of the people in India's democratic system.

Challenges Ahead

Reform is an essential element of democratic governance. But as it has been experienced, to introduce one is easier said than done. Reforms are an indicator of a progressive polity, and yet they are always difficult to come about. When even simple procedural amendments are difficult, it is obviously hard to bring any changes in the form of democracy or in the electoral system. Normally, politicians find comfort in status-quo-ism and hence, there is a fundamental reluctance towards course correction.

Besides, it is extremely complex under any constitution to switch over to another electoral system, once a particular method is already in practice. Implementation of reforms requires a strong political will. A strong desire to pursue reforms on the part of a leader is imperative. Only such a leader can plan a clear strategy and work on it ceaselessly. In the context of India, unless the political leadership accepts that systemic changes are necessary and develops a strong political will, the process of thinking about them will never get the requisite momentum. Again, it will require courage of conviction to pursue an agenda for reforms.

Against this background, it is noteworthy that politicians in India have never shown the requisite keenness to review the present constitutional framework and if necessary, bring in substantial changes. As has been said earlier, an attempt to review the functioning of the Constitution itself was publicly opposed. Political parties raised doubts about this exercise of the NDA government between 1999-2004.[2] Voicing apprehensions about the motives of the government, the CPI (M)[3] commented, 'It (the NDA Government) is going ahead with setting up of a Commission to review the Constitution, which is just a device for proposing changes in the secular character of the Constitution and for replacing the parliamentary system with a presidential form of government'. Politicians, who unmistakably swear by the Constitution and warn against reviewing its functioning, forget that even Dr Babasaheb Ambedkar, the architect of the Indian Constitution, had repudiated not just the claim to having authored the document, but the Constitution itself.[4]

This resistance to the introduction of some basic reforms in the constitutional framework is universal. Bill Clinton, in one of his observations about Lani Guinier, an ardent advocate of the Proportional Representation system in the US, had said the latter's advocacy of PR was 'very difficult to defend' and even 'undemocratic'.[5]

---

[2]This exercise on the 'Review of the Constitution' was in the eye of a controversy and had invited diverse opinions from varied quarters. Then President KR Narayanan had cautioned the government against 'revising' the Constitution or the parliamentary form of government and categorically stated that the Constitution has not failed us; rather we have failed the Constitution. This was followed by a clarification from the government that the proposed review would be very much within the framework of the parliamentary form of government and that the basic features of the Constitution would be out of its purview. Fierce opposition to the proposed review from some sources was based on the standpoint that the commission was simply a platform of the government for giving shape to its covert agenda.

[3]From the CPI(M) web site, http://www.cpim.org/.

[4]As quoted by Arun Shourie, *The Parliamentary System*, p.18.

[5]As quoted by Arend Lijphart, Patterns of Democracy: Government Forms and Performance in Thirty-Six countries, p.81., originally from *New York Times*, June 4 1993.

Although reforms are hard to come about, they are integral to any living society and polity. There are many instances in which nations have opted for a particular form of democracy and subsequently switched over to the other. In neighbouring Sri Lanka, several experiments were tried during the last three decades. Starting from a pluralist electoral system at the time of Independence in 1947 to executive presidency and PR in 1978, and to the present combination of run-off and preferential voting for the election of a president, Sri Lanka has come a long way. In far-off Australia too, parties and politicians have experimented with a variety of voting systems that they believed would advance popular democracy and pragmatic politics. Between 1911 and 1962, Australia introduced major reforms in their electoral system. Compulsion in the enrolment of voters was introduced in 1911, while FPTP was replaced with preferential voting for the House in 1918 and for the senate in 1919. In 1948, PR was introduced for the Senate.

Long Overdue Reforms

Political scientists and observers believe that India has chosen a sort of stability over growth. According to the Indian-born British economist, Meghnad Desai, 'To stay a peaceful and stable society India has to be a muddle and mess'. Quoting him, an article in *The Economist* commented,[6] 'A nation with more than a billion people, 29 states enjoying considerable autonomy, 33 major languages and 1650 dialects and six major religions, one of which is Islam followed by 13% of people, understandably, has to put staying together above everything. A slow moving but flexible democracy is the only way of holding all this together' (sic).

With changing times, people have become restive. They are not happy with just 'holding together' and are craving for change. This is reflected in noted industrialist Rahul Bajaj's write-up, which appeared in a major English daily in 2006. According to him, India requires both political and economic reforms together: 'Unless either

---

[6]As quoted in *The Economist*, London, 5 March 2005.p.15

of the two major political parties has at least 200 plus seats and coalition government has a majority in the Lok Sabha, the political system will continue to neglect the economy. Short-term political expediency and crisis management would absorb most of the energies of the government.'[7]

Several others have also stressed the need for political reforms. After half a century of the attainment of Independence and having given the present constitution a chance, it is worthwhile to ponder as to where we are exactly headed. As pointed out by many pro-reform thinkers at the National Seminar on Electoral Reforms held in Kolkata in 2001, the fact that, as 'We the people' have failed in achieving the goals set by the makers of the Constitution, what is needed is a fresh look at the present system. It is imperative to take a step further and examine factors that have led to this situation.[8] Many concur with this conclusion. The founder chairman of the software giant Infosys, NR Narayana Murthy, in December 2005, gave vent to his agony, saying that we require reforms since 'our institutions—from Parliament and legislatures to courts and distribution systems—have become pervaded with corruption.'[9]

As a consequence, popular faith in democracy is fast on the wane. An all-pervading cynicism has resulted in an absolute lack of popular initiative. A sense of utter contempt, almost bordering on a deep-seated hatred of the political class is visible when citizens voice their opinions. Jagdeep S Chhokar, a senior activist of the Association of Democratic Reforms, has quoted from a letter to the editor, after the general elections in 1999, which says:

> Thank God! The verbal cacophony, throwing of abuses and trading of charges by political parties with each

[7]Rahul Bajaj, 'Reforms take a back seat' in *The Times of India*, Mumbai, 20 January 2006, p.30.

[8]On the basis of the views expressed by the participants at the National Seminar on Electoral Reforms, held in Kolkata under the aegis of the Ministry of Culture, Government of India, in September 2001.

[9]NR Narayana Murthy's speech as reported in *The Times of India*, Mumbai, 29 December 2005. p.15.

> other is over...what democratic values this bunch of self-appointed leaders will propagate with such narrow-minded approaches? Our democracy ends the day we cast our vote...no wonder people showed fatigue and displayed lack of enthusiasm in the type of democratic exercise now repeatedly held to elect the begging candidates so that on being elected they can sit in power and loot us, and amass wealth and power for their dynasties (sic).[10]

Another instance of this discomfiture with the political machinery is available from the folk traditions of Maharashtra. A ballad, originally sung in a folk theatre programme named *Bapacha Bap*, in 1956, makes fun of the entire political class. The narrative suggests that God had once wrongfully sent a brainless creature to earth and how he became a political leader. These examples are a true reflection of utter public disdain about the entire electoral process that has singularly occupied centre stage in our democracy.

Unfortunately, widespread disdain about politicians has acquired centrality in public discourse too. In the April 2011 agitation led by Anna Hazare, ridiculing politicians had become a favourite pastime. While politicians have to seriously look into the reasons behind this widespread indifference, others must understand that mere disdain can take us nowhere. Practically, at all levels, this situation has generated a crisis of motivation and leadership. In this context I am reminded of an anecdote. In 2007, a group of newly-elected members of municipal corporations in Mumbai, Pune and Sholapur shared their experiences with me.[11] In the run up to the elections of the municipal corporations and district councils (Zilla Parishads) in Maharashtra, political parties had to organise stage performances by bar-girls in several districts like Ahmednagar, in order to ensure attendances at public meetings. In the cities,

[10] Jagdeep S Chhokar, *Electoral Reforms: Law Commission's Recommendations*, p.8.

[11] Based on a group discussion in Mumbai on 5 July, 2007 with the newly elected members of municipal corporations in Mumbai, Thane, Pune, Sholapur and other cities.

members of housing societies collectively and brazenly bargained for the repair of compound wall or similar sops, while one Municipal Corporation sitting member said, he had to outsmart his rival by actually completing the work of paving the courtyard of a housing society where the voters were preparing to auction their votes en bloc. These are all symptoms of erosion of popular faith in democratic values and by implication, the democratic system.

Several observers from abroad too believe that introducing reforms is the only way to salvage the situation. According to British political scientist Peter S Lyon, we (Indians) essentially have to do away with the populist character of parliamentary democracy by cleansing the entire body politic. Many have opined that parties in India must tighten their formal control and revitalise their organisations. Party operators and power brokers must not be given any patronage at all. If this is not done, the next generation will get more disillusioned.

A discussion about political reforms in India is not new. Many have advocated multiple reforms on several occasions in the past. Way back in 1981, Krishan Kant, a senior political leader who later became India's vice-president, had observed: While in the Fifties an MP or an MLA was considered as a representative of the people, in the Sixties they came to be known as their advocates and now people think that 'they elect their *dalal*s, or brokers'.[12] Krishan Kant is not the only one who chose not to mince his words. When the Centenary Session of the Indian National Congress was held in Mumbai in 1985, Rajiv Gandhi, the then prime minister and party president, had used the same term and denounced the tendency of party workers to function as power-brokers. As pointed out by Harold Laski, leaders of parties cannot escape the blame. In his *Grammar of Politics*, Laski has observed that the parliamentary leader has become 'submissive', instead of remaining 'authoritative'. He is a tool in the hands of power brokers.[13]

---

[12]Krishan Kant, 'The Present System, Its Central Point of Rot and Resurgence' (The text of GV Mavlankar Memorial Lecture delivered by him in 1981) p.5.

[13]As quoted by Rafiq Zakaria, 'Save India from this democracy', *The Asian Age*, Mumbai, 29 January 2003.

Krishan Kant had correctly diagnosed what ails our electoral system. According to him, there was an urgent need 'to break nexus between the individual and the constituency',[14] because of the fact that the present...

> ...election process has established and consolidated such individuals and interest groups all over the country. A party today is a loose alliance of such interest groups without any genuine commitment to ideology or national programme. Any individual, in order to get elected, has to play their game. This has divided the polity in such a manner that we have now dominant, corrupt social and political elite on one side and the people on the other. There is complete alienation between the two. This has led to uncontrolled corruption on the one hand and growing social tension on the other.[15]

WHY DID WE OPT FOR THE WESTMINSTER MODEL?

The question—whether India will adopt the parliamentary model or otherwise—was settled in 1928. The Motilal Nehru Committee set up by the All Parties Conference recommended, among other things, a parliamentary and federal structure for the government. It is a fact that when the Constituent Assembly of India decided to opt for the Westminster model and parliamentary democracy, some members like Brajeshwar Prasad[16] had opposed this step, describing it as being outdated. Again, between 1947 and 1949, the Constituent Assembly deliberated at length and considered the suggestion that India should adopt its ancient models[17] and modify them suitably while

---

[14]Krishan Kant, *op.cit*,p.10.

[15]*Ibid.*

[16]Constituent Assembly of India debates at http://parliamentofindia.nic.in/ls/debates/vol7p5b.htm.

[17]In his essay, 'Democracy in Ancient India', Steve Muhlberger, Associate Professor of History, Nipissing University, has referred to 'government by discussion' as one of the popular models of democracy in ancient India.

deciding about the political choices. However, traditionalists were greatly outnumbered by the opponents and it was forcefully argued that 'the only relevant experience India had at systematic political organisation as a nation was that of parliamentary democracy. Earlier experience was far too vague and fragmentary to draw upon.'[18] Political correctness, perhaps, dominated both the discussion and the decision. Some members of the Constituent Assembly did not forget to state that India should be adopting democratic institutions without compromising with our 'Indianness' and the country should accept every technique the modern world can offer to keep itself Indian.[19]

According to jurist MC Chagla, the preference for the Parliamentary democracy...

> ...was mainly due to (1) before independence we had been working through our Legislatures, both at the Centre and in the States more or less on the British model and so we were accustomed to the practices and conventions of that system and (2) an elected president as the head of the executive was too reminiscent of the kings and emperors who had ruled us in the past.[20]

In reality, however, with several hereditary politicians lining up, we often end up electing what Patrick French has described as a *Vansh Sabha,* instead of a true Lok Sabha.

INADEQUACY OF THE WESTMINSTER MODEL

Worried about the inherent weaknesses of the Westminster model and the parliamentary system under it, veteran politicians and thinkers

[18]Rajni Kothari, *Politics in India* p.102.

[19]*Ibid.* p.103.

[20]MC Chagla, in a broadcast on *Constitutional Aspect of Parliamentary Government*, on AIR on 16 January, 1973, as quoted by Jaswant B Mehta, in *Presidential System: A better alternative*, p.8.

like Rafiq Zakaria, have almost written off the present system. According to him:

> [The parliamentary system] might have served well in a country like Britain which is mature and highly experienced in parliamentary norms and practices, but for India it has become a curse. It should be scrapped if India is to be saved. I think our founding fathers committed the greatest blunder in adopting it; the parliamentary system has produced most of our ills. It is the *Gangotri* of corruption.[21]

The expectations from political parties in the West European countries and in countries like India vary greatly. Many believe that political parties as envisaged under the Westminster model fulfill the requirements of democracies in the West. However, the Westminster model cannot effectively deal with the problems that arise in countries like India and hence, the political leadership in these countries fails in dealing with them. Popular expectations in India are much higher than the sphere of usual activity of a political party as understood in Great Britain, from where this institution has been borrowed by us.

HISTORY OF THE EFFORTS FOR REFORMS

In so far as reforms are concerned, the track record of India is far from reassuring. Differences in all spheres are sharp and basic. In addition, the virus of populism also has cast its thick shadow on any discussion about reforms. Thanks to populism, any attempt to even remotely suggest the overhauling of our system is seen as tampering with what they call the 'basic principles of our Constitution'. In 1999, the way in which the NDA government's initiative for reviewing the functioning of the Constitution through a National Commission headed by Justice Venkatchalliah was opposed, has been explained earlier. Besides, it is also a fact that the report failed in attracting the attention that it deserved. The Government itself chose to put it

[21] Rafiq Zakaria, *op.cit.*

up only on the Internet. The first-ever serious attempt to review the Constitution not only remained abortive, but it also failed to generate any further discussion on its recommendations.

While numerous reforms are essential for an effective overhaul of our system, only those that will have a direct or indirect bearing on the functioning of our political parties and, thereby the democratic system, need to be focused.

Broadly, these changes include constitutional, electoral, political party and attitudinal reforms.

Reforms to Meet the Challenge of Political Instability

Sixty-five years after Independence, there is an urgent need for reviewing the functioning of India's Constitution. It is a fact that it is one of the most amended Constitutions of the world. It has been amended 99 times and the actual number of articles has gone up to 447 from 395, while that of schedules to 12 from 8.

Defections and the no-confidence motions tabled in an irresponsible manner are the two principal reasons for volatility. A comprehensive anti-defection law was first enacted in 1985 with a view to preventing political defections and to plug the loopholes. It was subsequently amended in 2003. Even after these enactments, unfortunately, defections have continued unabatedly. This ground reality has prompted many, like renowned journalist Inder Jit and Justice Rajinder Sachar, to demand a total ban on any kind of defections. Describing any defection as a rape of democracy, in a strongly-worded observation, Inder Jit says, 'A new and simple legislation should be enacted to punish not only an individual rape but also gang rape'.[22] Rajinder Sachar advocates the same, demanding 'a simple provision that if a legislator, either of a state assembly or of the Lok Sabha, having been elected on the ticket of a party joins another political party, his seat will automatically

---

[22]Inder Jit in Subhash Kashyap (Ed.) *National Resurgence through Electoral Reforms*, p.140.

stand vacated'.[23] Sachar further observes that such disqualification should not be attached only to the disobedience of party whip. Except for a confidence motion or the money bill, 'the member's right of free speech and voting should be protected'.[24] Yet another suggestion for the effective prevention of political defections is the 'right to recall', which exists in some of the states in the US and which was strongly advocated by Jayaprakash Narayan (JP). However, there are very obvious practical difficulties in introducing this system, which, many believe, may prove to be costlier than the ailment itself.

Defections erode the emotional bonds within an organisation and diminish the role of ideology. Earlier, most of the political parties were born out of a social or political movement. It was during these movements that activists used to develop camaraderie and fellow feeling. Today, precious little has remained in a political party that could bind an individual, making the very thought of defection dreadful for him. Nuances of the styles of functioning shape the organisational ethos of a party. This ethos determines the culture. At present, most of the major political parties have a similar organisational culture, hence no political party is truly alien to a politician. This factor certainly has made defections much easier.

In this context, it is noteworthy to look into the recommendations of the National Commission to Review the Working of the Constitution (2001). The Commission has clearly said that:

> The provisions of the Tenth Schedule of the Constitution should be amended specifically to provide that all persons defecting—whether individually or in groups—from the party or the alliance of parties, on whose ticket they had been elected, must resign from their parliamentary or assembly seats and must contest fresh elections. In other words, they should lose their membership and the protection under the provision of split, etc., should be scrapped.

---

[23] Rajinder Sachar, in Subhash Kashyap (Ed.) *op.cit*, p.129.
[24] *Ibid.*

> The defectors should also be debarred to hold any public office of a minister or any other remunerative political post for at least the duration of the remaining term of the existing legislature or until the next fresh elections, whichever is earlier. The vote cast by a defector to topple a government should be treated as invalid.

The Commission further recommends that 'the power to decide on questions as to disqualification on ground of defection should vest in the Election Commission, instead of in the Chairman or Speaker of the House concerned.'[25]

This disease of defection has always been a part of spirited discussions. However, the point often missed in such discussions is that at times, individuals are forced to defect for want of any space to voice their view, which may be contrary to the official view of the party. Undemocratic and irresponsible ways of conducting party affairs give a fillip to such tendencies. One cannot be unmindful of the fact that an elected representative also has his personal opinion and a party whip need not always bind him/her on each and every issue. In this context, suggestions pertaining to limiting the issuance of party whip merits discussion within the parties.

As a part of measures to overcome instability, it has often been suggested that the German system be emulated. Only such no-confidence motions should be allowed, wherein a motion of confidence for an alternate leader is built-in. When the government, under AB Vajpayee, lost in the Lok Sabha just by a single vote in 1998, this suggestion was discussed widely. The National Commission to Review the Working of the Constitution has also supported this alternative. The Commission has recommended an amendment in the Rules of Procedure for adoption of a system of constructive vote of no-confidence. It has also suggested that, 'For a motion of no-

[25]Report of the National Commission to Review the Working of the Constitution (Chapter 4, paragraph 4.18.1) at http://lawmin.nic.in/ncrwc/finalreport/v 1ch4. htm.

confidence to be brought out against a government, at least 20% of the total number of members of the House should give notice. Also, the motion should be accompanied by a proposal of alternative Leader to be voted simultaneously' (sic).[26]

Taking a cue from similar provisions in the French constitution, the fifteenth Law Commission has recommended in its 170th report[27] that a Constitutional Amendment be introduced, making it mandatory that any motion of no-confidence in the Lok Sabha should be accompanied by a motion of confidence in an alternate candidate (as Prime Minister). It has also suggested that once a motion of no-confidence or confidence has been discussed, no such motions should be allowed for a period of at least two years. From political analyst Dorab Sopariwala to senior BJP leaders like LK Advani, many have advocated the introduction of this provision for a 'Constructive Vote of No-Confidence'.

Of late there has also been a discussion about setting and ensuring some fixed term for Lok Sabha and state assemblies to ward off the threats to the stability of the incumbent government. A suggestion pertaining to constitutional provisions ensuring mandatory holding of simultaneous elections to the Lok Sabha and the state assemblies also made the rounds a few years ago. Bhairon Singh Shekhawat, the then Vice-President of India, and LK Advani had publicly mooted this idea that was endorsed by former Governor

---

[26] *Ibid* Chapter 4, paragraph 4.33.3

[27] Law Commission (170th) Report says, 'In our opinion, a new rule, Rule 198A should be introduced in the Rules of Procedure and Conduct of Business in the Lok Sabha providing that—'Rule 198-A (1) Once a no-confidence motion is taken up for discussion and voted upon as contemplated by sub-rules (3) and (4) of Rule 198, no fresh motion expressing want of confidence in the Council of Ministers shall be permitted to be made for a period of two years from the date of voting upon such motion.' Rule 198—(1) Once a no-confidence motion is taken up for discussion and voted upon as contemplated by sub-rules(3) and (4) of Rule 198, no fresh motion expressing want of confidence in such Council of Ministers shall be permitted to be moved for a period of two years. (3) No leave shall be granted under Rule 198 to a motion expressing want of confidence in the Council of Ministers, unless it is accompanied by a motion expressing confidence in a named individual. Only the motion expressing confidence in a named individual shall be put to vote.'.

of Maharashtra, PC Alexander. In an article written in 2003, Alexander demanded, 'The change in the election system should ensure that the citizen going to the polling booth can cast his votes for all the three tiers of representative government on the same day.'[28] He advocates this idea of simultaneous elections mainly to save on the huge expenditure that India, as a nation, has to incur for our elaborate electoral exercises.

Some experts have also advocated a switchover to the presidential system. Political scientists like Ramesh Babu recommend the presidential system mainly for the 'calendar stability' of the duly elected government. Besides, according to him, 'Since the President and the Vice-President are in effect elected by the whole country, national political integration can be achieved more quickly and in a more dynamic fashion... .'[29] Rafiq Zakaria has also strongly advocated this move. Under the presidential system, the 'chances of rogues and rascals getting into either legislature or government are minimal.'[30] Among other things, Zakaria also believes that the separation of powers in the presidential system is far better than what we have in the parliamentary system.

But one should not lose sight of the weaknesses inherent in the presidential system. Also, there is a powerful and convincing argument that since we are more familiar with the parliamentary system, it is much easier to introduce reforms in it than to move on to something new, which we have never experimented with.

In order to prevent the domination of crass populist tendencies, leading to a tyranny of the majority, political scientist Jurg Steiner has suggested practising 'amicable agreement' in place of the decision by a majority. In Switzerland, there is a strong and time-tested tradition of taking all interests into account while deciding on a particular issue, along with the formal majority voting.

---

[28]PC Alexander, 'A Case for Simultaneous Elections', *The Asian Age*, Mumbai. 26 June, 2003.

[29]B Ramesh Babu, *Thoughts on the American Presidential System and its Relevance to India*, p.21.

[30] Rafiq Zakaria, *op.cit.*

Resolving a matter amicably through compromises and making the proposition acceptable to all parties is at the core of this procedure. Such initiatives should be studied in depth and a replicable model must be evolved.

Against this background, the following measures are suggested:

- Defections at every level, and whether that of an individual or a group, should be banned, making vacation of seat by the defector mandatory. Even for an independent candidate, switching loyalties once declared should attract disqualification.
- A system of constructive vote of no-confidence should be introduced.
- A system of recognising only a pre-poll alliance should be in place. Issuing a joint public-declaration explaining the objectives of the alliance and the nature of understanding with a clear provision for dissolution under specific circumstances should be made mandatory. All post-poll alliances should be primarily considered illegal. The Election Commission of India should have the discretion of allowing such alliances, only when there is a constitutional deadlock and only after filing due affidavits about the common minimum programme and common policy perspectives.

Electoral Reforms

There are two distinct aspects of electoral reforms. To explore the possibility of extensive changes in the overall conduct of elections under the present FPTP system, it is also important to discuss the possibility of adapting other available alternatives like PR.

Discussions, reports and research projects on comprehensive electoral reforms have touched upon a whole gamut of issues.[31]

[31]This includes the reports submitted by the VM Tarkunde Committee (1974-75), Dinesh Goswami Committee (1990) Justice VR Krishna Iyer Committee (1994) and the 170th Report on the Law Commission on 'Reforms of the Electoral Law' (1999).

Unfortunately, very little of what they have suggested has been implemented. Considering the scope of this book, the analysis here is limited only to such factors that have contributed to the technique-orientation, which is inherent to the entire electoral process. These factors range from the use of money and muscle power, manoeuvring tactics leading towards a strategic division of opposition votes to routinely adopting propaganda tricks.

Winning elections has become a technique mainly because of an elected representative's understandable attempt to reduce the volatility of the electoral situation. An aspirant works to this end, starting from ensuring party nomination or re-nomination. Although the relevance of political parties is consistently diminishing in the period between two elections, party labels still carry importance at the time of elections. Today, party nominations are decided in an arbitrary way and there are allegations about auctions of party nominations. Taking advantage of this process, leaders wantonly promote a culture of sycophancy, reducing objectivity in candidate selection. That the nomination-seekers go to any extent for winning the hearts of selectors goes without saying. All this has greatly contributed to making this process absolutely opaque, and at times, influenced by extra-political reasons.

An overall democratisation of party functioning is essential in order to reduce the effect of this unreasonable exercise.

Here comes the question of laying down proper procedures for selecting aspirants. In this context, what the Conservative Party in UK had established in 1948 is perhaps worth emulating. On the basis of what is known as The Maxwell Fyfe Committee's[32] report, the Conservative Party in the UK laid down specific grounds for the selection of candidates, the list for which started with 'personal character'.

---

[32]This committee had suggested a Standing Committee to assess a candidate on the following grounds:

1. Personal character. 2. Party loyalty. 3. Past record and experience. 4. Political knowledge. 5. Speaking ability and 6. Financial arrangements. (For reference, AG Noorani, *India's Constitution and Politics*, p.505.

Vote bank politics is basically played on two counts. It ensures that the community to which a candidate belongs, votes en bloc in support of the respective candidate. It also guarantees that the votes of other communities are effectively fragmented. To secure the first aspect of making a community vote en bloc, identity issues come handy. From a Common Civil Code to quota for Muslims, the Congress has always refused to take a genuinely secular position on such matters, mainly because of the apprehension of losing the support of the Muslims. As a result, the Vishwa Hindu Parishad[33] mooted the idea of creating a Hindu vote bank to counter the attempts of the Congress. Concern for losing the OBC vote bank is the real cause of the brouhaha created by a section of politicians on the issue of quotas for OBCs.

Since identity issues are a part of societal life, it is hard to ensure that they are not touched upon in an electoral campaign. The least that can be done to prevent competitive de-secularisation of electoral politics is to stop emotive and identity issues from dominating electoral campaigns. To this end, serious attempts should be made to educate the voters about matters that concern their welfare. At the municipal level, vote bank politics is also played by giving protection to unauthorised slums. Reforms in municipal administration can prevent all this. For example, the system can make the officials accountable for a vacant piece of land where the threat of unauthorised occupation is always alive. While humanitarian considerations may not allow this to happen, it is worth considering a denial of voting rights to all those who are not legal occupants of their place of residence.

To reduce the local electoral malpractices, it is crucial to introduce extensive reforms in campaigns. Starting from the process of voter registration, the entire exercise of the elections should be monitored. This may also help to overcome the pressures of electability which undermine the element of a candidate's competence.

[33] http://www.hindu.com/2006/02/09/stories/2006020905531200.htm for a news item quoting Pravin Togadia of the VHP on the Hindu vote bank.

Irregularities in voters' lists leave scope for manipulations. False voting or impersonation is the starting point of all possible misdeeds. A post-poll survey conducted by the Hyderabad based *Lok Satta Times* in 2001 pointed out that up to 21 per cent of the votes cast may have been bogus.[34] The demands of organisations like *Lok Satta* merit serious attention at the national level. These involve making the voter identity cards mandatory. Although this has been done partly, existing rules need to be firmly implemented. The organisation has also demanded conducting a re-poll in a situation where the tendered votes in a polling station exceed 1 per cent of the valid votes.

With an alert and proactive Election Commission of India, an element of deterrence seems to have been effectively introduced. No matter how vigilant these authorities may become, unless individuals and citizen groups come forward, illegal deeds supported by money and muscle power may not be curbed absolutely. It is true that electoral malpractices and irregularities may not guarantee success in an election. But it is equally true that the incapacity to muster money and muscle power may lead to defeat for sure. This situation has already forced law-abiding citizens to abandon the political arena, leaving the field open for anti-social and unscrupulous elements.

Measures such as the Code of Conduct of the Election Commission of India have been in vogue for quite some time. While the focus of this Code of Conduct is mainly on preventing the use of public money or facilities for partisan purposes, that itself is not enough. With a more positive and truly democratic approach, the following measures, with a clear focus on educating the masses and bringing transparency, could be introduced:

- Giving incentives to the elected representatives for filing a report to the electorate and publishing it every year.
- The details of candidates' assets must be published in

[34] *Lok-Satta Times*, Hyderabad, Jan-Feb. 2001

the local newspapers and should be aired on local TV channels.

- Mandatory publication of a manifesto by contesting parties at respective levels followed by a compulsory Action Taken Report (ATR) on the manifestos by every political party. Even parties that have lost the elections could be asked to give information about their efforts to follow up on their promises.
- Mandatory publication of a constituency manifesto by each contesting candidate in every election at all levels, followed by a publication of an annual ATR.

Many believe that providing state funds for electoral campaigns could effectively prevent the growing influence of money power. TN Seshan,[35] former Chief Election Commissioner of India, had supported this idea. In the Nineties, the Inderjit Gupta Committee[36] too had recommended partial state assistance to the parties, initially to be given in kind. The committee also suggested the creation of a separate election fund through the contributions of central as well as state governments.

Ensuring genuine representativeness as an outcome of the election process and reducing the fragmentation of polity is the other area in which the fifteenth Law Commission of India has made a set of suggestions in its 170th report, which was submitted in 1999. As observed by one of the leading lights of the ADR, Jagdeep Chhokar, the politicians in the present system are dividing society and thereby, the nation, simply because it gets them elected. And they have been doing so by continuing to split political parties into smaller factions, thereby also fragmenting the electorate and

[35]TN Seshan, 'I vouch for Indian democracy', *The Indian Express*, Mumbai, 22 March 2004, p.8.

[36]Inderjit Gupta Committee on state funding of elections presented its report to the government in 1998. The report suggested state funding to the parties in the form of kind rather than cash and among its recommendations was the allocation of ₹600 crore each, both by the Centre and collectively by the state governments for funding elections.

the polity at large. This fragmentation of the polity seems to call for the replacement of the phrase 'Unity in Diversity' with 'utility in diversity', at least for the politicians.[37]

Statistical records prove this danger of multiplicity of parties, due to unabated fragmentation of polity. For example, in the general elections to the Lok Sabha in 1998, as many as 177 parties put up their candidates. As shown by the chart[38] below, only three parties namely the BJP, CPI (M) and the Congress secured more than 5 per cent of the 368.38 million votes cast.

Votes Secured by Parties (%)	No. of Parties
More than 5%	3
1.01—5.00%	14
0.51—1.00%	5
0.11—0.50%	47
Below 0.05	138

Two important suggestions of the Law Commission, in its 170th Report, pertaining to the prevention of further fragmentation of our polity, also merit serious consideration. The Commission has suggested that only those political parties which secure at least 5 per cent of the total votes polled nationally, be allowed a representation in Parliament. The other, and one of the most controversial recommendations, is that of debarring independent candidates from contesting elections to the Lok Sabha.

Campaign reforms are also a part of the electoral reforms. In this context, reducing wasteful and ostentatious election expenditure is also crucial. Even after sixty-five years of parliamentary democracy in India, precious little has been done to

[37] Jagdeep S Chhokar, *Electoral Reforms: Law Commission's Recommendations*, p.9.

[38] From an article by Dorab R Soparjwala, ('It's Broke-so we'd better fix it') *The Times of India*, Mumbai. 16 May 1999.

curb unaccountable use of money in elections. According to *Lok Satta Times*, 'In India, the expenditure in legislative elections is often 10 to 15 times the legal ceiling prescribed.'[39] Political parties indulge in ostentatious campaigning; hence, they spend heavily during the run up to the elections. The whole emphasis is on creating an atmosphere and not on educating the electorate. About this, PC Alexander wrote:

> Election time is collection time for the candidates and enormous sums are collected as so called voluntary 'donations' and 'contributions'. The expenditure incurred by the political parties, hardly justifiable in a developing country, is possible to a great extent because Explanation 1 to section 77(1) of the Representation of Peoples Act, 1951, gives the candidate an easy escape route. This is also because the accounts of political parties are rarely audited by impartial agencies.[40]

In this context, it is important to review the impact of a provision in the law, introduced in 2003, allowing industrialists to donate money to political parties and get a tax rebate. This has helped bring the nexus between political party/ies and corporate house/s to the fore. Things have become transparent as all such transactions are now in the public domain.

Party Reforms

There could be two distinct approaches to party reforms. Parties should initiate reforms themselves for a more purposeful organisation within. A constitutional framework should be provided to ensure a more professional, methodical and trustworthy organisational functioning of parties.

---

[39] *Lok-Satta Times*, May-June 2001.

[40] PC Alexander, 'A Case for Simultaneous Elections', *The Asian Age*, Mumbai, 26 June, 2003.

As far as the first approach is concerned, there are instances—albeit very rare—of parties introducing reforms in their organisational functioning. Mahatma Gandhi firmly believed in the ethical and disciplined functioning of all Congressmen, especially party legislators.[41] He had also approvingly welcomed a draft declaration to be signed by all those holding public offices, mooted by one Brijlal Nehru.[42] However, no institutional set-up to ensure a disciplined, ethical and value-oriented functioning of party organisation was suggested during his times. As a measure for facilitating greater representation for women and other weaker sections, the Congress accepted the recommendations of the Karunakaran Committee in 1998 and decided, in principle, to reserve 33 per cent of the party's posts for women and 20 per cent for the scheduled castes, scheduled tribes and minorities.[43]

The CPI (M) is known for insisting upon some kind of financial control over its elected members. Its party constitution says, 'Salaries and allowances drawn by communist legislators and local body members are considered to be Party money. The Party Committee concerned shall fix up the wages and allowances of the members.'[44]

The BJP, in November 1982, had officially adopted a code of conduct for its MPs and state legislatures, abhorring the practice of entering into the well of the house. But later, it could not adhere to this code. The BJP's Ajeevan Sahayog Nidhi, a scheme for one-time sumptuous contributions for the party coffers, to be collected by cheques from party well-wishers, can also be mentioned as an honest attempt at introducing reforms. The party had also officially decided that its office bearers should desist from participating in functions organised by caste-based organisations. In January 2008, the BJP

[41]MK Gandhi, 'Indian National Congress', in *India of My Dreams*, p.288.
[42]MK Gandhi, Chapters 7 and 8 in Section 3, 'Members of Legislatures', *Gandhiji Expects*. p.15, 16, 17.
[43]News item in rediff.com at http://ia.rediff.com/news/1998/dec/09cong1.htm.
[44]As mentioned at the website of the party at http://www.cpim.org/.

had amended the party's constitution so that at least 33 per cent representation could be given to women at various levels.

Such examples of voluntarily introduced internal or organisational reforms by the parties are rare and, at times, just a token. Rarely have political parties publicly discussed these amendments, much less assessed their success or limitations. As a consequence, these steps have remained only a few experiments here and there, without any serious attempt at institutionalising them.

There is a fairly long history of formal and governmental attempts at introducing systemic reforms for the functioning of parties. The fifteenth Law Commission, in 1960, had undertaken a thorough review of the Representation of People Act, 1951. The report had very forthrightly suggested some legal framework concerning the functioning of political parties in India. The Commission had strongly recommended introduction of 'internal democracy, financial transparency and accountability in the working of political parties by law'. It also pointed out that, 'A political party which does not respect democratic principles in its internal working cannot be expected to respect those principles in the governance of the country.'[45] The commission had proposed that a new section, titled 'Organisation of Political Parties' and matters incidental there, to be added to the Representation of People Act 1951, for the purpose of ensuring regular holding of elections and transparency of financial affairs. The Law Commission had also recommended that non observance of these provisions should attract de-recognition of a political party.

Several politicians have also argued for a legal framework to ensure democratic functioning of parties. According to Atal Bihari Vajpayee, 'Internal democracy within political parties is an important pre-requisite for a healthy democratic culture at the national level. Unfortunately, free debate, accountability and regular organisational

---

[45] As mentioned at http://www.lawcommissionofindia.nic.in/lc170.htm as on 2 January 2006. For details, see Sections 3.1.2.1, 3.1.3 and 3.1.3.1 of the Law Commission Report.

elections have become an exception rather than the norm among our political parties.'[46] From Vasant Sathe to PA Sangma and from Sugata Roy to Roda Mistry, politicians from diverse ideological moorings have stressed the need for greater democratisation of parties.[47]

There is an urgent need to bring political parties under a well-thought out legal framework. Aware of the deepening rot in the system, two Chief Election Commissioners in the past, RVS Peri-Sastri and TN Seshan, tried to compel the political parties to function democratically. Unfortunately, their efforts either remained half-hearted or were opposed indirectly. A case in point is the Shiv Sena, which hurriedly conducted a membership drive and elected its working president in July 2002, simply to abide by the diktats of the Election Commission of India.

Many, like noted journalist Inder Jit, have mooted the idea for a law governing the functioning of political parties on the lines of the West German Basic Law,[48] which, according to him, was a recognition of two basic points. 'First, political parties themselves must function democratically before they could be expected to run the system democratically. Second, blind trust in the free play of forces could prove disastrous.'[49] The law on political parties in the German Constitution covers a wide range of issues. It has a total of forty-one Articles under seven different sections, comprising

---

[46] Atal Behari Vajpayee, *Challenges to Democracy in India*, the text of the 13th Desraj Chowdhary Annual Memorial Lecture delivered in New Delhi on 11 November 1996.

[47] Proceedings of the National Seminar on National resurgence through Electoral Reforms, as documented by Subhash C.Kashyap, *National Resurgence through Electoral Reforms*, p.6.

[48] The Basic Law, adopted on 23 May 1949 for the first time, provided political parties constitutional position. It stipulated—a) The political parties shall participate in the forming of the political will of the people. They may be freely established. Their internal organisation must conform to democratic principles. They must publicly account for the sources of their funds. b) Parties which seek to impair and abolish the free democratic basic order or endanger the existence of the Federal Republic of Germany shall be unconstitutional.

[49] Inder Jit in Subhash C Kashyap (Ed.), *op.cit*, p.6.

constitutional status and functions of the parties, internal organisation and nomination of candidates for election. Even in a relatively small country like Bulgaria, a comprehensive law, governing the functions of political parties was passed in 2001. Chapter four of this Act is aimed at maximum transparency of the party's financial sources. An important aspect of this legislation is that parties are given the right to collect funds in a controllable way. It also protects the party from the financial pressure of conglomerates. Under this legislation, the financial control over political parties provides for utmost transparency, strict order and unified criteria for each party. There is no reason why, if not the political parties, at least the intelligentsia and the civil society should not be demanding a legislation to regulate political parties in India. There is evidence to suggest that proper institutionalisation of intra-party democracy goes a long way in evolving a stable party system. As pointed out by Kanchan Chandra,[50] when criteria for entry and advancement in a political party are not clear, incorporating newly moblised backward caste groups and marginal sections becomes difficult. In this situation, such groups tend to form a new political party, contributing to the fragmentation of the party system. And fragmentation of polity has its own consequences. Arun Shourie was right when he cautioned his fellow countrymen,'[A] society so splintered will not be able to stand up to an all out assault by one determined to crush freedom...In region after region, the splintering has already delivered power into the hands of local toughs...Each round of elections enfeebles the polity further'.[51]

Some individuals believe that any kind of legal compulsion for the introduction of intra-party democracy is not advisable. The traditional pattern of party organisation, named by Rajni Kothari[52] as the 'Congress System', is perhaps peculiar to the Indian situation. According to him, this system means 'laying out of the infrastructure of politics vertically downward all the way, and horizontally across

[50] *Ibid.* p.6.

[51] Arun Shourie, *Prerequisites of Freedom*, Nani A. Palkhiwala Memorial Trust, 2005, p.25.

[52] Rajni Kothari, '*Context of Electoral Change in India*', p.14.

such a large and heterogeneous population' and 'more effective pattern of control and opposition (within the party)'. Considering the way parties function in India, it can perhaps be argued that this is the inevitable part of mainstreaming and greater legitimisation of parties seeking a nationwide mandate. The argument advanced by Pratap Bhanu Mehta against making internal democracy mandatory, needs to be understood in this context; he has argued that 'we are free not to vote for them, but we cannot silence their voices'[53]. Mehta has also opposed giving independent commissions more powers to disqualify political parties on this count. He feels that giving such commissions carte blanche powers to decide about the legitimacy of political parties on the count of intra-party democracy 'is both, normatively and prudentially unsound'.[54]

Interestingly, Rajni Kothari himself has argued that the functional efficacy of the Congress type of politics cannot be taken for granted. He has voiced apprehensions that the factional and coalitional structuring of individual and group relationships in the Congress system 'may prove dysfunctional to the fulfilment of political and economic goals'. Kothari sounds prophetic when he further points out that this may lead to a two-fold crisis of performance and legitimacy. All this reinforces the point that parties are the Achilles' heel in India's political structure and unless they are strengthened, the polity will continue to pass through one crisis or the other.

How can one influence party organisations and party functioning through constitutional mechanisms? Benjamin Reilly has advocated a 'top-down' approach, wherein he mainly focuses on 'increasing party discipline and cohesion in parliament as a means of stabilising party politics, in the hope that more disciplined parties will lead to a more structured party system overall'.[55]

---

[53] Pratap Bhanu Mehta, 'Reform political parties first', *The Seminar*, January, 2001, Issue 497, p.41.

[54] *Ibid.*

[55] Benjamin Reilly, 'Political engineering of Parties and Party Systems', in his paper that could be accessed at www.allacademic.com/meta/p63997_index.html.

Notwithstanding the differences of opinion about the ways and means of strengthening political parties, there seems to be a greater realisation about the need for such steps. In India, it is high time that we think of introducing a comprehensive legislation governing the functioning of political parties, on the lines of the Political Parties Act (1967) in Germany.

There are many who firmly believe that key reforms like a completely democratic way of arriving at decisions and full and open debates on policy options, regular filing of accurate receipts and disbursements, right to information for the public and fair and democratic choice of candidates by members of their representatives for elective positions would bring about a great change.

At a meeting of the Community of Democracies at Seoul in November 2002, organised by the Washington-based National Democratic Institute (NDI), it was strongly recommended that 'Organizations such as the World Bank, the UNDP and the IMF should adopt measures that support political party systems. While supporting economic development and good governance, political systems are often neglected. Support for programs that build professional capacity in political parties is especially critical.'[56]

Arun Shourie has argued that in a representative democracy, 'we must shift from representativeness to effectiveness', emphasising that a people's representative 'is to be elected because he is best equipped to weigh which, among competing proposals and options, is best for them. And not for them in particular but for the country as a whole'.[57] Here comes the aspect of capacity-building of politicians and precious little is being done on this front in India.[58] Not only in India but also almost all over the world, a person elected is also considered to be endowed with the ability to govern in whatever limited sense of the term. Commenting upon how the ineptness of

[56] www.ndi.org/ndi/library/1512_ww_communityofdemoc_final_11202.txt.

[57] Arun Shourie, *The Parliamentary System*,p.242.

[58] Rambhau Mhalgi Prabodhini in Mumbai is one such foundation that works for the capacity building of elected representatives from ministers to parliamentarians, members of legislative assemblies, municipal councillors, etc.

politicians is tolerated, jurist and thinker, NA Palkhiwala, had once sarcastically observed, 'One job for which you need no training or qualification whatsoever is the job of legislating for and governing the largest democracy on earth'.[59]

'While it is difficult to ensure that parties give tickets only to trained party workers, bodies to which representatives get elected certainly can frame rules making post-election training mandatory. It may be mentioned here that the department of cooperation of the Government of Maharashtra has made training compulsory for the directors elected to the cooperative banks.[60] Besides, can political parties not take a conscious decision to make training a pre-requisite for those seeking re-nomination? Initially this model can be adopted vis-à-vis those who aspire for organisational positions in the party. Later it can be applied to all those who seek the party's nominations in a run up to the elections.

Leadership Crisis

Ineffective management within the political parties has triggered a leadership crisis in India. Three distinct leadership patterns can be observed in the contemporary political situation of the country. A dynastic leader supported by a team of hand-picked, close confidants has always led the Congress. The BJP and the communist parties have experimented with collective leadership with varying degrees of success. The regional parties have a clannish organisational character. The party chief's succession plan runs on dynastic lines. At the centre of this scenario is the usual tug of war between charisma and collectivism. The secret of the success of leadership provided by individuals like Jawaharlal Nehru, Indira Gandhi, Rajiv Gandhi, Atal Bihari Vajpayee, Jyoti Basu, Bal Thackeray, MG Ramchandran, NT Ramarao and Lalu Prasad Yadav lies primarily in their personal charm. In comparison, experiments in providing effective collective

[59]NA Palkhiwala, 'Constitutional Changes and the Presidential System', Convocation Address, University of Madras, September, 1979 in *We The People*. As quoted by Arun Shourie in *The Parliamentary System* p.75.

[60]*The Economic Times*, Mumbai, 25 December 2007.

leadership under the charge of a not-so-charismatic person have been less successful.

Charisma or collectivism, pitfalls are on both the sides. Rajani Kothari[61] has summed up this crisis. Observing the scenario in the Congress after Nehru's death, he feels that collective leadership 'led to a greater vulnerability of the leadership to public pressures expressed through the different channels' although at the same time, 'such a "syndicating" of men of power and the consequent spread of their coalitional networks ultimately lend stress on a consensual and on the whole quiescent political culture...'. Besides, there is the question of dynastic succession in parties. While regulating the functioning of voluntary organisations, many government agencies in India put a condition that family members or blood relations cannot be a part of the managing body of a public charitable trust. Are political parties in India of any lesser importance that similar conditions or guidelines cannot be stipulated in their context? That to form a party in India is easier than forming an NGO should not surprise anyone.

Party Finances

The present arrangement of party finances also needs to be reviewed. Raising funds through an appeal to the public is now a thing of the past. Large but clandestine corporate donations and personally accumulated funds by leaders through all kinds of corrupt practices are the principal fountainheads of finance today. If the tax-monitoring authorities honestly try to check the sources of party income and the expenses incurred, several unpleasant truths will come to the fore. In fact, indulging in 'envelope culture' by the members of municipal corporations is so well established today that according to a rough estimate, at least 70 per cent of the elected members of municipal corporations in Maharashtra (and elsewhere too) either do not (require to) work to earn their livelihood or work only for the sake of formality. Since 1949, in the UK, political parties are required to

[61]Rajani Kothari, *Context of Electoral Change in India*, p.11.

'publish annually full and adequate statements of their accounts'[62]. Why can this not be replicated in India?

All in all, it is urgently required that a comprehensive law regulating and disciplining the functioning of parties is formulated. Such legislation should cover the following aspects of party functioning:

- Establishing a political party: The process of forming a new political party must be made more serious and elaborate. It should be mandatory for the party to publish its annual report.
- Recruitment: The party membership's register should be necessarily maintained at the state and district levels.
- Internal democracy: Elections for party office bearers should be conducted under a framework which is to be laid down by the Election Commission of India.
- Transparency: The annual accounts of the party, both at the state and national levels should be published.
- Human resource development: On the lines of foundations supported by parties in Germany (stiftungs), efforts should be made to establish training and research centres for and by parties with a partial financial assistance from the government. The possibility of making comprehensive training mandatory for all first-timers, whether the people's elected representatives or party office bearers, should also be explored. Serious steps should be taken so that no elected official could seek re-nomination without undergoing training during his first tenure.

By the time all these reforms are given a serious thought, an independent organisation called 'Political Party Watch' should be established urgently. The Association of Democratic Reforms has already started this kind of an initiative but it needs to be strengthened and institutionalised. This structure will monitor parties on certain important counts.

---

[62]For details, see www.opsi.gov.uk/acts/acts2000/en/00en41-g.htm.

Attitudinal Reforms

Deeper analysis of several crises affecting democracy in India and elsewhere leads us to the conclusion that indifference on the part of the people is at the core of this predicament. To a considerable extent, this apathy emanates from lack of enlightenment. The situation has worsened during the last sixty-five years. Initially, it was hoped that the democratic system would produce an enlightened citizenry. Later, the political class realised that its interests are best served by an illiterate electorate and hence, efforts to educate people were seen as detrimental to its political pursuits.

For any democracy to be successful, it is necessary to educate the citizens or at least ensure an adequate arrangement for civic education. Unfortunately, in the recent past, the democratic process in India has become less deliberative. Over the years, institutions like legislatures have rapidly deteriorated in their ability to deliberate on issues and oversee the policy-making and implementation aspects of governance. Besides, elections too have not provided occasions for a long-drawn-out debate on complex issues. As is very obvious, all these factors have had a cascading effect on the entire democratic process. Since elections in India are no longer 'a contest of ideas', what is being promoted is further communalisation of the party system, whereby voters are most likely to vote according to their caste or some other community affiliation. If one looks at the newspaper reports of electioneering in the Sixties and compares them with those of the Nineties, it wouldn't be difficult to make out how brazen the caste-and community-dominated thinking has become. Repeated references to caste combinations such as MY (Muslim-Yadav) KHAM (Kshatriya-Harijan-Adivasis and Muslims) indicate the deep-seated, caste oriented thinking of the politicians as well as opinion-makers. An attitudinal change is also required amongst the opinion-making classes.

Non-professionalism and the resultant casual approach has made the entire democratic process flippant. Most of the political parties do not have a mechanism to conduct meetings at various levels regularly. Those who have such a system, leave little scope for deliberations on policy matters. No wonder then, many leaders are unaware of their party's manifestos and many parliamentarians do not have a clear idea about the issues they vote for or against. In the 2004 elections to the Maharashtra State Assembly, the Congress had declared year 2000 as the cut off date for regularisation of slums in Mumbai. After attaining power, the party's chief in the state audaciously announced that the mention of the year 2000 was a printing mistake.[63] As emphasised by Pratap Bhanu Mehta, the only way out of this sorry situation is 'through changing the culture of political parties in India'.[64]

Any amount of reforms in electoral laws or even amendments to the Constitution will be insufficient to produce the desired effect unless systemic efforts for people's education and enlightened citizenry are undertaken. As explained elaborately by former union minister, Jagmohan, certain amendments in the Constitution have fallen short of expectations. Notably, amongst these is the provision by which it became mandatory for every candidate to declare, before the elections being contested by him/her, the details of any criminal case or cases which concerned him. Even after enforcing this amendment, the fourteenth Lok Sabha saw that about a hundred such candidates got elected. 'About thirty of them had such serious charges as murder, dacoity, rape, kidnap and extortion pending against them'.[65] As analysed by Jagmohan, the problem all along was the electorate—the stuff they were made of. Even prior to this change, the voters knew about the involvement of some candidates

[63]As referred to in the report of the Indian People's Human Rights Commission (IPHRC) prepared by Justice (Retd.) RB Mehrotra and JB D'Souza, former Chief Secretary, Government of Maharashtra, who led an unofficial judicial enquiry into the lathi charge by the Mumbai police on 6 April 2005, on a *morcha* taken out by people whose homes had been demolished by the State and municipal authorities in Mumbai in December 2004. At http://dupb.blogspot.com/2005/05/fact-file-about-slum-demolitions.html.

[64]Pratap Bhanu Mehta, *op.cit.*p.41.

[65]Jagmohan, 'A call for a Vedantic State', in *Pragya Bharati*, Hyderabad, January, 2006 p.24.

in illegal activities. But most of them were willing to ignore this fact. These voters were:

> ...either beneficiaries of the criminal activities or considered cast, creed and other parochial factors more important. Morality, righteousness, concern for the health of the polity or the future of the country mattered little in their calculations. Clearly, the outcome of the amendments could not be different from what it turned out to be. In fact, the number of MPs involved in criminal cases increased in the fourteenth Lok Sabha as compared to their number in the thirteenth. Some of them even became ministers in the Union Cabinet, holding important portfolios.[66]

In the assembly elections of 2004 in Maharashtra, an NGO, the Maharashtra Election Watch, with the help of *Lok Satta,* analysed the affidavits of all the nominees. They represented all the major political parties in the state. The findings revealed that of the 1,625 candidates, 366 had a criminal background. This means that 22.5 per cent of the candidates had criminal cases pending against them.[67] Considering the fact that Bhai Thakur of Vasai, Pappu Kalani of Ulhas Nagar and Arun Gawli of Mumbai and several others with criminal backgrounds have made it to the state legislature, it speaks volumes about the penetration of such elements in politics.

An absence of enlightened public opinion has also contributed—directly or indirectly—to the decline in the quality of business transacted in our legislatures and in the parliament. The waning of institutions like legislatures is both the impact of as well as the reason for unenlightened public opinion. The parameters of business in the legislature and especially that of a member's performance have little to do with the support that he may garner

[66] *Ibid*.p.25.
[67] http://www.loksatta.org/poffice.htm.

in his constituency. As one would expect, a member of parliament has to have some understanding of legal issues, foreign affairs or defence. But this will hardly please the electorate in his constituency. What will determine his electoral performance is, perhaps, his response to clogged drains and bad roads. Absence of an enlightened public opinion and absolute lack of efforts for public education, added to a dearth of mechanisms to make elected representatives accountable to the citizens, promotes populism.

Jagdeep Chhokar has quoted US Supreme Court judge, Felix Frank, who had once said, '...an active citizenry is an essential condition for democracy to succeed...Democracy involves hardship—the hardship of unceasing responsibility of every citizen. Where the entire people do not take a continuous and considered part in public life, there can be no democracy in any meaningful sense of the term'.[68]

Public education may reduce bitterness towards politics. Those who indulge in the luxury of cynicism forget that, after all, it is we who choose these politicians. Underscoring the fact that in a democracy, one cannot have two sets of laws, senior journalist and former MP Pritish Nandi, had pointed out:

> Every time we cheered and clapped watching *Deewar*,[69] we encouraged the hero worship of crime, we taught our children to glorify wrongdoers in the name of social justice. Today, Mayawati is doing the same ...[70] Why are we blaming them? We made heroes out of them...[71]

One crisis leads to another. Due to unenlightened public opinion and an ignorant and docile citizenry, incapable

[68]Jagdeep S Chhokar, 'Education for Citizenship', *The Times of India,* Mumbai. 22 March 2006.

[69]A popular Hindi film of the Seventies effectively portrays how a gangster acquires prosperity.

[70]Mayawati, then Chief Minister of Uttar Pradesh.

[71]Pritish Nandi, 'The Great Betrayal', at www.rediff.com/news/aug/27nandy.htm.

representatives often return to the houses of legislature, making it easy for bureaucrats to quietly tighten their grip and add to the erosion of institutions, particularly of the Parliament. As a result, we have a prime ministerial system of government instead of the parliamentary one. In the Indian context, during the Nehruvian era, Parliament and parliamentary business enjoyed a place of prominence. Nehru took special care to establish the importance of parliament. This concern gradually diminished with the prime ministers' presence in Parliament becoming less frequent. In the words of researcher and political scientist Kuldeep Mathur, 'Consequently, the role of parliament in providing inputs to policy through discussions on the financial proposals of the government has considerably eroded. The members do not have research assistance and are driven more by the political consideration of their constituencies'.[72] It won't be a surprise that during 1985 to 1995, the financial approvals of only a few ministries, seven to be specific, were debated. The Demands for Grants for as many as eleven ministries were not taken up for detailed discussion even once and most of the time more than 85 per cent of the budget was passed without any argument.[73] Since 1995, the situation has worsened. A study undertaken by the Parliamentary Research Services clearly reveals that in 2011, just six per cent of the parliamentary bills were presented and passed by the house in which they were introduced in one single day. In the same year, in Haryana, all the bills were cleared after a day-long discussion. Corresponding figures for this phenomenon in West Bengal are 91 per cent and for Bihar, 96 per cent. What is urgently needed, therefore, is an overhaul of the Rules of Business in the Parliament as also in the state legislatures and, for that matter, in all elective bodies.

---

[72]Kuldeep Mathur, 'Decline of a Centralizing State: Changing Nature of Political Power in India', at www.planningcommission.nic.in/reports/sereport/ser/vision2025/polipower.pdf.

[73]Sandeep Shastri, 'Department Related Standing Committees in the Indian Parliament: An Assessment', *The Indian Journal of Public Administration*.xliv, 2, April-June 1998 p.184-200.

In 1996 Atal Bihari Vajpayee had observed:

> Neither Parliament nor the state Vidhan Sabhas are doing with any degree of competence or commitment what they are primarily meant to do: legislative function...Barring exceptions, those who get elected to these apex democratic institutions are neither trained, formally or informally, in law making nor do they seem to have an inclination to develop the necessary knowledge and competence in their profession...serious debate has ceased to take place in our elective bodies, which have come to resemble *akharas*.[74]

It is tragic that all these *akharas* are flourishing at a very heavy cost to the public exchequer. As per the analysis by a Delhi-based think-tank called Liberty Institute, it costs the nation ₹37,000 per minute to keep the Parliament functioning.[75] The number of sittings of the Lok Sabha too has come down from 677 in the first (1952-57) Lok Sabha to 332 in the fourteenth (2004-09) Lok Sabha[76].

Capacity Building

One way of changing the prevalent situation is by revisiting the issue of 'crisis of purpose' that is haunting our polity today. But unfortunately, there are hardly any political parties that are seriously engaged in organisation building, training the cadres and honing leadership talents of the younger politicians. An honourable exception is the BJP. At the grass roots, almost all the parties have a fairly spirited rank and file. In an ideology-driven party organisation like that of the BJP, even ministers participate in training with

---

[74] Atal Bihari Vajpayee, *Challenges to Democracy in India*, The Text of the 13th Desraj Chowdhary Annual Memorial Lecture delivered in New Delhi on 11 November 1996.

[75] Barun Mitra, 'The Easy Guide to How Much Money you spend on Parliament', *The Indian Express,* Mumbai, October 27, 2004.

[76] 14th Lok Sabha Study Report http://mpa.nic.in/Statbook12.pdf.

due seriousness. Between 2002 and 2011, BJP conducted at least three workshops for the ministers belonging to states governed by the party. Close to an average of 100 participants participated in these. While questions about the efficacy of such activities could always be asked, yet the fact remains that each time minister-delegates leave such training camps, they unmistakably insist that the party should hold at least one such workshop every year and thereby 'enhance the chances of we—the ministers—remaining on the track'.

Systemic Change?

Many political analysts, thinkers and several constitution experts have squarely blamed the FPTP system for the present-day ills. To many, it results in the election of those candidates and parties whose success depends on a minority of votes cast, which makes the whole exercise seem unrepresentative. *A Handbook for Electoral System Design*, prepared by the Stockholm based IIDEA (International Institute for Democracy and Electoral Assistance) has clearly brought out several disadvantages of the system and one can easily conclude that India provides an example of how FPTP can prove to be perilous. Some of the key disadvantages are:

- Exclusion of minorities as well as women from fair representation.
- Encouragement to the development of political parties based on clan, ethnicity or region.
- Exaggeration of 'regional fiefdoms', where one party wins all the seats in a province.

Commenting upon the Indian experience of the FPTP, the IIDEA handbook says, 'The nature of the system meant that small changes in vote share often had a dramatic impact upon the shape of the resulting parliament.'

A brief overview of the electoral performance of the Congress, India's oldest political party, as given in the chart here, brings the weakness of FPTP into focus.

Year of General Election	Percentage of Total Votes Polled by the Congress	Number of Seats Obtained
1971 won	43.7	352
1977 lost	34.52	154
1980 won	42.7	353
1984 won	48.10	405
1989 lost	39.53	197
1991 won	36.80	232
1996 lost	28.80	140
1999 lost	28.30	114
2004 won	26.53	145
2009 won	28.52	206

It is the same case with Britain. In the four elections between 1979 and 1992, the Conservative Party won an average of 42.6 per cent of the total vote but 56.0 per cent of seats. The Labour Party won 32.4 per cent votes and 37.8 per cent of seats. The Liberal Democrats and their predecessors won 19.9 per cent of votes but only 2.9 per cent of seats.[77] This disproportionality is considered to be inherent to the majoritarian system.

Several of the problems associated with democracy in India are, in fact, products of the FPTP system. To quote Mahesh Chandra Sharma, 'The ills of the present system of parliamentary democracy that was fashioned after the British model at the time of independence are becoming evident with each passing day.'[78] Domination of the electability factor, pressure of electoral compulsions and the resultant competitive indulgence in electoral malpractices, greater chances of victory of those candidates who have been opposed by a majority

[77] *Encyclopedia of Democracy*, p.415.
[78] As told in an interview with the author.

of the electorate—thanks to the built-in mechanism to ensure strategic division of votes—and the ability to give over-representation to the majority community at the cost of scattered minorities, are widely recognised as systemic flaws of the FPTP. There are scores of examples pointing towards these flaws. During the Lok Sabha elections of 2004 in sixty constituencies in Uttar Pradesh, the percentage of votes obtained by the winning candidates was between 20 to 39 per cent. In another ten constituencies, it varied from 40 to 49 per cent.[79] With enough built-in scope for developing a constituency as a personal or dynastic fiefdom, we have witnessed how the strangleholds of dynasties in constituencies like Rae Bareli (Nehru-Gandhi), Gwalior (Scindias), Baramati (Pawars), to mention a few, continue for decades together.

Another serious factor that calls for a systemic change is the fact that the parliamentary system promotes fragmented politics. Consequently, castes and community loyalties become the foundations of parties. This also influences the politics of larger parties with a national appeal and they too give in to the pressures of caste considerations. All this has affected the electorate's voting behaviour. Candidates are generally selected on caste lines and citizens vote on caste appeal. States like Uttar Pradesh, Bihar and Tamil Nadu are already in the grip of caste politics and others like Karnataka, Maharashtra, Rajasthan and Gujarat are not far behind. In a situation like this, the electoral system has been almost totally subverted by money and muscle power, not to forget the vote bank considerations of caste and communities. Although casteism and communalism may have taken a back seat in the country's social fabric, they get unabated support from the electoral process.

A Case for Proportional Representation

At the beginning of this book, it was mentioned that the quest is basically for a system that will ensure a greater amount of political stability with reduced frequency of elections, ultimately helping the

[79] http://www.janadesh.org/files/3_10majorproblems.html.

incumbent governments take courageous decisions. Also, this study is aimed at searching for a system that will substantially reduce the element of 'technique' from the electoral exercise, thereby reducing the scope for vote bank politics. Besides, the systemic solution was also expected to allow at least some consideration to factors other than the candidate's electability, thereby creating a situation that will encourage honest, dedicated and hard-working individuals to enter in politics. It would be enlightening to investigate how PR fares on these expectations.

Mixed Member Proportional Representation (MMPR), also known as Mixed Compensatory Proportional Representation (MCPR),[80] is a well entrenched system in Germany. It perfectly blends two distinct mechanisms, allowing the election of one part of representatives of local districts by the FPTP vote in single-seat constituencies, and at the same time, thanks to compensation mandates, provides a fully proportional outcome. Of the various systems, MMPR seems to be one of the most popular. As has been mentioned earlier, countries like Albania, Bolivia, Lesotho, Mexico, New Zealand, the Philippines and Venezuela have adopted it at the national level. In the UK, MMPR is used for the election of the Scottish and the Welsh regional assemblies. Often described as a system that

[80]Through an illustration, MCPR could be explained as follows:

- 50 per cent of the seats in the Lok Sabha would be elected via constituency-election, just like under the FPTP. For convenience, this 50 per cent of seats would be labeled as the 'Constituency List'.
- The remaining 50 per cent of seats in the Lok Sabha would be elected via PR. These seats would be allocated according to the respective shares of the state vote received by each party. For convenience, this 50 per cent of seats would be labeled as the 'Parties List'.
- Each voter would cast two votes. The first vote would be for their local member of the Lok Sabha. This vote would relate to the Constituency List. The second vote would be for a preferred party. This second vote would relate to the Parties List.
- The ultimate number of seats won by each party will be a combination of seats drawn from the Constituency List and Parties List. This figure will be calculated using several adjustments to ensure fairness in distribution of seats.

combines the 'best of both worlds', MMPR allows voters to think both locally as well as nationally.

From Jayprakash Narayan (JN), to psephologist Dorab Sopariwala, many individuals have been advocating the switchover to MCPR or PR. To put it simply, under this system, voters are expected to cast two votes, one for a candidate in their constituency and the other for a party of their choice. Party votes later decide the allocation of seats to various contesting parties. Advocates of PR believe that as compared to the present Westminster model, PR is more likely to help improve the quality of democratic governance and, in effect, arrest the growing indifference towards the democratic process, leading to cynicism and eventual lack of faith in democratic ideals. After reviewing the relationship between democratic representation and electoral system in India, a researcher, TM Joseph, strongly recommends that 'the German model is well placed to feature strongly as it ensures stability, allows constituency representation and provides outcome far more proportional'[81] than our present system.

The conviction about the advisability of the PR system emerges from several reasons. One of the strongest arguments in its favour is that it generates higher voter turnout than majoritarian system.

Organisations like Janadesh, a platform for the National Campaign for Political Reforms, have been very strongly advocating that India should switchover to PR. Claiming that, under this, parties are in almost no pressure to be the biggest and loudest voice and hence there is less expenditure on elections. Advocates also argue that it is best suited to reduce corruption. 'In the top 20 least corrupt countries, 17 follow one form of PR or the other', claims a pamphlet published by Janadesh.

The major points of comparison mentioned in the chart here reveal why PR merits a serious consideration, as an alternative to the present FPTP, in the specific context of India.

The distinctive features of FPTP and PR are obvious.

---

[81]TM Joseph, 'Democracy and Representation in India: Does Electoral System matter?' in *Gandhi Marg,* October-November, 2006, p.321.

While under the FPTP, individuals get prominence and parties get relegated to the background and hence it is more prone to the promotion of hero-worship, under PR, the organisational identity of parties becomes crucial. Again, the electoral process under the FPTP is more likely to be hijacked by money and muscle power, leading to a growing number of tainted politicians. PR is more capable of challenging moneyed and patronage politics. FPTP promotes a perceptible challenger party and other parties are denied representation due to it, commensurate with their popular base. Similarly, FPTP is also considered more prone to promoting dynastic politics as against PR. Again, in the electoral campaign, since the PR system is not totally candidate-centric, there is always greater likelihood of issues becoming more decisive under the PR.

Even under the Westminster system, competent and honest persons who prefer to remain away from direct electoral politics for obvious reasons can easily enter the legislatures via the upper houses. But, as past experience shows, parties have largely abused this particular provision of the Constitution. The upper houses of legislatures in India are often used as back-door entry points for veteran politicians who have either failed in the direct elections or who are not confidant of facing the electorate. Under Article 80 of the Constitution of India, the President in the case of Parliament and as per Article 171 (5), the Governor in the case of state Legislatures, is authorised to appoint eminent persons 'having special knowledge or practical experience in respect of such matters as the following, namely literature, science, art, cooperative movement and social service'. But this provision has also been abused and crass politicians who have nothing to do with literature, performing arts, and sports, etc. have been appointed simply to keep the political flock together. For example, since 1990, in Maharashtra, of the thirty-six individuals appointed, only three were truly away from partisan politics and belonged to disciplines such as arts and literature. Besides, PR also enables the promotion of greater gender justice as demonstrated by Norway, where the proportion of women members in their house of representatives increased from 6.7 per cent in 1957 to 15.05 per cent in 1973.[82]

Jayprakash Narayan (JN) is a staunch supporter of proportional representation. According to him, 'Combination of dependence on local mafias for election and the compulsions of survival in power are at the root of the (present) crisis'.[83] Therefore, he suggests switching over to PR. To him, it is a system which gives 'honest and competent candidates a decent chance of getting elected, and reduce the dependence of parties on criminals and mafia on grounds of "winnability"'.[84] Atal Bihari Vajpayee has also openly come forward in support of the PR system. Pointing out that with its inherent flaws, the present FPTP 'weakens the representative character of elective bodies'.[85]

PR has also been recommended in the 170th Report of the Law Commission of India (1999). The report says, 'We feel that a combination of FPP (FPTP) and the list systems...may best meet our needs'.[86] In order to find a solution to this crisis through changing the electoral system, the Commission reviewed all the 212 parliamentary electoral systems listed in The Global Distribution of Electoral Systems (as presented by the Administration and Cost of Election Study Project undertaken by the UNDP and others), in order to assess what might be the most suitable for us. After an elaborate analysis, it recommended a combination of both the present FPTP system and the list system. As claimed by Janadesh, several political parties, including the CPI (M), the DMK, the MDMK, the Indian Union Muslim League and the Shiromani Akali Dal have also supported PR.[87]

---

[82] http://economics.about.com/cs/issues/ for 'Proportional Representation versus First-past-the-post'.

[83] Jayprakash Narayan (JN), '*Defining Moment—Challenge and Opportunity*' an appeal issued by Lok Satta

[84] *ibid*

[85] Atal Bihari Vajpayee, *op.cit.*

[86] For details visit http://www.lawcommissionofindia.nic.in/lc170.htm.

[87] A pamphlet by Janadesh, a forum promoted by *Lok Satta*, Maharashtra.

Dorab Sopariwala has listed out the positive aspects of this system. He observes, '[T]o be represented in the Lok Sabha, a party must get (1) more than ten per cent of the votes nationally, plus (2) more than ten per cent in at least eight out of 15 states that have ten or more Lok Sabha seats'.[88] He has also argued that the list system under this full proportionality will reduce the importance and appeal of castes and communities. Also, with well-distributed and balanced lists, he feels, 'We may be able to move away from the politics of personalities to the politics of policies'.[89]

PR could perhaps be described as the most likely answer in this quest for systemic solutions to India's democratic deficit. As compared to FPTP, PR will provide greater political stability and more certainty about the schedule of elections. PR provides for a simultaneous voting for an individual as well as for a party and this element is more likely to reduce the technique element that has gripped our electoral system. With the provision of the list system, chances for consideration for the ability of a candidate are in a way reinstated. This will automatically encourage entry of good, well-meaning, quality people in politics. Since PR is considered to be a system that facilitates greater number of well-meaning and quality persons, populism is less likely to rule the roost. This will certainly facilitate courageous but unpopular decision-making. The PR system will also offer incentives such as ensuring intra-party democracy, transparency in financial transactions and discourage parties to take up emotional issues to influence the masses.

Apart from switching over to PR, what can also be given a serious thought is adopting a model where we have a 'polity of concentric circles of multitier governance with power spread out and shared in a bottom-up rather than top-down scenario.' This system would provide for only one poll—for village Panchayats in rural areas and urban local bodies in cities—in five years. All the other bodies, including a district council, state legislature and even

[88]Dorab R Sopariwala, 'It's Broke—so we'd better fix it', *The Times of India*, Mumbai. 16 May, 1999.
[89]*Ibid.*

the national parliament and president would be elected indirectly through the chain of elected representatives. Apparently, this system, which has its origin in Gandhian concepts, may sound impracticable but still one should not reject it outright.

Implementation of Reforms

Problems associated with the functional failure of our systems are so very common and so oft repeated that every lack of action about the micro and macro issues leads to a suspicion about the desire to overcome the problems. Thus, many believe that politicians, regardless of the party that they belong to, have absolutely no political will to introduce systemic reforms. Since the diagnosis about what ails our democratic system differs from person to person, there is no unanimity about the solutions. And even if one achieves a semblance of unanimity, crass cynicism and the resultant lack of motivation takes out the punch from any agenda for reform. Disillusionment at the popular level leads to further disenchantment, depleting the requisite climate for pushing systemic changes. Possibly, this is the reason why persons like NR Narayana Murthy condemn the entire political class, alleging that the vested interests of the politicians make them pro-status quo.[90]

Systemic alterations require some kind of change in the existing institutions and it is here that the political will is put to test. Political scientist and thinker, Atul Kohli, rightly observed the scenario of our political parties, 'Differences with party leader are regarded as anti-party activity and here is no scope for dissent which is an integral part of the democratic process. Therefore, powerful leaders in India have often proved to be enemies of institutions such as political parties'.[91]

While the quest for systemic solutions to the innumerable crises that have plagued our present political system will no doubt continue for long, the solutions that we seek should be firmly rooted

---

[90] NR Narayana Murthy's speech *op.cit.*

[91] Atul Kohli, *Democracy and Discontent: India's Growing Crisis of Governability*, p.402.

in the Indian soil. In *Young India,* dated 26 June 1924, Gandhiji had written:

> My Swa-raj (self rule) is to keep intact the genius of our civilization. I want to write many new things but they must all be written on the Indian slate. I would gladly borrow from the West when I can return the amount with decent interest.[92]

As very brilliantly analysed by eminent journalist Mark Tully, the crisis is not in the system, but the mindset that governs the system. He says:

> The characteristic genius of the Indian mind is not to shake the beliefs of the common man but to lead them by stages to the understanding of the deeper philosophical meaning behind their beliefs. But the Western world and the Indian elite who emulate it ignore the genius of the Indian mind. They want to write a full stop in a land where there are no full stops.[93]

Political and democratic reforms are easier said than done. From the Arab countries to neighbouring Nepal and from Guatemala to England, the pace of reforms has been far too slow. Consensus-building has always remained a big hurdle for all such efforts. Since reforms are the only solution, they need to be resolutely evolved and implemented. Let us look at the example of Georgia. Regardless of the difference of opinions about the quality of democratic governance under the Saakashvili regime, a tiny country like Georgia could earn laurels for the reforms implemented by the government. Acclaiming the success of the Georgian reforms, *The Economist* commented that Georgia has practically reinvented itself. According to it, the country now is 'less corrupt than most former Soviet republics and

[92]RK Prabhu, (Compiled) MK Gandhi, *India of My dreams*, p.8.
[93]Mark Tully, *No Full Stops in India*, p.13.

one of the easiest places in the world to do business, according to the World Bank. Its liberalised economy has weathered Russian embargoes, and the state held together during the war with Russia. Its police do not take bribes and electricity is no longer a luxury. Most important, people are no longer surprised by such success. The biggest transformation is in their minds..... And yet the mental shift which has occurred in Georgia will make it hard to turn the country backwards.'[94] If Georgia can make miraculous changes through systemic reforms, why cannot India?

In 2011, in a decisive verdict by referendum, Britons had rejected the Liberal Democratic agenda for reforms in the electoral system. The British experience underscores the fact that it is extremely hard to educate people about reforms and seek their support. Thanks to the lack of political education, achieving consensus on key democratic reforms in India is several times more difficult than elsewhere, but at the same time, the urgency of introducing reforms is manifold. In India, we just cannot ignore the fact that our achievements through democratic governance have been far too less than what this nation deserves. We have a plethora of challenges in making India a resurgent republic. People are hungry for a better quality of life through better-managed systems. We can ignore the unrest within, only to our peril. Unless we make our political democracy deliver, and deliver fast and effectively, complex issues concerning the consolidation of social and economic democracy cannot be resolved.

What is more worrisome is that the delay in fixing the system may further add to our social tensions, frustrate huge sections of aspiring India and even jeopardise our spiritual democracy! It is high time that the enormity of the crisis is realised by all, and measures like political reforms are debated, discussed and a consensus is evolved. Sooner than later, India needs to unlock its democracy—now chained to the archaic, outdated aspects of the system—and keep pace with the fast-growing aspirations of its GenNext. Future generations have huge stakes involved in this transformation.

---

[94] *The Economist*, August 19, 2010.

They will curse the present generation lest we fail in realising these changes. Let us not forget that introducing political reforms will add to the functional quality of our democratic governance. Better governance will lead to a better quality of life. When India has systems to depend upon, cynicism will evaporate, bringing new hopes and dreams to her people. These unflinching aspirations, after all, are the key to India's pride of place, globally. Introducing democratic reforms, by far, remains the surest and, perhaps, the only way towards making India a true superpower!

Bibliography

A: Primary Sources

1. Documents

Report of the National Commission to Review the Working of the Constitution at http://lawmin.nic.in/ncrwc/finalreport/v1ch4.htm as on 28 May 2007.

A Report of National Institute of Urban Affairs about the impact of 74th amendment www.niua.org/.../74caa_v1/Impact%20of%20the%2074th%20CAA-Consolidated%20Report%20Vol%20-%20I_summary.pdf as on 1 May, 2007.

A monograph, *Political Parties and Election Symbols*, published by Election Commission of India in February 2007.

170th Report of the Law Commission (India), http://www.lawcommissionofindia.nic.in/lc170.htm as on 2 January 2006.

New Zealand's Change to MMP, a report prepared by Electoral Commission of New Zealand. http://janda.org/c95/news%20articles/New%20Zealand/ZNswitch.htm as on 11 January 2006.

ANC Submission on Future Electoral System to the Electoral task Team. (17 October, 2002) at http://www.anc.org.za/ancdocs/misc/electsub.html as on 11 January 2006.

Report of the Royal Commission on Electoral System (New Zealand) http://www.aceproject.org/main/english/es/esy_nz.htm as on 31 January, 2006.

Report of the The Indian People's Human Rights Commission (IPHRC) prepared by Justice (Retd) R.B. Mehrotra and J.B.D'Souza, former Chief Secretary, Government of Maharashtra, who led an unofficial judicial enquiry into the *lathi* charge by the Mumbai police on 6 April, 2005, on a *morcha* taken out by people whose homes had been demolished by the State and municipal authorities in Mumbai in December 2004 at http://dupb.blogspot.com/2005/05/fact-file-about-slum-demolitions.html as on 2 January, 2007.

Assessing and Analysing Governance in India: Evidence from a New Survey, a report on democracy and governance in India prepared by the Overseas Development Institute (UK) prepared by Julius Court, at http://www.odi.org.uk/wga_governance/Abstracts/Governance_in_India_abs.html as on 1 May, 2007.

A Report on Global Corruption Barometer at the Transparency International website at www.transparency.de/fileadmin/pdfs/Korruptionsindices/Global_Corruption_Barometer_2005_Report.pdf as on 7 May 2006.

CSDS National Election Study Report at http://www.lokniti.org/projects.htm#nes as on 12 May 2005.

Voting Turnout from 1945 to 1977: a

Global report on Political Participation, International IDEA, Stockholm. 1997.

Discussion document prepared for the National Policy Conference of African National Congress (ANC) in October 2002, at http://www.anc.org.za/ancdocs/misc/electsub.html as on 31 January 2006.

Constituent Assembly of India debates at http://parliamentofindia.nic.in/ls/debates/vol7p5b.htm as on 2 February 2006.

2. Party Documents

Challenges to Democracy in India (The Text of the 13th Des Raj Choudhary Annual Memorial Lecture delivered by Atal Behari Vajpayee, in New Delhi on 11 November, 1996) published by the BJP.

Communist Party of India (Marxists), *On Party Programme* (Party Education Series), published by HS Kang, New Delhi, September 2003.

CPI (Marxists): *Report on Implementation of Organisational Tasks*. (Adopted by the Central Committee at its meeting in September 2006), November 2006.

Manifesto of the BJP led National Democratic Alliance (NDA), March 2004.

Manifesto of the Indian National Congress, March 2004.

Prabhat Jha (Ed.). 2007. *Sankalpa*. Published by Dr Mukherjee Smruti Nyas, (associated with the BJP), New Delhi.

Tasks Ahead, BJP (National Head Quarter, New Delhi) Publication: July 2004.

Prakash Karat. 2007. *The Role of the Left-led Governments and our Understanding*. CPI (M) Publication, New Delhi May 2007

3. Interviews

AB Bardhan, General Secretary, Communist Party of India, New Delhi. 8 February 2004.

Andrew Imlach, then researcher with the Commonwealth Parliamentary Association, London. 1 August 1998.

Dr Mahesh Chandra Sharma, ex-Member of Parliament and then President of BJP Rajasthan, New Delhi. 1 February 2004 and 23 December 2006.

Dr Wolfgang Weeg. Senior functionary, Social Democratic Party, (SPD) party. Bonn, Germany. 8 August 1998.

Helmut Scholz, senior functionary, Party of Democratic Socialism. Bonn, Germany. 14 August 1998.

Jayprakash Narayan (JN), Founder of Lok-Satta, Hyderabad. 27 July 2006.

Justice (Retd) Chandrashekhar Dharmadhikari, Mumbai. 27 June 2007.

K. Govindacharya, former General Secretary, BJP, New Delhi. 8 February 2004.

Peter Lyon, then Director, Institute of Commonwealth Studies, London. 30 August 1998.

Pippa Norris, McGuire Lecturer in Comparative Politics, at the John F. Kennedy School of Government, Harvard University, Boston. 29 January, 1999.

Shivraj Patil, veteran Congress member and former Home Minister of India, New Delhi. 10 February 2004.

Swapan Dasgupta, senior journalist in New Delhi. 2 December 2004.

Vasant Sathe, veteran Congress member and former Union Minister, Gurgaon, Haryana. 9 February 2004.

4. Focused Group Discussions

With the activists of Shiv Sena on 3 July 2003.

With the activists of Bharatiya Janata Yuva Morcha on 28 May, 2005.

With the activists of Maharashtra Nav Nirmaan Sena at Pune. 11 September 2005.

With the elected representatives of the Kalyan-Dombivali Municipal Corporation, Maharashtra. 2 June 2006.

B. Secondary Sources

1. Books

Almond, Gabriel and Sidney Verba . *Civic Culture* New Jersey, Princeton University Press, 1965.

Barker, Earnest. *Reflections on Government* London and New York, Oxford University Press, 1942.

Broder, David S. *Democracy Derailed-Initiative Campaign and the Power of Money* New York, Harcourt, 2000.

Burns, James MacGregor. *Leadership for a New Century: A Blueprint for a More Participatory Democracy* Bill Bradley's (Ex-Member of US Senate) keynote address in JMB Academy of Leadership, University of Maryland, 1998.

Canovan, Margaret. *Populism* London, Harcourt, Brace Jovanovich, 1981.

Chhokar, Jagdeep S. *Electoral Reforms: Law Commission's Recommendations* Ahmedabad, Ahmedabad Management Association, 1999.

Croly, Herbert. *Progressive Democracy* New York, Macmillan Publishing Co, 1914.

Dahl, Robert A. *On Democracy* New Delhi, Affiliated East-West Press Pvt. Ltd, 2001.

———. A *Preface to Democratic Theory* Chicago, University of Chicago Press, 1956.

deSouza, Peter Ronald and Sridharan E. (Ed.) *India's Political Parties* New Delhi, Sage Publications, 2006.

Diamond, Larry et al. (Ed.). *Consolidation of the Third World Democracies* Baltimore, Johns Hopkins University Press, 1997.

DiClerico, Robert E. and Allan S Hammock (Ed.). *Points of View: Readings in American Government and Politics* Boston, McGraw Hill, 1998.

Downs, Anthony: *An Economic Theory of Democracy* New York, Harper and Row, 1957.

Duverger, Maurice: *Political Parties: Their Organisation and Activity in the Modern State* London, Methuen and Company Ltd, 1951.

Gallagher, Michael, Michael Laver and Peter Mair. *Representative Government in Modern Europe* Boston, McGraw Hill, 2005.

Gandhi, MK. Compiled by RK Prabhu. *India of My Dreams* Ahmedabad, Navjeevan Publishing House, 12th ed. 2006.

———. *Collected Writings*, Vol.1 Ahmedabad, Navjeevan Publishing House, 1997.

———. Compiled by HM Vyas. *Gandhiji Expects* Ahmedabad, Navjeevan Publishing House, 1965.

———. *Collected Works* New Delhi, Publications Division, Government of India, 1958-1965.

Golwalkar, MS *Bunch of Thoughts* Bangalore, Jagran Prakashan, 2nd ed. 1980.

Guha, Ramachandra. *India after Gandhi* London, Picador/Macmillan, 2007.

Huntington, Samuel P. *The Third Wave, Democratization in the Late Twentieth Century.* Norman, OK, University of Oklahoma Press, 1991.

Kant, Krishan. *The Present System its Central Point of Rot and Resurgence* The text of GV Mavlankar Memorial Lecture delivered in 1981. Ahmedabad, Harold Laski Institute of Political Science, 1981.

Kashyap, Subhash (Ed.). *National Resurgence Through Electoral Reforms* Delhi, Rashtriya Jagriti Sansthan and Shipra Publications, 2002.

Kavanagh, Dennis. *The Blair Effect: 2001-*

2005 Cambridge, Cambridge University Press, 2005.

Key, VO Jr. *Politics, Parties and Pressure Groups* New York, Thomas Y. Crowell Company, 1942.

Kirkpatrick, Jeane Jordan. *Dismantling the Parties: Reflections on party reform and party decomposition* Washington DC, American Enterprise Institution for Public Policy Research, 1979.

Kohli, Atul (Ed.). *The Success of India's Democracy* New Delhi, Foundation Books Pvt. Ltd., Cambridge University Press, 2004.

———. *Democracy and Discontent: India's Growing Crisis of Governability* New York, Cambridge University Press, 1991.

Kothari, Rajni. *Politics in India* Boston, Little, Brown and Co, 1970.

———. *Context of Electoral Change in India—General Elections 1967* Bombay, Academic Books, 1969.

Kulkarni, AG. *A study of Political Parties in Maharashtra with Special Reference to the Period 1947-62-67* unpublished thesis, University of Pune 1968.

Ladd, Everett Carl. *Where Have All the Voters Gone?* New York, London, W. W Norton and Co, 1982.

Laski, Harold. *A Grammar of Politics* New Haven, Yale University Press, 4th ed., 1937.

Lawson, Kay and Peter H Merkl. (Ed.). *When Parties fail.* Princeton, Princeton University Press, 1988.

Lawson, Kay (Ed.). *How Political Parties Work? Perspectives from Within* London, Praeger, 1984.

Lijphart, Arend. *Patterns of Democracy: Government Forms and Performance in Thirty-Six Countries* New Haven and London, Yale University Press, 1996.

Lipset, Seymour Martin (Ed.). *The Encyclopedia of Democracy* Washington DC, Congressional Quarterly Books, 1995.

Lively, Jack and Adam. *Democracy in Britain-A Reader* Boston, Blackwell Publishing, 1994.

Lohia, Ram Manohar. *Marx, Gandhi and Socialism* Hyderabad, Navhind, 1963.

Manglapus, Raul S. *Will of the People: Original Democracy in Non-Western Societies* New York, Greenwood Press, 1987.

Mehta, Jaswant B. *Presidential System: A Better Alternative* Mumbai, National Forum for Presidential Democracy, 1998.

Babu, Ramesh B. *Thoughts on the American Presidential System and its Relevance to India* Ahmedabad, Harold Laski Institute of Political Science, 1982.

Luce, Edward. *In spite of Gods* London, Little Brown, 2006.

Maisel, Louis and Joseph Cooper. (Ed). *The Impact of the Electoral Process—Sage Electoral Studies Year Book Volume 3, 1977* Beverly Hills, Sage Publications, 1988.

Malhotra, GC. (Ed.). *Fifty Years of Indian Parliament* Lok Sabha Secretariat, New Delhi, 2002.

Masani, Minoo. *The Essence of Democracy* Ahmedabad, Harold Laski Institute of Political Science, 1989.

McLean, Ian (Ed.). *The Concise Oxford Dictionary of Politics* New York, Oxford University Press, 1996.

Mechery, FA and Maneesha Tikekar. *Constitution, Polity and Society – A study of Indian political system* Bombay, Macmillan India Ltd, 1987.

Mehta, GL. *Harold Laski Revisited* Ahmedabad, Harold Laski Institute of Political Science, 1960.

Modak, Ashok, et al (Ed.). *Left Front Rule in West Bengal: Genesis, Growth and Decay* Mumbai, Rambhau Mhalgi Prabodhini, 1997.

Mody Nawaz, Raman S Kannamma and Louis D'Silva, (Ed.) *Revisiting Indian*

Democracy Mumbai, Allied Publishers, 2001.

Moraes, Frank. *India Today* (Book) New York, The Macmillan Company, 1960.

Munshi, KM. *Indian Constitutional Documents-Volume 1: Pilgrimage to Freedom* Bombay, Bharatiya Vidya Bhavan, 1968.

Narayan, Jayprakash. *Bharatiya Rajya Vyavastha Ki Punarrachana: Ek Sujhav (Hindi)* Varanasi, Sarva Seva Sangha-Prakashan, 3rd ed., 2002.

Neumann, Sigmund (Ed). *Modern Political Parties* Chicago, The University of Chicago Press, 1956.

Noorani, AG. *India's Constitution and Politics* Bombay, Jaico Publishing House, 1970.

Patel, HM. *The First Flush of Freedom—Recollections and Reflections* New Delhi, Rupa and Co., 2005.

———. *Democracy at Work in India* Ahmedabad, Harold Laski Institute of Political Science, 1961.

Patil, Shivraj V. *Emerging Vision of India* London, Jain Vishwa Bharati, 1996.

Phatak, Narhar Raghunath. *Adarsha Bharat Sevak: Gopal Krishna Gokhale Yanche Charitra (Marathi)* (Biography of Gopal Krishna Gokhale) Mumbai, Mauj Prakashan, 1967.

Szajkowski, Bogdan (Ed.). *Political Parties of the World* London, John Harper Publishing, 6th ed., 2005.

Prabhu, RK and UR Rao. (Ed). *Mind of Mahatma Gandhi* Ahmedabad, Navjeevan Trust, 3rd ed., 1967.

Prasad, Bimla (Ed.), Jay Prakash Narayan. *Socialism, Sarvodaya and Democracy, Selected Works of Jayprakash Narayan* Bombay, Asia Publishing House, 1964.

Randal, Wicky (Ed.). *Political Parties in the Third World* Beverly Hills, Sage Publications, 1988.

Reilly, Benjamin. *Democracy in Divided Societies* Cambridge, Cambridge University Press, 2001.

Right, William E. *A Comparative Study of Party Organization* Columbus Ohio, Charles E. Merrill Publishing Company, 1971.

Roy, MN. *Politics, Power and Parties* Calcutta, Renaissance Publishers, 1960.

Sartori, Giovanni. *Comparative Constitutional Engineering: An Enquiry into Structural Incentives and Outcomes* New York, New York University Press, 1994.

———. *Democratic Theory*, Indianapolis, 2nd revised edition, Liberty Press, 1978.

———. *Democratic Theory* Calcutta, Oxford and IBH Publishing Co., 1965.

———. *Democratic Theory* Detroit, Michigan Wayne State University Press, 1962.

Saward, Michael. *The Terms of Democracy* Cambridge, UK, Polity Press, 1998.

Schumpeter, Joseph A. *Capitalism, Socialism and Democracy* New York, Harper & Row, 3rd ed., 1950.

SDSA Team. *State of Democracy in South Asia: A report* New Delhi, Oxford University Press, 2008.

Shourie, Arun. *The Parliamentary System: What We Made of It, What We can Make of It* Delhi, ASA/Rupa, 2006.

Subramanian, N. *Ethnicity and Populist Mobilization: Political Parties, Citizens and Democracy in South India* Delhi, Oxford University Press, 1999.

Sukathankar, YN. *Human Nature and Politics* Ahmedabad, Harold Lasky Institute of Political Science, 1960.

Taggart, Paul. *Populism* Buckingham, Philadelphia, Open University Press, 2000.

Tully, Mark. *No Full Stops in India* New Delhi, Penguin Books, 1992.

Upadhyay, Deendayal. *Political Diary* Mumbai, Jaico Publishing House, 1968.

Bhave, Vinoba. *Democratic Values* Varanasi, Sarva Seva Sangha-Prakashan, 3rd ed., 2002.

Vora, Rajendra and Suhas Palshikar. (Ed). *Indian Democracy: Meanings and Practices* New Delhi, Sage Publications, 2004.

Wattenberg, Martin P. *The Decline of American Political Parties 1952-1996* London Harvard University Press, 1984.

Zimmerman, Joseph F. *The Referendum: The People Decide Public Policy* London, Praeger, 2001.

2. Articles

Acharya, Shankar. 'Dump populism, let India grow'. At http://www.rediff.com on 28 December 2005.

Agarwal, Subhash. 'Democracy counts', in *Developments* Magazine, issue 39, 2007.

Alexander, PC. 'A Case for simultaneous elections', *The Asian Age*, Mumbai. 26 June 2003.

Amy, Douglas J. 'What is PR and why do we need this reform?' at http://www.mtholyoke.edu/acad/polit/damy/BeginningReading/whatispr.htm on 12 December 2005.

Andrews, Edmund L. A dispatch in *International Herald Tribune*, London, 16 September 1998.

Appleton, Andrew M. and Daniel S Ward. 'Measuring party organisation in the United States: An assessment and a new approach'. *Party Politics,* Vol.1, Issue 1, January 1995.

Maira, Arun. 'Can argumentative India be governed?' *The Economic Times*, Mumbai, 19 December 2005.

Bajaj, Rahul. 'Reforms take a back seat,' *The Times of India*, Mumbai, 20 January 2006.

Beetham, David. '*In for the count*' at http://www.redpepper.org.uk/dem/x-nov98-beetham.htm on 16 January 2006.

Bhowmik, Subir. 'Ethnicity, ideology and religion: Separatist movements in India's North-East' http://www.apcss.org/Publicatio"ns/Edited%20Volumes/ReligiousRadicalism/PagesfromReligiousRadicalismandSecurityinSout as on 2 February 2007

Brass, Tom. 'The agrarian myth, the new "populism" and the new "right",' *Economic and Political Weekly*, Vol. Xxxii.No.4.25 January 1997 PE-27.

Brunell, Peter. '*Building better democracies: Why political parties matter?*', at www.wfd.oeg/upload/docs/WFDBBD5:noprice.pdf as on 18 January, 2006.

Chandra, Kanchan. 'Elections as auctions,' *Seminar* 539, July 2004.

Chandra Mohan, C. 'Drawbacks of a perpetual election mode,' *The Financial Express,* 7 August 2003.

Chatterjee, Partha.'Beyond the nation? Or within?' *Economic and Political Weekly*, 4–11 January 1997, Volume xxxii.No.1 and 2.

Chhokar, Jagdeep S. 'Education for citizenship', *The Times of India,* Mumbai. 22 March 2006.

Court, Julius. 'Assessing and analysing governance in India: Evidence from a new survey' at http://www.odi.org.uk/wga_governance/Abstracts/Governance_in_India_abs.html as on 1 May 2007.

Dhanagare, DN. 'Civil society, state and democracy: Contextualising a discourse'. *Sociological Bulletin*, 50(2), September 2001.

Dewey CJ. 'Images of the village community (1972): A study in Anglo-Indian ideology', *Modern Asian Studies*, Vol. 6, No. 3 (1972).

Diamond, Larry. 'The global state of democracy', *Current History*, Volume 99, No. 641 Philadelphia, USA, December 2000.

Dionne, EJ Jr. 'The third way is vogue on both sides of the Atlantic,' *The International Herald Tribune*, London, 11 August 1998

Dutta, Anuradha. 'Sacrificing Ideology,' *The Pioneer*, New Delhi, 15 December 2005.

Ganguly, Amulya. '*The degeneration of Indian political class*' at http://news.monstersandcritics.com/india on 26 August 2006.

Ganguly, Sumit. 'India's unlikely democracy: Six decades of independence', '*Journal of Democracy*', April 2007. Volume 18, Number 2.

Geremek, Bronislaw. 'Democracy: A receding tide?', *The Economic Times*, Mumbai, 23 February, 2004.

Grant, Jorden. 'Politics without parties: A growing trend?' *Parliamentary Affairs*, Vol. 51, No. 4, 1998, Oxford University Press.

Jagmohan. 'A call for a vedantic state', Pragya *Bharati*, Hyderabad, January 2006.

Jain, LC. 'We have to pay for our democracy' at http://www.humanscape.org/Humanscape/2004/Nov/wehave.php as on 1 May 2007.

Jenkins, Rob. 'Civil society versus corruption', '*Journal of Democracy*', April 2007, Vol. 18, No. 2.

Joseph, TM. 'Democracy and representation in India: Does electoral system Matter?' *Gandhi Marg*, *(Hindi)*, October-November, 2006.

Kashyap, Subhash C. 'Parliament, reform thyself', in *The Tribune*, Chandigarh, 24 September 2005.

Katz Richard S. and Peter Mair. 'Changing models of party organisation and party democracy: The emergence of the cartel party', *Party Politics*, Vol.1, No.1. January 1995.

Kochanek, Stanley A. 'The Indian national congress', *The Journal of Asian Studies*, August 1966.

Koole, Ruud. 'Cadre, catch-all or cartel? A comment on the notion of cartel party', in *Party Politics*, Vol. 1, No. 4, 1996.

Kurian, NJ. 'Growing inter-state disparities', *Seminar* (Issue 509), 10 January 2002.

Ladner, Andreas and Michael Brandle. 'Does direct democracy matter for political parties?' An Empirical Test in Swiss Cantons, *Party Politics*, Vol.5 No.3.

Madhukar. CV. 'House this for debate?' *The Indian Express*, 3 January 2007.

Maira, Arun. 'Can argumentative India be governed?', The *Economic Times*, Mumbai, 19 December, 2005.

Malhotra, Inder. 'Polls spell populism in India' http://sify.com on 29 October 2003.

Mathur, Kuldeep. '*Decline of a centralised state: Changing nature of political power in India*', at

http://planningcommission.nic.in/reports/sereport/ser/vision2025/polipowr.pd as on 2 May 2007.

Mehta, Pratap Bhanu. 'Parliament and judiciary: Where should the line be drawn?' *The Economic Times*, Mumbai, 31 January 2006.

———. 'Sense and consensus', *The Indian Express*, Mumbai, 28 August 2005

———. 'Where's the party?' *The Indian Express*, Mumbai, 29 June 2005.

———. 'The maturing voter?' *Seminar*, Issue 533, January 2004.

———. 'Reform political parties first', *The Seminar*, Issue 497, January 2001

Mitra, Barun. 'The easy guide to how much money you spend on Parliament', *The Indian Express*, Mumbai, 27 October 2004.

Muhlberger, Steve. 'Democracy in ancient India' at http://www.infinityfoundation.com/mandala/h_es/h_es_muhlb_democra_frameset.htm, as on 2 January 2007.

Nandi, Pritish. 'The great betrayal' at

www.rediff.com/news/aug/27nandy.htm as on 12 November 2006

Narayan, Jayprakash (JN). 'India together' at http://www.indiatogether.org/2007/nov/med-mediaind.htm as on 29 November 2007.

———. 'The idea of India in danger', *The Economic Times,* Mumbai 21 February 2003

Ramswami, Cho. 'Coalition politics and the death of ideology,' *VIGIL, 20th Anniversary Souvenir,* August 2003, Chennai

Riddell, Peter. 'Lets do it, lets start flirting with PR', in *Timesonline*, 19 May, 2005 on http://www.timesonline.co.uk/article/0,1053-1617884,00.html

Ridley, FF. 'Crusaders and Politicians', *Parliamentary Affairs*, Oxford University Press Vol.51, No 3, July 1998.

Reilly, Benjamin. 'Political engineering of parties and parry systems' www.allacademic.com/meta/p63997_index.htm as on 7 May 2007.

Rousseas, Stephen W and James Farganis. 'American Politics and the End of Ideology' http://www.writing.upenn.edu/~afilreis/50s/end-of-I-farganis.html as on 4 June 2005.

Rosenberger, Sieglinde. 'The other side of the coin: Populism, nationalism and the European Union', Harvard International Review, at http://hir.harvard.edu/articles/1210/2/ on 4 October 2005.

Runald, Jurgan. 'Constitutional debates in Philippines: From presidentialism to parliamentarism?',Asian *Survey*, May/June 2003, Vol.43, No.03.

Sarangi, Prakash. 'The party system in India', at http://www.mssu.edu/projectsouthasia/tsa/VINI/SarangiPFVhtm as on 4 June 2006.

Sen, Sumanta. 'Caste for higher things' in *The Telegraph,* Kolkata, 19 May, 2007.

Seshan, TN. 'I vouch for Indian democracy', *The Indian Express*, Mumbai, 22 March, 2004. p.8.

Shastri, Sandeep. 'Department related standing committees in the Indian parliament: An assessment', *The Indian Journal of Public Administration.*Xliv, 2, April-June 1998.

Shourie, HD. 'The basic functioning of political parties in India', in *Liberal Times,* Vol. IX/No.1, 2001, (Freidrich-Naumann Stiftung. Regional Office South Asia).

Sinha, Sanjay. 'Electoral compulsions versus growth', *The Economic Times*, Mumbai. 17 May 2007.

Sopariwala, Dorab R. 'It's Broke—so we'd better fix it', *The Times of India,* Mumbai, 16 May, 1999.

Suri, KC. 'Parties under pressure: Political parties in India since independence' at http://www.lokniti.org/WPS-1.pdf as on 2 January 2006.

Tan, Alexander C. 'Party change and party membership decline', *Party Politics* (Vol.3 No.3) 1997.

Tismaneanu, Vladimir. 'The first post-communist decade', *Romanian Journal of Society and Politics* Vol. 1, No. 1.

Torres, Vladimir. '*The impact of populism on social, political and economic development in the hemisphere*' at www.focal.ca/pdf/VT_The_Impact_of_Populism.pdf as on 19 November 2005.

Walgrave, Stefaan and Michiel Nuytemans. 'Media and political agenda setting: The Belgian case' (Belgium, 1991-2000) at http://www.allacademic.com/meta/p61500_index.html as on 24 December 2007.

Yadav, Yogendra. 'Party Games', *The Indian Express*, Ahmedabad, 21 March 2007.

Zakaria, Rafiq. 'Save India from this democracy', *The Asian Age*, Mumbai, 29 January 2003.

Webb, Paul D. 'Are British political parties

in decline?' *Party Politics*, (Vol.1, No.3), July 1995.

Zakaria, Rafiq. 'Save India from this democracy'. *The Asian Age*, Mumbai, 29 January 2003.

3. Websites

http://www.nipissingu.ca/department/history/muhlberger/histdem/vanhanen.htm as on 12 November 2004.

www.freedomhouse.org as on 12 November 2004.

Second Treatise, Chapter 11, at http://www.blupete.com/Literature/Biographies/Philosophy/Locke.htm, as on 11 January 2006.

Burke, Edmund. *Speech to the Electors of Bristol*, 3 November, 1774 at http://en.wikipedia.org/wiki/Edmund_Burk as on 12 May, 2006.

http://www.parliament.uk/commons/lib/research/rp2000/rp00-002.pd as on November11, 2005

Mass Society, Wikipedia, at http://en.wikipedia.org/wiki/Mass_Society as on 15 October 2007.

Public Affairs Centre at http://www.pacindia.org/blogs/whats-wrong-with-democracy-in-india as on 26 December 2007.

'Constituent Assembly of India', at http://lawmin.nic.in/ncrwc/finalreport/v2b1-2ch3.htm as on 2 January 2007.

http://www.india-today.com/itoday/20000918/chidambaram.shtmlas on May 3, 2006

http://www.indianexpress.com/story/204383.html as on July 13, 2007

www.ids.ac.uk/logolink/resources/downloads/Recite_Confpapers/PRIA Policy_Paper_Urban1.pdf as on May 1, 2007

http://www.eci.gov.in/ElectoralLaws/OrdersNotifications/Registration_of_Political_Party.pdf as on May 2, 2007

http://www.hinduonnet.com/2004/03/28/stories/2004032800971300.htm

http://loksattaparty.blogspot.com/2006/10/birth-of-lok-satta-party.htm as on May 2, 2007

www.lokniti.org/WPS-1.pdf as on May 2, 2007

http://www.guardian.co.uk/india/story/0,2077646,00.htm as on May 11, 2007

http://www.thehindubusinessline.com/2004/06/15 as on May 11, 2007

http://www.carnegieendowment.org/files/Mehta.pdf. As on May 11, 2007

http://www.inq7.net/opi/2004/may/02/text/opi_rsdavid-1-p.htm on May2, 2007

http://spot.colorado.edu/~mcguire/rptheo.html. as on May 2, 2007

http://epicproject.org/ace/compepic/en/VE02 as on July 14, 2005

Inter American Development Bank Press Releaseathttp://www.idea.int/news/inthenews/2006_mar.cfm as on 5 June 2006.

http://www.idea.int/vt/survey/voter_turnout1.cfm

http://www.idea.int/vt/country_view.cfm? as on March 2, 2006

http://en.wikipedia.org/wiki/Negative_voting as on January 2, 2007

http://www.gfk.hr/press_en/crisis.htm on July 16, 2005

http://www.david-kilgour.com as on January 11, 2006

www.loksatta.orgon July 1, 2005

The Hindu at http://www.thehindu.com/2006/09/17/stories/2006092707590500.htm as on 17 September 2006.

http://www.inq7.net/opi/2004/may/02/text/opi_rsdavid-1-p.htmon May2, 2004

http://www.swachid.com/gandhian%20thoughts.htmir as on May 2, 2007 http://www.worldproutassembly.org/archives/2007/05/the_political_d.html as on May 2, 2007

http://www.austin.cc.tx.us/1patrick/his1302/populism.html as on January 2, 2006

http://hir.harvard.edu/articles/1210/2/ as on October 4, 2005.

The Hindu, 19 October 2004 appearing at http://www.hindu.com/2004/10/09/stories/2004100905511100.htm

http://www.rediff.com/news/2005/oct/28loud.htm as on November 11, 2005

http://www.umanet.org/cms.cfm?fuseaction=articles.viewThisArticle&articleID=45&pageID=159

http://www.jfklibrary.org/Historical+Resources/Archives/Reference+Desk/Speeches/JFK/JFK+Pre-Pres/002PREPRES12SPEECHES_55OCT27.htm as on May 2006

http://www.liveindia.com/freedomfighters/JBKripalani.html as on May 2,2007,

http://www.bjp.org/

http://www.aph.gov.au/Library/Pubs/rp/1999-2000/2000rp23.htm as on January 31, 2006

http://www.rediff.com/news/2003/may/27inter.htm on May 27, 2003

http://vicepresidentofindia.nic.in/content.asp?id=132 as on February. 8, 2008

http://janda.org/c95/news%20articles/New%20Zealand/ZNswitch.htm on January 16, 2006

http://www.bransdle.demon.co.uk/vote/listPR.html on January 18, 2006

http://www.anc.org.za/ancdocs/misc/electsub.html as on January 11, 2006

The Independent online, published on 7 June, 2005 at http://news.independent.co.uk/uk/politics/article224786.ece

www.citizensassembly.bc.ca/resources/Weekend%20Session%20Readings/Weekend5Session2McLeayPrint.ppt as on January 31, 2006

Paul Harris http://janda.org/c95/news%20articles/New%20Zealand/ZNswitch.htm on January.31, 2006

Reilly, Benjamin, '*Political Engineering of Parties and Party Systems*', the text of a speech at APSA website at http://www.bt.undp.org/Democracy/Political Engineering as on 2 January 2006.

http://ias.berkeley.edu/southasia/democracy07/docs/vrao.ppt as on May 2, 20006

http://www.indiaenews.com/politics/20071127/82934.ht as on December 25, 2007

http://www.cpim.org/ as on January 2, 2006

http://www.hindu.com/2006/02/09/stories/2006020905531200.htm as on 9 February, 2006 A news item quoting Pravin Togadia of the VHP on Hindu vote bank

http://ia.rediff.com/news/1998/dec/09cong1.htm as on May 7, 2007

www.ndi.org/ndi/library/1512_ww_communityofdemoc_final_11202.txt as on May 7, 2007

www.opsi.gov.uk/acts/acts2000/en/00en41-g.htm as on May 2, 2007

http://dupb.blogspot.com/2005/05/fact-file-about-slum-demolitions.htmlon January 2,2007

http://www.loksatta.org/poffice.htm, as on November 12, 2006

http://www.janadesh.org/files/3_10majorproblems.html as on January 7, 2006

'Proportional representation versus first-past-the-post' at http://economics.about.com/cs/issues/ as on 2 January 2007.

http://mpa.nic.in/Statbook12.pdf as on 7 June 2013.

Index